"Mr Chelsea."

PAUL DAVIS

Enjoy!

Paul Davis

PROSPERO

A Life in Rock n' Roll and Architecture from the King's Road to Tokyo

PAUL DAVIS

"MR. CHELSEA"

The Author; Sunday morning street portrait, Montmartre

CONTENTS

神苑拝観の皆様へ

臥龍橋を渡られる場合は
池に落ちないよう足元に
充分注意して下さい。
万一の事故等について
責任を負いかねますので
予めご了承下さいませ

社務所

PLEASE, MIND YOUR STEP.

When crossing 『臥竜橋』,

be careful of the footing sufficiently.

Understand beforehand because the

responsibility can not be assumed

about the accident in case and so on.

1 OUT OF THE CORNER

It is September 1960, in the leafy London suburb of Dulwich village. I am aged nine years and five months. My apparently excellent prep school has many practices for which 50 years later it would have been either prosecuted or closed, if not both.

I am in class 4C, whose teacher is Miss Usher. She is Australian, with a slim figure, a pale complexion and she wears intense pink lipstick. She always dresses in white blouses paired with a dark blue pleated skirt which shows her delicate calves joining the slingbacks on her tiny feet. Almost all 4C have a crush on her as she is certainly the prettiest of all the teachers. The boys can't help but notice that Miss Usher's blouses, although demure in design, often reveal a lacy white bra through slightly gaping buttons. Miss Usher looks down her sharp thin nose at us through eyes of palest grey blue. She has high cheekbones and a finely shaped chin, but her lips are straight and mean. She seems to enjoy marking our little pale blue spelling books with big red crosses, especially mine.

I am half deaf, but Miss Usher either does not know or does not care. She is cold and lacks empathy. Maybe the strident manner she adopts to control the class is a mask for her inexperience. She addresses me from behind her raised desk.

'Davis, spell geography'.

I don't hear her. She moves down the aisle of desks towards me.

'Davis, spell geography', she repeats.

I haven't heard her or noticed her approach. A rap from her ruler on the back of my hand brings her to my attention. She leans over me, her steely cold eyes glaring down at me.

'Stand in the corner you little dunce!'

Without even knowing what my misdemeanour is, I obediently face the wall in this familiar spot, my back to the room. I am close to tears, humiliated and alone. Should cold, unkind and pretty become one and the same in my young mind?

Some days, when Miss Usher's short temper is even shorter, I am evicted from class and made to stand in the windowless corridor. I pray to become invisible because if the deputy head walks past, the chances of a beating are both probable and painful. The swish of a thin bamboo cane on my naked backside is felt by my whole body, like a sharp burn, or the cut of a knife on my innocent skin. Luckily, I'm often absent from school with tonsillitis. I'd rather be safely ill in my comfy bed. Alone in bed is better than alone in the classroom corner.

In the spring of '61 at the Brompton Hospital on the Fulham Road in SW3 (almost 40 years later I would be appointed to prepare its Masterplan for redevelopment), I had an operation to remove my tonsils and adenoids. It was hard to swallow. My throat felt like coarse sandpaper and the only food I could eat was

Opposite:
Kyoto stepping stones; advice for life

5

vanilla ice cream. Even when I was still groggy from the anaesthetic, I felt something was different. I was aware of sounds I hadn't heard before: footsteps in the hospital corridor, bus wheels on the rain-drenched road outside. I could hear the door handle turning in the latch, the scrape of the chair on linoleum as Mum brought it closer to the bedside. For nine years, my life had been muffled as if my hearing had been smothered under the bedclothes, rendering all sound dull and indistinct. Now the operation had had the unforeseen side effect of unblocking my hearing, and my world was pulled into sharper focus. As I convalesced, all my senses seemed more awake. I felt more alive.

As I climbed the stairs to my bedroom back at home, I saw a raven perched on the landing window ledge staring in at me. I was scared by his intense shining black eyes, even though I kept a sketchbook whose pages were full of pencil drawings of raptors and owls. The raven stood there, motionless, a silken sentinel, every day for a week. On the seventh day, as I passed the window, I noted with relief that the raven wasn't there. As I climbed into bed, there was a piercing squawk from the top of my wardrobe and his black eyes drilled into mine. I froze, as the dark apparition leapt and flew twice around the room. Then it disappeared through the open window. I lay in bed numb, unnerved; that was the last I saw of it. The raven had gone, and I felt as if it had taken my deafness with it. Life had started anew.

During the summer term, I spent less time standing in the corner. In the playground, shrill laughter and shouts in unbroken voices filled my ears. 'Ready, steady, go!' I was quicker off the mark. I felt free of Miss Usher, too; she had become invisible to me.

Below:
Haircut for speech day, aged 10

That autumn term I was in a new class with a different teacher, Miss Caster. Where Miss Usher had been slim and cold, Miss Caster was buxom and motherly. I admired her wavy golden hair, her rosy cheeks and the scarlet lipstick she wore on her plump smiling lips. My recovered hearing brought me confidence. Now that words had sound, my spelling improved. I could follow verbal explanations; I had no problem with sums. My homework was now covered in blue ticks instead of red crosses.

For the first time I was given top marks. I was first not last. With Miss Caster's exuberant support, I passed my 11+ exit exam. We weren't wealthy enough for Dulwich College fees, but my score was high enough for a scholarship to Alleyn's College of God's Gift, a direct grant grammar which was just down the road. At the time, it seemed a bit second-best, but Alleyn's turned out to be first best for me. That is serendipity; life unfolding without expectation and choosing the road on your behalf.

Alleyn's school was almost exactly one mile from our house; down College Road, through Dulwich Village, past the toy and sports shops, the grocer's (then still ration-book regulated), the out-of-bounds Greyhound pub, then puffing up the steep hill to school. For the next seven years, I would cycle this route, changing along the way from the pre-teen innocence of an 11-year-old to the streetwise arrogance of an argumentative 18-year-old hippy. These were years of huge change and growth, full of laughter, learning, misbehaviour, winning and losing, failure and achievement. I changed from virgin to randy youth, from bullied victim to proud athlete.

Alleyn's was founded by Edward Alleyn, Christopher Marlowe's principal actor. He made a fortune as a brothel owner and entrepreneur, and was the drinking companion of King James I. In 1619 he purchased the manor of Dulwich for five thousand pounds. Through 350 years, a tradition of excellence had been upheld in school play productions. Aged 15, I joined this tradition, playing a knight in Hamlet with just five lines, which I somehow managed to deliver even though my knees were shaking.

The same year, I discovered the art room. It was painted white, with tall windows that captured the sky. It had distressed wide wooden floorboards and large paint-stained tables which were arranged at right angles to maximise the north light. Around the walls on wide shelves stood antique busts of Roman emperors, skulls of animals and even a human skull, which we nicknamed Yorick. The colourful, more mature works left behind by departed sixth formers hung as targets for us to aspire to.

Above:
Winning the relay race

This space, huge to me, was a blithely creative, slightly cluttered mess. It was a place of freedom and self-expression amongst the rigorous discipline of a 1960s direct grant school with advancing aspirations. Although at first overawed, I knew instantly that this was the room that would become my refuge and release, where I could find myself and excel.

Chris Lawrence was art master. He had long jet-black hair which he wore swept back, and a meticulously shaped goatee beard. He drove a midnight blue Jaguar XK150 convertible. Here was a schoolteacher out of a more romantic mould. His dress sense was predictably flamboyant. He could see that a small group of his pupils were stage-struck and enthusiastic to have their eyes opened. We were gripped with creative teenage trial-and-error energy, and he encouraged our efforts to make our drawings big and bold. We sculpted and carved anything we could find. We screen printed in wild colours and painted in oil on huge canvases.

We experimented and pushed ourselves in all directions, while Chris introduced us to the new wave of Pop Art, the Abstract Expressionists and event 'happenings'. I was excited by Frank Stella and Bridget Riley's optical exploits whether in colour or black and white. M.C. Escher's early lithographs of Italian hill towns, his illusory architecture and inventive geometric pattern-making inspired pure adolescent wonder. Slides of these artists' work became an integral part of our projected light show. More studiously, preparing for History of Art A level, we explored the work

Above:
Frank Stella
Hyena Stomp
I-Wei Huang/Dreamstime.com

Above right:
Andrea del Sarto:
Working sketch

of artists through the millennia. At the time, my own favourite artists were Fra Angelico, Piero della Francesca, Michelangelo, Andrea del Sarto and Albrecht Dürer. A legion of later artists has since fought for inclusion on my list of favourites for their use of space, light, line, colour and composition. They have stimulated my imagination, as have their renditions of all subjects, whether landscape, architecture, or the human form.

Chris Lawrence was soon superseded by Peter Major. Peter had dark orange hair and a Saxon full-face matching beard. Observing my growing interest in architecture, he sent me off around the different eras of school buildings to sketch staircases. This was great training and advanced my ability to understand and conceive in three dimensions. My carving in wood, soft aerated concrete blocks and stone improved. Inspired by Giacometti, I started making kinetic sculptures on wire frames, wrapped in rough plaster of Paris. 'Two lovers dancing' spun slowly around on an old wind-up record player at the end-of-year art show. I also learnt to make complex castings in resin with metal filings; once burnished, they shone lustrously with a gun-metal patina. The best, though hardly groundbreaking, won the annual senior art prize. Armed with the generous book token, I headed to Zwemmer's, the world famous art bookshop on Charing Cross Road, which was a favourite haunt of mine. I cashed in the token for a huge two volume complete works of Michelangelo that has been my companion in life for over 50 years.

Peter encouraged me to go to London art galleries on free afternoons, so I escaped from school to visit the newly opened Institute of Contemporary Arts in Nash House on The Mall. The ICA was like an adult play centre and, ever the enthusiast, I immediately signed up to form a Contemporary Arts Society at school. As a result, I gained preferential or free access to all events at the ICA. The Mall's opening exhibition in 1968 was *Cybernetic Serendipity*, featuring TV screens connected to the earliest computer art and graphics along with a mosaic floor of changing coloured lights. It was a seminal exhibition and included a series of live music and light performances. The most memorable and influential to my receptive ears and eyes was by Soft Machine, with lighting by Mark Boyle. I was there with Philip and Gus. It was the most advanced and colourful psychedelic light show my closest friends and I had seen.

1969, my last year at school, was the 350th anniversary of the Foundation. Legend has it that Edward Alleyn had a vision of his worldly misdeeds, whilst playing Faustus in the first production of Marlowe's most eloquent play. To make amends in the eyes of God, Alleyn gifted an endowment to fund a school and almshouses for the poor children and elderly of the manor. To celebrate the anniversary, the main school production was to be *Doctor Faustus*. Simon Danischewski, a close friend from the year below, and I were asked by the headmaster if we would take on the two formidable roles of Faust and Mephistopheles. There was fierce competition between Alleyn's and neighbouring Dulwich College, so the school's reputation would depend on us. The pressure was on, and we determined to deliver a performance beyond our individual abilities. We were given extra tuition and acting coaching by Mike and Chris Croft, former teachers at the school who had started the National Youth Theatre. My role as the fallen angel, tempting Faustus to the Dark Side, brought me out in front of an audience of several hundred people. My effort was rewarded by the warmth of the applause. Amazing to think of these days, but *The Times* came to review the production and gave us a glowing notice. It was a huge boost to my personal confidence. My father carried that cutting in his wallet until the day he died, proud of his little dunce who had found his way out of the corner.

Below:
Me as Mephistopheles, 'Icily calm and watchful, treated the play's poetic splendours with affection and clarity'
The Times, 1969

2 THE KING'S ROAD

Philip Vernon lived just down the road at 5 Frank Dixon Way. His dad Russell was Architect to the Dulwich Estate, while his mum Ruth was always welcoming and almost seemed to enjoy having kids mess up her elegantly designed and furnished home. Philip and I were in the same nursery class at Dulwich College Preparatory School and as small boys we collected toy soldiers and Dinky military vehicles like most post-war baby boomers. Out in the corner of his big garden where we were free to play as we liked, we cut a military trench where we would plot daring attacks wearing his dad's old tin helmets along with wooden rifles we made ourselves. When we tired of that game, we energetically dug the trench deeper and longer, roofed it over to become a submarine deck, and mounted a huge upside-down terracotta pot as the conning tower which had a hole in the base big enough that our heads could pop through. We must have looked like Bill and Ben the Flowerpot Men from the popular children's show of that time. The Vernon house had bay windows to the ground floor and linked onto an old high brick garden wall that ran around its perimeter. As we grew bigger and more adventurous, our favourite game was to circumnavigate the whole property without touching the ground. We moved from the walls to the roofs of bay windows and then clung to first floor windowsills as we pushed our ten-year-old commando ambitions to the limit. We never fell from a great height, but we learnt a lot about roofs, lead flashings and risk-taking.

In our early teens, we spent winter evenings joining both of our Scalextric sets together to make longer tracks and then we built our own slot racing track in the apex roof space above Philip's attic. We laid a dense fibreboard floor over the ceiling joists, and then flitched and saw-cut the central structural spine beam to link the two sides of the long, narrow space. Then we chiselled the slot grooves, painted the track with a rubberised sand-infused paint for grip, glued copper tape to both sides of each groove, and made final electrical transformer connections. We had designed and built our own 40ft-long (12m) slot racing track. Landscaping, pits and grandstands followed, as well as our own customised kit electric slot racing cars. My favourite was a Revel 289 AC Cobra. The real ones had been tracked at 190 miles per hour on the M1 motorway testing for the Le Mans 24-hour race. The stuff of legend to 12-year-old car buff boys.

As we grew older, the Vernon attic became a creative hang-out for Philip and me, along with his mate Gus Thomson, whose mum Jean made ends meet by taking in lodgers and doing watercolour architects' drawings for Russell's firm (which I admired greatly, particularly for the way that the addition of colour brought the places she illustrated to life). Others from Alleyn's joined us, as well as several boarders

Opposite:
One of many changes to
Granny Takes a Trip
King's Road shopfronts
Photograph: Mirrorpix/Getty Images

Right:
Revell 289 AC Cobra kit;
still going after 58 years

Below:
The Times, June '64
The stuff of legend

MOTORWAY USED AS LE MANS TEST TRACK

The Cobra waits among the lorries at a lay-by on the M1 for a clear road to test its speed

Cobra reached 190 mph on the M1

By Maxwell Boyd

Cars preparing for next week's 24-hour race at Le Mans have been using the M1 as a test track, clocking up speeds approaching 200 m.p.h.

Police forces patrolling M1 know that the test runs are taking place but so far they have turned a blind eye towards them. Since the road is derestricted, they can take no action from the point of view of speed alone and as no accidents have occurred and as no reason to intervene.

Manufacturers say they are forced to use the motorway—they have been "motorway-testing" various high-performance cars for some time because there is no suitable private track.

Since certain design features function only at the highest speeds, most manufacturers feel it

is essential that their cars should be tried out "on the limit" at least once before Le Mans, where the larger-engined cars regularly reach 180-200 m.p.h. on the Mulsanne straight. One of these is A.C. Cars of Thames Ditton, Surrey, whose Cobra for Le Mans reached about 190 m.p.h during an early morning run on M1 last week.

Out-of-date track

A.C. take every possible precaution in the interests of safety during these tests. The car is driven by an experienced and skilled racing driver and the tests are conducted between 5 a.m. and 7 a.m. when traffic on the road is at its lightest. An efficient silencing system prevents the exhaust noise from causing annoyance.

A.C. would rather use a private track, but technical progress has outstripped the facilities of the Motor Industry Research Association's 11-year-old proving ground at Nuneaton, the only one available to manufacturers. The maximum lap speed that can be reached on its 2.8-mile high speed track is approximately 155 m.p.h. and the maximum flat-out speed about 165 m.p.h. Nowadays, a standard production Jaguar E-type can take these facilities almost to their limit.

The M.I.R.A. authorities would like to build a separate high-speed proving ground, but are unable to do so unless the industry itself supplies the money. A M.I.R.A. spokesman said: "The industry brought the proving ground into existence to stop cars being tested

on the open road. They ought to let us go ahead and build another track."

On hearing that cars were being driven at 190 m.p.h. on M1, an astonished A.A. spokesman said: "Obviously manufacturers must be able to test their cars at these speeds, but facilities should certainly be available to do it in private."

Britain's lack of high-speed facilities was dramatically emphasised at the Indianapolis 500 race a fortnight ago when a smashed suspension put world champion Jim Clark out of the race. It had been shattered by pieces of flying tyre tread. A senior tyre technician told me: "The tyre disintegrated simply because its design could not be tested at the speeds demanded."

from Dulwich College, escaping from their dormitories only a few hundred yards away to enjoy unlimited hours of conversation, amplified music, coffee and Marmite toast; and, as we grew older, booze, joints and the company of girls. Amongst them was Phil Targett-Adams, a tall, reserved boy who was always playing his guitar. His father had been head of the British Overseas Airways Corporation (BOAC) in South America and they had moved around the region, living, amongst other exotic places, opposite Batista's villa in Cuba at the time of the Revolution. Phil's mother was Venezuelan, and he later adopted her maiden name Manzanera when he joined Roxy Music.

Another favourite meeting place for this growing gang was the crypt of All Saints Church, on Rosendale Road in Dulwich. We would detour to walk past a house with a huge eye painted over the front window. Soft Machine were living there, and it was from the first floor window that Robert Wyatt, the brilliant drummer, would later fall during a party and tragically break his back. It was at the youth club that I met Maggie, who was two years older than me, and became my first proper girlfriend. She and her best friend Susie both attended the church services as well as hanging out with the irreligious gang at Philip's. She joined us as we started to roam further afield, over the river to Central London, and more excitingly to Chelsea and the King's Road.

My first trip to this Mecca of nascent hippy fashion was in early '66. Philip and I soaked up the atmosphere and window shopped before leaping into Bricks corner boutique. We emerged dressed in our new gear feeling pretty hip. A photographer for *Esquire* magazine asked to take a string of shots as we leant self-consciously against the shop window. Did any of them ever appear? I don't think so, but maybe they're buried in their archive somewhere.

My glamorous 20-year-old cousin Gillian had been living with us in Dulwich whilst studying at St Martin's College of Art. Her boyfriend Peter was an architect with a basement flat on Cheyne Walk down by the Thames Embankment. He drove an Aston Martin DB4 like there was no tomorrow. I would sit sideways in the cramped back seat to watch out of the rear window for the speed cops (there were no cameras back then). On an outing to Silverstone, I acted as pit man (or boy). Peter was somewhat average in the first race and was given a beneficial handicap for the last race, a temporary holding of the Tourist Trophy. He won, collected the impressive silver cup, huge laurel wreath and a magnum of champagne. Later that evening, after a road race back to Chelsea, we arrived at our much frequented local, The Builders Arms on Britten Street. Carrying the spoils of the day, we entered to raucous cheers from our friends and the many regular drinkers. A heroic night ensued and imprinted a naively optimistic notion of life as an architect.

Some weekends, I would stay over on Cheyne Walk with Maggie. For her 18th birthday, we hit Mary Quant's shop and bought a dandelion yellow satin mini-dress with a bold keyhole neckline. Maggie looked like a brunette Twiggy with the same cute haircut of the time. Gillian and Peter invited us to their favourite night club to celebrate. Arriving back at the flat, we watched the sunrise over the three bridges of Chelsea for the first time.

One Stop record shop had the best American West Coast import albums. I was standing outside contemplating the next addition to my collection when a tall guy with beyond shoulder-length sandy coloured hair and matching suede jeans strolled up beside me. Comparing notes on favourite groups, I plucked up courage to ask him where he got his cool jeans.

'Mexico,' he replied in a slow drawl.

'Are you in a band?' I asked.

He was Henry Verstine, the guitarist in Canned Heat. We chatted about favourite albums. I bought Bob Dylan's *Highway 61 Revisited* and Henry wandered off with a shoulder bag full of blues records. Undaunted by the encounter but deflated at not being able to copycat purchase similar trousers, I headed for the Chelsea Antique Market where I treated myself to a pair of claret suede jeans and bib front sailor's blue serge bell-bottoms. They became an integral part of my personal long-term image. My mother was not impressed by how tightly they fitted.

The day before my 15th birthday, 28 May 1966, Bob Dylan was playing at the Royal Albert Hall in Kensington. Philip and I had tickets in the arena, only about 20 rows back from the stage. We had been listening to every one of Dylan's albums over and over and were word perfect on pretty much all his lyrics, from protest songs like *The Lonesome Death of Hattie Carroll* to my favourite love song *Love Minus Zero, No Limit*. That change was on the way was evident from the more radical image of Dylan in a midnight-blue and pink floral satin shirt on the cover of *Highway 61*, not to mention that album's electric arrangements. Rumours of a new double album were rife, but *Blonde on Blonde* was still a few months from release. In the eyes and ears of his dedicated folk music fans, Dylan had deserted his roots by 'going electric'. The folkies had idolised Dylan as the spokesperson of his generation with his bluntly spoken acoustic protest songs and were angry at him for going commercial. Dylan and The Hawks were at the end of a year-long world tour that had mostly been met with booing and organised walk outs. In Manchester the week before, one member of the audience had cried out 'Judas'.

In '66, TV was still only black and white, and a lot of grey. Arriving at Prince Albert's cultural extravaganza for the first time, we strode excitedly up the impressively civic grey stone steps from Prince Consort Road. The colourful red brick, terracotta and stone-arcaded coliseum of a compressed wedding cake filled the skyline. The grand, temple-like entrance further raised our anticipation of the evening ahead. Then we entered the arena, which was enveloped in red and gold, its gently sloping first tier topped by three galleries of encircling boxes, conjuring images of overblown Victoriana. Above these exclusive grandstand miniature parlours rose yet more tiers of steeply sloping seats. The whole concoction was topped by the ribbed dome supported by a heroically scaled ambulatory of silhouetted columns framing Venetian arches. Blown away by this rich architectural experience, we slid into our seats close to the stage with its backdrop of the castle-like organ casing.

Dylan was smaller than expected, dressed in a high-lapelled, brown and grey-check suit with drainpipe trousers, his hair frizzed in the profile that would become a legendary silhouette. Solo, he commanded the stage, wandering around, fidgeting

with guitar and mic, exhibiting a kind of confident anxiety. Hearing *Visions of Johanna* for the very first time, the poetry of the song and its narrative held the entire audience in reverent silence. It was the stillness before the storm.

The second set with the Hawks, later known simply as 'The Band', was what the fuss was about. Some of the audience shouted abuse. Philip and I loved the exuberant, raucous energy of Robbie Robertson, Garth Hudson, Rick Danko and co. Guitars, Hammond organ and drums resonated in the awful acoustics of the Albert Hall. Dylan bounced across the stage, buoyed up by the joy of his electrified music. He was having a whale of a time.

Right:
The Royal Albert Hall:
A colourful wedding cake
Colosseum
© I-Wei Huang
Alamy stock photo

Dylan was our little gang's first musical hero. His lyrics helped to open our questioning adolescent minds. The times were indeed a changin' and he gave voice to the protest movement, whether political, racial or social. Blues and folk music had narrative soul, but Dylan brought a new level of poetic allegory, storytelling and depth of character into his lyrics. He altered the potential and perception of what a pop song could be. It was no longer just a two-minute jingle. One track, a story of racial injustice told with dignity and passion; another, a love song with a new depth of poetic imagery; then a lengthy tale of desultory street life in downtown New York City. His words flowed through his albums and each new release moved further beyond its predecessor.

An artist moves on, keeps questioning his work, seeking new methods of expression, new moods, colours, forms. Picasso moved from period to period, Frank Lloyd Wright moved from one era and place of influence to another. It is hard to think of a great painter, author, architect, poet or musician who does not search, evolve, and move on. It is the very nature and purpose of art and artist to keep searching for better. On 28 May '66, Dylan was exercising his right as an artist, moving to the next era of self-expression. His performance was full of energy, experiment and rhythm; it was occasionally cacophonous, joyous then reflective, lyrically inventive, and just as polemical as before. Dylan was being himself, a song writer, performer and artist moving onwards. It was a useful lesson for adolescent would-be artists.

To the cry of 'Judas', he had simply retorted 'I don't believe you, you're a liar', and got on with being who he wanted to be. To all of us, our first major music concert is an important memory and influence; we were lucky that ours was that special gig. Were we aware that his words and music would become a soundtrack to our lives? Oblivious, that night we bounced through the streets of Kensington singing all the way home.

Back then, there was a lot going on in music all over London and, of course, Liverpool, though I only ever saw the Beatles on TV, not live at the Cavern. There was a less publicised basement club in Great Newport Street just off Charing Cross Road, Studio 51. It was a great place to hang out. Some of our friends from Alleyn's were blues music devotees, especially Steve Gamgee and Chris Turner. Steve was cursed with blotchy acne and barely said a word unless expounding his encyclopaedic knowledge of early blues musicians and their songs, which he expressed by playing outstanding acoustic guitar. Chris played exceptional harmonica and even as a (white) schoolboy played on albums with Sonny Terry and Brownie McGhee as well as Champion Jack Dupree.

Steve and Chris liked to play on the Sunday afternoon open-stage blues jam sessions in the unlit basement that was Studio 51. In the gloom of the small, low-ceilinged room was a rudimentary stage and lights with several mikes and diverse instruments ready to go. Steve and Chris would play a few blues songs early on, with Chris often concluding with a more than energetic *Train*, a classic trad harmonica instrumental, his wild hair almost as expressive as the speed of his mouth on the harp. Dave Kelly and the John Dummer Blues Band played as the resident group.

Tony McPhee and Jo Ann Kelly, Dave's brilliant sister, were part of the regular line up. Jo Ann Kelly could have been a rival to Janis Joplin. Super cool Long John Baldry would often show up with his silky blonde hair almost scraping the ceiling, and add his gravelly voice to the vocals. On other occasions, John Mayall, Alexis Korner, or Champion Jack Dupree would drop in to play. One Sunday, a guitarist who had just walked away from Cream after storming America joined the crowded stage; his name was Eric Clapton. A couple of times the afternoon jam was further complemented by a young Rod Stewart who was just making a name for himself. Sundays in the late sixties were great, even more so because the gigs cost nothing.

One Sunday in March '68, we joined the anti-Vietnam march to Grosvenor Square. The atmosphere amongst the crowd was angry but peaceful. When the mounted police moved in the mood changed to scary, and we swiftly made our way back to the haven of Studio 51.

Back then, most gigs were in the back rooms of pubs, sports club halls and colleges. Each week our group of friends would see emerging bands that would become legends in the following decades. The Bromley Court Hotel had a ballroom that hosted the Bromel Jazz Club. The hotel, converted from a mansion in the '30s, and requisitioned in the war, was still pretty run down. The Bromel Club had hosted big name blues musicians and then become a hangout for mods. By '66-'67 it was a venue for breaking bands like the Spencer Davis Group, the Rolling Stones and local boy David Bowie. As schoolboy hippies, we didn't fit in with the tailored mohair suits and scooter gangs who were capable of violent intimidation. To hear the live music, we ran that gauntlet.

One night as we walked to Susie's house from the station, a gang of drunken skinheads took exception to our dress code of bandanas, military jackets and long hair. Philip was smart enough to do a runner, while Maggie slipped inside a red phone box and seven heavies set upon me and Gus. Gus helped get two off me only for them to be replaced by three others. I was knocked semi-conscious to the concrete pavement as a steel toecap booted my eye and broke my cheekbone. The pain brought me to, and I began to scream; that was the right move. The skinheads disappeared into the housing estate opposite and the street fell silent. Maggie had rung 999 and a police car and ambulance arrived. The hospital doctor patched me up and told me I was lucky not to lose the sight in my right eye.

Jimi Hendrix released his first UK single, *Hey Joe*, just before Christmas '66. His deep plaintive voice and the tightly clipped then soaring guitar made the record an instant favourite of mine. It still is.

The first gig on the first Jimi Hendrix Experience tour was at the Bromel Club on 4 January '67. It was half empty, but the sound level, animation and passion of Hendrix's playing were beyond anything we had witnessed at the time. Jimi and Noel Redding (bass) were both tall and nearly touched the low-panelled ceiling, as did their Marshall amplification stacks. Mitch Mitchell (drums) was as wildly focused as Keith Moon of The Who. Hendrix's long fingers moved with easy alacrity along the neck of his white guitar, which he played left-handed behind his back and then with his teeth. Kneeling over his guitar, he seduced it sensuously. Dressed in purple velvet trousers, open frilled shirt, neck chains and bandana, every inch of his lithe body, spirit and soul expressed a new level of freedom, individuality and mystery. As Van Gogh's connection of soul, oil paint and canvas were a pure outpouring of light and colour, so Hendrix's complete immersion in and coupling with his guitar encapsulated the art of the new electric music. He spoke in a rounded, gently punctuated, slightly staccato, mellow voice that was immediately identifiable.

As word spread, with his first single climbing the charts, he played the Bromley Court Hotel again on 8 February. Fortunately, we had decided to arrive early and were at the front of the queue for our seven shillings and sixpence entry ticket. That night, it was packed out and we were right at the front, sitting on the wooden floor waiting to be blown away again. Hendrix rose to the packed room and was utterly explosive. Bill Wyman, the laid back Stones bass player, who was in the audience, looked incredulous.

Whenever the Jimi Hendrix Experience were playing in or around London, our group of friends would skip anything to be there. Polly Lucas was a close friend of mine within our partying, gig-going group. She had been seriously upset by her parents' divorce and now had to live between the homes of her mother and two elder brothers. She struggled to trust and accept love. We shared an adolescent melancholy and a passion for art. Our favourite song was Tim Hardin's haunting *Hang on to a Dream*. 'What can I say, she's walking away…'. I can still picture her tall figure walking towards me, her long auburn hair flowing, wearing faded jeans and a snug shrunken woolly jumper. Polly's father was Professor of Film at the Royal College of Art. He had a flat in Albert Hall Mansions overlooking Hyde Park which was a great place to hang out. The apartment was full of art and books which Polly and I relished; we explored ideas together during our budding teenage intimacy. Her father was rarely there, so it felt like our own space. Another great luxury was that he held a debenture box in the Albert Hall. His taste ran to classical music, so when a rock concert was on, his box was available for Polly and friends. Free access to the Albert Hall for gigs and a 50-yard walk to crash out afterwards was an adolescent dream.

On 18 February '69, Hendrix and Soft Machine played a surprisingly lacklustre double bill. Only a week later, on 24 February, at short notice we heard Jimi was playing again. This time, he was on form and filled the auditorium with energy and panache. What we didn't know at the time was that this would be the last Jimi Hendrix Experience performance in Europe.

A year later, I had a holiday job working on a concrete gang, building the new Swiss Embassy on Bryanston Square. It was dangerous, hard work erecting the formwork and pouring the fluid concrete high up on the scaffold of the multi-storey skeletal structural frame. The site was just around the corner from Montagu Square where Hendrix had been living in a flat borrowed from John Lennon. On 18 September, as I walked up to Marble Arch tube station, the *Evening Standard* billboard announced, HENDRIX DEAD. I sloped home, despondent at the loss of a hero. When a person changes how you perceive and feel about life, their memory stays alive inside you.

My schooldays ended in June '69. A week later on 5 July, Chris Turner's electric blues band Screw was one of the support acts for an open-air concert in Hyde Park; the Rolling Stones were headlining the event. Arriving early to set up, their extra-large hired white transit van parked close to stage right. As other bands trucks arrived and the crowds built up, Screw's transport was isolated and immoveable. Its roof served as a perfect private grandstand for the whole of the most memorable Hyde Park open-air concert. A perfect start to end of school summer holidays.

That autumn, Philip and I both headed to university to study architecture, he at Leeds and I at Nottingham. Other friends had gone elsewhere, or were travelling, making music, working, or had just drifted away. School was over, the next act had begun, and I embraced new opportunities with enthusiasm. I found university life to be a transformative and expanding stage. It was also an era of student unrest; another pool for me to dive into. I forged new friendships, and the course was demanding. There was a coin telephone box in the Union building, from where I used to call Susie, who had now become my regular girlfriend, though I had known her as a friend for years. We wrote endless long romantic letters about how our lives were moving on. Susie was studying gemology at the Sir John Cass college and working at Mappin & Webb in the City.

Our friendship circle was inevitably finding wider orbits. Back in Dulwich, two of my closest friends Brian and Polly were going out together but I only saw them sporadically while I was away in Nottingham. If only I could turn the clock back, I would have tried to spend more time with them. It hurt even more deeply not to learn from Brian until a year after the tragedy that she had been murdered on Sydenham Hill Station. We had often waited there for trains together, laughing and flirting. Her case was never solved. The loss of a young friend carries a particular pain for any of us. A hand never again to hold, a voice unheard but not forgotten.

3   ULTRAMARINE LIGHT SHOW

Many of our friends were musicians and played in electric bands. Neither Philip, Gus nor I were musicians, but we were immersed in the new music. We had heard talk and seen pictures of the Pink Floyd gigs at All Saints Church Hall at Powys Grove in the autumn of '66. News reached us of Mark Boyle doing light shows with Soft Machine at the UFO Club in Tottenham Court Road. We had seen his light show on our one visit to the old ICA in Dover Street. These were music and light happenings that later became the stuff of internet folklore.

Later, on seeing the Bauhaus exhibition at the Royal Academy in September '68 we were further inspired to experiment with our fathers' slide projectors. Moholy Nagy's photograms and light machines left a deep impression on us, also Gerhard Richter's liquid crystal work using Polaroid filters shown at Better Books in Charing Cross Road was a catalyst for more experimental ideas.

Our first foray into performing a light show in public was a self-promoted gig held at All Saints crypt in Dulwich in support of our friends Brian Barnett and Ian Haigue's band, Savage Rose. We used a 16mm movie projector with hand-painted loops, which gave a great sense of expressionist movement. Still slides, evoking Yves Klein and Jackson Pollock, added to the layering of colourful abstract pure light. By the simple technique of using multiple projectors with spinning colour wheels, we created a sense of considerable movement. It sounds, and was, rather basic compared to the gigantic computer controlled live music shows of today. But Philip, Gus and I had a lot of creative fun playing with coloured light in motion.

Through '67, we advanced our techniques as well as our ideas and imagery, acquiring numerous, and various, projectors. The original upright Tutor 1 & 2 were the most powerful (1000 watt) and accessible for liquid slide projection. Fortunately, these had become surprisingly cheap, as educational establishments had switched to the new Kodak carousel projectors and the old Tutors were considered redundant. Projected slides of artwork by Joseph Albers, Bridget Riley and Frank Stella's *Magic Squares* came alive with colour wheels slowly turning in front of multiple layered beams of projected light. Polaroid filters rotated in front of patterned and stressed clear plastic sheets and gave subtle evolving coloured geometries. Our own experiments with colour slide photography added to our visual vocabulary and we built a greater diversity of themes. We took micro photographs of metallic materials and structures in nature and close-ups of body parts, Islamic patterns, flames, sunsets, and time-lapse moving fairground lights. These all took on new perceptions when their scale was enlarged by projection to cover 20ft-high stage backdrops.

We saw Mark Boyle's light show again on Friday 15 December '67 at the Middle Earth Club in a Covent Garden basement (decades later my firm would

23

be appointed as executive architects to CapCo who owned the whole area). Pink Floyd were headlining but Syd Barrett was sadly in acid meltdown and my vague recollection is that David Gilmour played on some tracks. The first of very few gigs with five members? I stand to be corrected on that, but Boyle's lighting mixed effective moving liquid slides with multi-coloured silhouetted shadow lighting on the simple white backdrop, especially animated by Nick Mason's wide armed drum style and Roger Waters's lanky torso.

Our experiments with liquid slides did not match Mark Boyle's work until we discovered Winsor and Newton's Vitrina glass paint. This had the right viscosity to stay within the sandwiches of glass slides and to heat up to boiling point with a quick blast from a cigarette lighter. The intensity of Vitrina colours was excellent, as was the translucency. A chemist friend mixed bespoke aniline dyes for us. When a tiny dusting of bicarbonate of soda or effervescent Eno powder was added, these gave a chemical reaction releasing air bubbles into the projected liquid layers of vibrant colour.

Gus was the most electronically practical of our little gang and he built an organ keyboard hooked up to clusters of coloured stage footlights. He would play the keys in time with the music, which gave the musicians effective moving shadows on the

Right:
Ultramarine liquid projection '69

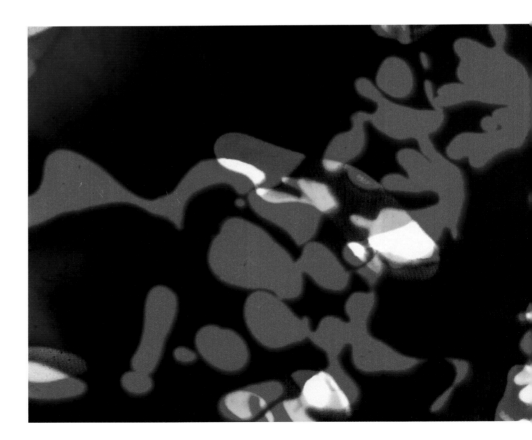

back-stage screen while front lighting the players. Olafur Eliasson used precisely the same technique at an art installation at the Tate exhibition in 2019.

Soft Machine and Mark Boyle performed again in '68 as part of the *Cybernetic Serendipity* exhibition where we also encountered John Cage and Iannis Xenakis. The latter introduced us to the connections between music, mathematics and architecture.

By '68, whilst still at school, Philip, Gus and I had adopted the name Ultramarine and were working semi-professionally for bands and colleges around London. Our meagre fees allowed us to build or buy more equipment as well as pay for petrol and drinks. We nearly bought a disused lighthouse lantern with huge cut-glass prismatic lenses from Laurence Corner, the big military surplus warehouse near Warren Street, but it weighed over half a ton and the idea of taking it home on the tube was beyond even our teenage idiocy. I've always had a bad habit of impulse buying great discounted deals.

There was an end of year *Summer Miscellany* in '68 at Dulwich College, where we did the light show for Phil Targett-Adams's first public appearance with school mates Bill and Ian McCormick with Charlie Hayward on drums (subsequently part of Phil's 801 band). The show ended with the school insignia being symbolically

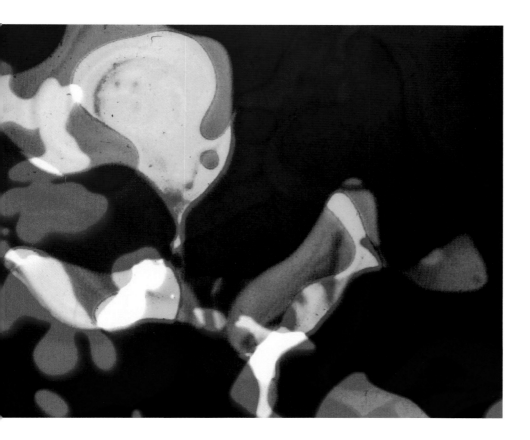

set alight while the band played The Doors' number *Light my Fire*. Phil had left Dulwich College without much love for his old school.

Our favourite venue, the Middle Earth Club, had become a centre for the underground music culture. An aggressive bust by the police put an end to it, but thanks to John Peel (the doyen DJ of 'underground' music), it re-emerged at the unconverted Roundhouse, a semi-derelict railway turntable building in Camden Town. In September '68, Jefferson Airplane and The Doors were to perform a double-bill, double-set all-nighter. After Friday school, we changed into our most colourful hippy gear of former military uniforms, tie-dyed collarless shirts and torn bandanas, and set off north. Arriving early, we bought our 30 shilling (£1.50) tickets on the door and then had time to explore the raw industrial structure that was to become the venue for so many amazing gigs. Before the building filled with fans, we had plenty of teenage hours to waste amongst the cast iron columns, red brick arches and hidden spiral staircases. The emptiness and hard surfaces resonated as we listened to the echoes of our own voices.

Jim Morrison, dressed in black leather, performed *The Unknown Soldier*, leaping, falling, then lying on stage and slowly speaking the lyrics as the Doors' music built to a searing crescendo. It needed only the simplest of follow spot lighting to achieve a dramatic impact.

The Airplane, by contrast, had brought their resident light show, Headlights, from San Francisco. They were miles ahead of anyone operating in the UK at the time, using multiple layering of photos, graphics, positive and negative patterns, all cleverly interwoven. They projected movie loops as well as overhead projector liquids in shallow glass dishes and strobe lights. This proved an explosive influence on our subsequent development of lightshow technique, inevitably aided by us being stoned.

We left Camden Town at seven in the morning and changed into our school uniforms on the train back to Dulwich in time for Saturday morning school. Not surprisingly, I fell asleep during an 'A' level English lesson and was rewarded with 100 lines to be written in detention.

'I must not fall asleep in class'.

I didn't care. Five decades later, I still hold clear, colourful visual memories of the most creative and sensuous lightshow London would witness for years to come. Whenever I hear the Doors' *Light My Fire* or the Airplane's *White Rabbit*, a silly grin crosses my face as I can almost feel I'm back, sitting on the cold, concrete floor of the Camden Town Roundhouse.

As our light show became better known around the club, college, and university circuit, we did shows for Mott the Hoople, Yes, Family, Jon Hiseman's Colosseum, T Rex and many other bands. Being non-musicians, it gave us the opportunity for involvement and not just as spectators. We had a lot of fun. For The Faces, with Rod Stewart and Ronnie Wood, we lit the support band, but when The Faces started their energetic and glamorous performance, we just used stage lighting since the psychedelic projection seemed irrelevant. Just after I had started studying Architecture at Nottingham University in the autumn of '69, our gang had a gig to light The Who. We did a great show for the warm-up band, and then before The Who came on to play their rock opera, *Tommy,* we asked Roger Daltrey what he wanted us to do to light them. His exact words were:

'Just put all the f...ing light on me, forget the psychedelic stuff.'

So that's what we did.

The best show we ever did was for Pink Floyd at Nottingham in late '71. By this time, we had become increasingly professional. To accompany *A Saucerful of Secrets*, we had sequenced specially-taken photographic slides of microbes and galaxies using the latest NASA pictures from space. We also projected our own macro-lens colour slides, all overlaid on exploding liquid slides with heat and chemical reactions. The expression of changes of scale and dimension was visually exciting and effective. The Floyd were playing their cosmic music and we helped to make the event a more complete sound and light happening.

After '72 Philip and I concentrated on becoming architects. The evolution of our light show had given us the opportunity for visual expression and active involvement in the music scene. The connections between the mathematics of musical scales integrated with light and diverse aspects of geometry seemed integral to an approach to architecture; how rhythm, chord structure, quiet space and tempo, patterns in sound and orchestration all relate music and architecture through shared mathematical concepts and even language. Sound, light, shade, colour, space, and form are all part of the artist's palette, whatever their medium. We were learning through practice the often quoted saying that 'Music is fluid architecture and architecture is frozen music.'

Gus was working for Midas building the top mixing desks for touring bands. He met Supertramp on some of their frequent visits to discuss mixing consoles. They asked him to join their crew as projection and mains man. He moved to LA and was on the road with Supertramp and then Delicate, their lighting and PA hire company, for more than 20 years. As we were to discover later, when friends move on, new doors often open.

4 INSPIRATION vs. POLITICS

The very first task in year one at Nottingham University School of Architecture was to build a series of different Pythagorean and polyhedral solid shapes (cubes, spheres, cylinders, tetrahedrons and, more ambitiously, octahedrons) out of different materials. Our bunch of new students set up in the well-equipped departmental workshop and positioned the shapes on a 600mm x 600mm base board. Each student's output was given a number and passed to another student to prepare a drawing of the model. This drawing was then given to another student to prepare a written description as precisely as possible. Then the written description was passed on to the next student who had to recreate the original model in the workshop. It was like an architectural game of Chinese Whispers.

Our first 'crit' of the year was then to reunite the original model with the end result of the communication exercise and judge how the starting point had changed through the process. Mostly the two were unidentifiable from each other. It was a clever initial exercise. We all had a lot to learn.

The lecture programme at Nottingham was broad-based and intellectually challenging. It felt like university should feel. The subjects we covered ranged from law, through structures and mechanical services, to history, landscape, philosophy, and sociology. Town planning and diverse world vernacular architecture particularly grabbed my attention.

I was not the first young architecture student to be enthralled by the fluid discipline of traditional Japanese tatami mat houses. In these buildings, defined by the rigorous application of mathematics and proportion, the room sizes are governed by a grid of different numbers of woven bamboo mats, roughly 1.8m x 0.9m in size. Fine timber-framed paper screens slide open and close, thereby allowing one room to merge into another. At once, they define rooms and then allow the whole footprint of a house to open into a flowing open plan. Each room is a distinct square or rectangle, with any storage element forming a continuous wall between rooms so that the perception of the space itself remains a perfect whole. The organisation of habitable pure mathematical shapes that flow from one to another represents one of the most highly evolved and sophisticated models of domestic design; the all-important sequence of small spaces that become the plan of a dwelling. The perimeter connection between internal rooms, via veranda to natural landscape or garden, set another fundamental concept adopted across contemporary western architecture. They are something of truly elegant resolution from which to learn.

The Barcelona Pavilion by Mies van de Rohe in 1929 was a high point of Modern Movement interpretation with the same abstract clarity of vision and fluidity of space and light as the Japanese house. I struggled to enjoy the mechanical

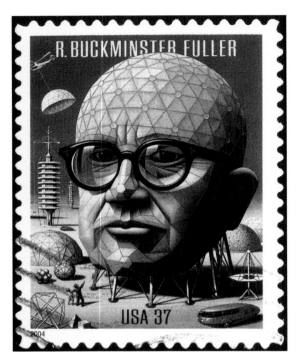

Above:
Buckminster Fuller inspired with his futurist structures alongside early warnings of climate change. His book, *Utopia or Oblivion* was essential student reading back in '69. I still have my original copy

pragmatism of Walter Gropius and the Bauhaus. This had created many elegant, simplified forms in reaction to the exuberance of Victorian decoration but regrettably those forms provided the potential of mass adoption for 'shoe box' architecture. This solved the politicians' problem of delivering housing to the legion of returning veterans of World War II, but in the hands of less-inspired architects, the reality was already turning into the ghettos of the urban dispossessed.

Even then, I was too much of a romantic to be swayed by that Brutalist approach to design. I was fascinated by the diversity of architecture that had grown out of extremes of climate and landscape; how man had learnt and adapted building materials and forms to create comfort anywhere on the planet. I became especially intrigued by the hot-dry-climate buildings and cities of North Africa and Iran, an interest that would soon inspire me to travel.

A curiosity for geometry led me to a fascination with the structure of flowers and the natural unique hexagonal shapes of snowflakes. I had a book with thousands of black and white microscope photos of snowflake patterns. Gus and I had taken transparencies of them and projected them onto flowers with hexagonal petal configurations as part of our light show.* Other influential books for me were *The Grammar of Ornament* by Owen Jones and *Arabic Geometric Pattern and Design* by J. Bourgoin. An ageing but totally engaging Buckminster Fuller gave a lecture at Manchester University which architecture students flocked to as if to a pop hero, to learn first-hand about his polyhedral dome structures. Fuller was a futurist thinker, inventor and architect who had conceived modular housing, the eco-efficient streamlined Dymaxion car. His super-efficient geodesic domes were the largest free-spanning structures in the world at the time. His latest book, *Utopia or Oblivion: The Prospects for Humanity* was in every student's shoulder bag and years ahead of its time in raising warnings about man-made climate change.

Keith Critchlow had just published his first book, *Order in Space*, which pushed the boundaries and meaning of geometry in ancient eras of architecture and had become essential reading for students searching for the spiritual root and historic meanings of the subject they were studying. I learnt that he was a lecturer at the Architectural Association school in London and contacted him. In my role as President of the Architectural Students Union, I arranged for him to come to the Peak District to set out the grid of lines that defined the megalithic stone circle at

---

* Keith Critchlow's seminal book *The Hidden Geometry of Flowers* (2011) defined the intuitive idea that we had played with when we projected pure mathematical shapes onto flowers with the same petal geometry. He died in 2020.

Arbor Low. His own name came from a less well-preserved stone circle in the same area. On 6 June '71, Critchlow, his friend Alan Hacker, the renowned clarinetist, and a gaggle of Nottingham students gathered in the early morning for the easy climb. Alan was in his wheelchair which proved a bumpy ride. Having walked the scene several times, we began our examination of the 4,000 year old circle of 50 large stones and fragments. Keith had sketched the ancient geometry onto an original drawing by Professor Alexander Thom which dated from 1911. Under Keith's directions and armed with big balls of string, pegs and mallets, we students set out the lines. From his wheelchair in the centre of the circle, Alan Hacker and two friends accompanied our intense antics with ethereal improvised music. The layout of the stone circle proved to be aligned to the movements of the moon and especially the sun's seasonal solstices and equinoxes. After lots of calculations, Keith's conclusion was that the elliptical 'Cove Stone' centrepiece was based on 8,15,17 Pythagorean paired triangles more than a millennium before the existence of the great Greek philosopher and mathematician. With the cosmic geometry completed, we lit a campfire barbeque and mused on man's search for understanding in the universe.

The hexagonal and octagonal patterns in Islamic geometry can extend in a variety of repeating shapes to infinity. To refine the precision of my drawing at differing scales, I would see how far I could sketch and extend these almost meditative patterns. Like snooker on a full-size table, the slightest inaccuracy of angle loses you the point. The next inevitable diversion was into three-dimensional geometry. *Polyhedron Models* by Magnus J Wenninger described the 75 known 'uniform' polyhedral structures. Starting with the Platonic and Archimedean solids, I built cocktail-stick models of each and ultimately graduated to the complex stellated dodecahedrons and icosahedrons.

Geometry was not the only idle obsession amongst new friends at university or long-standing friends in Dulwich. I often consulted the *I Ching* or Chinese *Book of Changes* as a way of finding answers to issues or ways to assist decision making. A selection of one out of 64 nuggets of ancient wisdom, or hexagrams, is made by throwing three coins. The one I most often seemed to choose was no. 56, 'The Wanderer'; while the most frequent phrase that arose within other hexagrams was 'Perseverance brings success'. Certainly, one thing that the lengthy timeframe of architectural projects has driven home to me over the years has been that I should do my best to temper my inherent impatience with perseverance.

A more flippant and humorous approach to undergraduate decisions was via *The Dice Man*, a popular paperback of the early '70s. Simply set yourself a series of options on what to do next, allocate each choice a number one to six, and then throw a die. The answer was rarely what one hoped for, but the game was the source of more laughs than life-changing actions. How strange and compelling youthful obsessions can be before the constricting realities of adult life crowd in and take over.

Below:
An evening playing with cocktail sticks

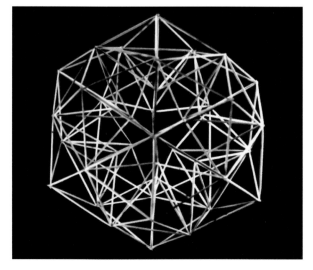

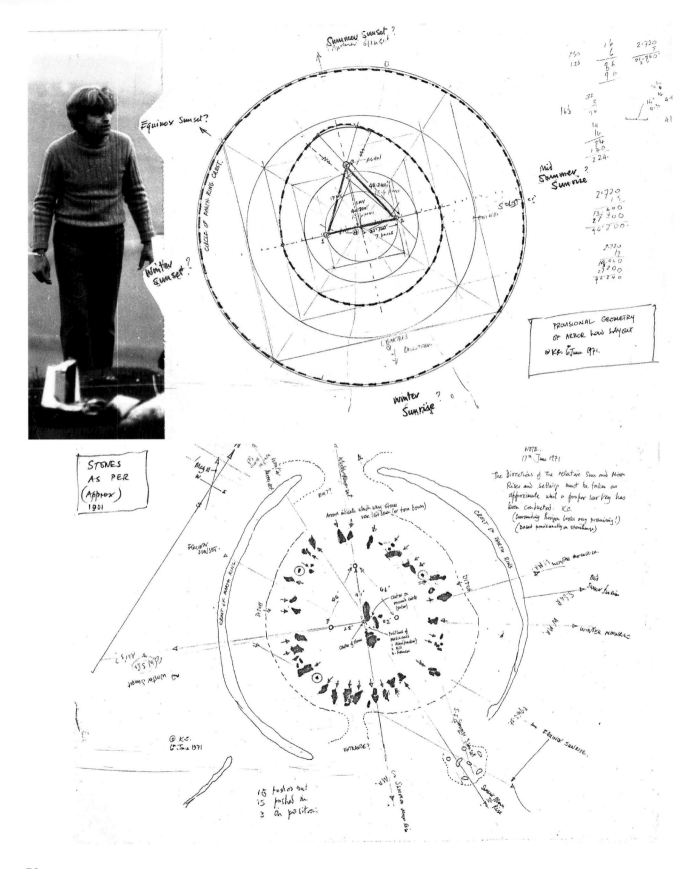

Opposite:
Keith Critchlow and the sketches he
made at Arbor Low on 6 June '71

Left and above:
Alan Hacker, clarinet, and student
architects at Arbor Low

Shortly after the Arbor Low outing, several of the Nottingham School of Architecture students headed to the RIBA conference in Bristol. For some long-forgotten reason, I had been elected as student representative on the RIBA Council. My speech was somewhere between a radical polemic on the future of housing and a clumsy reworking of 'The Emperor's New Palace'. It may well have irritated the more grown-up and experienced delegates, but after a genial conversation at the event, I was more than surprised to receive a long letter from Max Fry, who had collaborated with Walter Gropius and Le Corbusier. Over the following year, we corresponded about the future of architecture. He wrote about the need for patience and perseverance and how architecture is about long-term vision. To Fry, who had worked extensively in Africa, it was important to hold close geographical, cultural and social context in design. His letters inspired me and helped me retain the passion of my beliefs. It was an act of extraordinary generosity towards a critical young student.

Right:
A gift photo from Keith Critchlow. One of several complex polyhedral structures built for the AA Carnival

A key topic of the conference was the direction architectural education was heading, further highlighted by what appeared to be the imminent demise of the Architectural Association (AA). Internal political strife and external pressures to conform with university protocols had brought the notoriously maverick but influential school within weeks of closure. My school friend Simon Danischewsky had been accepted into the AA the year after I had started at Nottingham. Having heard that he was disillusioned about the future, I went to visit him. He had five weeks to go before his Part I final folio submission. With not much to show for three years' work, he was about to give up and was contemplating what to do next. I convinced him that he might as well make the most of these few weeks and that I would lend a helping hand. Over the following month, the two of us worked together to produce a substantial folio of drawings. He submitted it, and to our joint amazement, he passed RIBA Part I; elsewhere, this was equivalent to a three-year university level qualification. Whilst the AA has produced many high-profile alumni, I was flabbergasted by its lack of academic rigour compared to the standards of other schools of architecture.

Simon, ever the extrovert, was elected to organise the annual AA carnival, an event well known for its creative excesses in just about anything and everything. He asked Philip, Gus and me to help. Our light show exploits had moved into working with a group of contemporary dancers and the *Stockhausen Improvisation Band*. Although they looked like half a full orchestra, it was composed of a mixture of competent and not-so-able musicians. The improvised output was off the wall, though it all seemed like good fun at the time. We made plans for different 'happenings' in each area of the Bedford Square buildings, with all manner of music, performance, structures and lighting. It was almost called off at the last minute when someone suggested that the District Surveyor might visit to check regulatory compliance. We assumed that he might just condemn the slide we had installed from a first floor window into the basement courtyard two floors below. Most exciting was building a series of larger-than-life polyhedral structures completely filling some of the major rooms and a 16ft (5.5m) diameter rhombicosidodecahedron that we suspended across the internal courtyard. Keith Critchlow turned up to see what we were up to. He subsequently gave me an A2 mounted photograph of the one with the longest name before we hung it between the buildings.

The AA was one of the three schools that I applied to for Part II studies to complete my training in London. The interview was with a strangely constituted panel which included one of the cleaning staff. Given the mess that we had left after the carnival, I wasn't surprised when a letter of rejection arrived in the post. What I didn't mention at the interview was that two of us had done enough work in one month to pass their three-year course. Perhaps I should have done.

It was surprising that I had survived and completed Part I at Nottingham after the events of the spring of '71, when the big issue at English universities was the keeping of secret political files by departmental heads. Was England starting an era of McCarthyism? Was the keeping of political files a covert government directive or university policy? Students were suspicious and concerned, if not slightly paranoid.

Certainly, there was more than an air of dissatisfaction with traditional authority and the Establishment.

During a sit-in at Warwick University, secret files on political affiliations had been exposed and had become a focal issue across UK universities. To rebuff incipient unrest, the Senate of Nottingham University issued a statement saying that they did not keep political files on students. However, the girlfriend of one of our gang was working as a secretary in the philosophy department. She had taken a photocopy of a file and letter of reference written to the University of the Sorbonne, to which another friend, Nigel, was applying for his PhD. It was blatantly political and condemned any chance of him being accepted to study there. We knew that the university authorities were lying. How many secret files had been recorded and were hidden from us?

An Extraordinary General Meeting of the student union was called. Even though the Nottingham students were comparatively conservative, thousands turned up, the largest attendance ever. I was just one of many who were angered by the authorities. Trust, truth and fair play were part of my belief structure, even if not that of our university. Perhaps remembering my teenaged acting performances, I found the confidence to get up on stage and address this huge gathering. By late evening, after long open debate, the motion to occupy the Senate building was passed. We had to move very quickly since we knew that additional security staff had been drafted in, just in case.

A few of us ran to different sections of the grand classical Portland stone Senate building. I found a lower ground floor sash window unlocked, raised the lower sash, and as I rolled in, a security guard tried to ram it shut on me, ripping the metal buttons from my Levi's shirt and bruising my ribs. But I was in, and a few others were too. We opened the main front doors and hundreds of students poured up the steps and inside. The sit-in had begun. What now? Organise, prepare a statement of our demands, and issue a press release...

The next day some of the national press turned up and we recorded which papers were represented. The atmosphere was overwhelming. We were more than 1,000 disillusioned and angry young men and women for whom the authorities of our institution had denied us the truth.

When the early-edition newspapers arrived late on the second evening, I spotted a straight, short-back-and-sides guy that I knew from the Conservative Association sitting on the steps in tears. I sat beside him with my arm around his shaking shoulders.

'I've just read the *Daily Telegraph* piece on what we're doing,' he said. 'It doesn't recognise the facts, it's not true...they didn't even bother to come and see why we're here.'

After six days of rough sleeping, debate, and discussion amongst the student body and with the authorities, we finally left the Senate building, exhausted but with some hope of change during the Easter holidays. Some hope! Two days before the start of the summer term 11 of us received letters from the university summoning us to an interview. The evening before, we gathered in the student union bar, anxious and angry, but resolute that none of us would agree to whatever was put to us without reference to each other. A fretful night ensued, not knowing what awaited us.

Next morning, we met outside the chancellor's grand office to be called in one at a time at 15 minute intervals. Nigel went in first, ten of us waited. Half an hour passed, it seemed longer. Nigel emerged robust but pale. He had been asked to sign a legally binding document effectively giving up freedom of speech or gathering with others with any political intent. He had refused. One by one, we entered and sat alone opposite an intimidating line of university grandees. One by one, we emerged without putting pen to paper. We regrouped that afternoon and drafted our own written response reasserting our rights to free speech. We submitted it and heard nothing, but we knew we were 'marked'. Further sanctions and manipulation of files and performance seemed probable, if not inevitable.

Above:
Me aged 19.
Troublemaker?
Surely not!

That summer term, our second-year major project was to design a new house for the recently arrived departmental head, Professor John Tarn. Residential design was already my passion. When visiting school friends in their houses, I had observed the relationship between different family patterns and behaviours. I had noted how the context of a home both reflected and impacted on domestic lifestyle. The space was both an image of the family within and at the same time giving the potential for interaction. The quality of residential design could change lives. At the 'crit', architecture students pin up their drawings and orally present their designs to the tutors and their peers. Some were very good. Others displayed a youthful lack of vocabulary or experience of life. 'I'd like to live in Paul's house,' the new Prof. commented at the end. I finished that term on a high, having found, too, a man who would prove to be a much-needed ally.

Post second-year, summer vacation work was always a 'measured drawing', ideally of something that had not been measured before. Many people borrowed drawings from fifth year mates, traced them and then submitted them as their own. To avoid that practice, this particular year, the brief was more specific: the subject had to be something that had NEVER been measured. This suited me perfectly. I was going to North Africa in search of vernacular architecture; with the intention of finding something previously unmeasured, as the brief defined.

I had saved some cash for my trip from working on the concrete gang the previous year. Philip Vernon, my childhood and teenage mate was coming with me. We took the train from London and arrived in Naples on Thursday 29 July 1971 with £50 each. Our plan was to cross North Africa and reach Spain to meet up with his family and my girlfriend Susie in the second week of September.

5 MY GRAND TOUR

The train delivered us to Naples soon after midnight. A little apprehensive but unafraid or unaware of the realities of that city, we found a flatbed train truck down by the docks. A precarious bed for our first humid night in Italy. As soon as the sun had risen, we hitched to Positano, an elegant resort town that dramatically steps down the steep 45deg cliff to the Mediterranean Sea. The town was full of the international rich. Moving swiftly beyond the edge of town, we found a tiny cove beneath a vineyard and lemon grove and set up our discreet lightweight tent.

That night, we swam in the warm sea. As we dived off a rock into the water, it glowed with tiny electric phosphors like multi-coloured fireflies on the dark metallic surface. It was a magical night with stars sparkling above and below. When the sun woke us, we picked grapes and squeezed fresh lemons for our breakfast.

We moved on through a huge plain with high, sun-scorched hills to Padula. This cubist stone construction was the first hill town I had ever seen. I was riveted by its complex evolution, an intensity of tightly packed structures, steps and small courtyards; dense, with no wasted space. The cubic forms reminded me of Escher's early drawings of hill towns. The structures and interlocking forms were a perfect exemplar of the efficient use of the limited resource of land, teaching me first-hand that 'density' should not be confused with 'overcrowding'.

In Lagonegro, at the end of a mountainous single-track railway line, we found that a partially collapsed road bridge across the wide gorge had caused the isolation and decline of the ancient hill town economy; the impact of broken infrastructure is more costly than repair. Nonetheless, in the sole remaining restaurant, we had a gargantuan spaghetti and a litre of red wine for 500 lire; almost nothing, even then. Local musicians started to play, velvety robust red wine flowed bounteously and was generously shared; young and old danced and sang. A pretty French couple came over to us, we peeled off our English restraint and joined in dancing on the tables. The room resonated with laughter, staccato stomping, singing and more wine. Beyond midnight, as the lights from the old town faded, we stumbled back with our new friends to brew coffee. They played acoustic guitar and sang songs. We marvelled at the stars, the moon, the romance of the night, the joy of youth, and most of all, our freedom, living in the moment.

One lucky fast hitch took us to the toe of Italy and the ferry to Sicily. Inland, at the hill town of Castiglione, where a Norman castle topped steep and winding streets, we met a young lawyer called Charles de Montfort, whose surname was a direct reminder of the Norman conquest of the island in the eleventh century. Before that, the Moors had had control of Sicily and advanced many aspects of the sciences and agriculture to make it the granary of the Mediterranean.

Right:
Picturesque density:
An Italian hill town

We wound our way across Sicily, passing the otherworldly black lava landscape of Mt. Etna, then across the arid landscape to Enna, that sits defensively on top of a steep outcrop of rock commanding a narrow pass. Here we found a warm welcome and slices of pizza from huge trays for only a few lire. It's hard to imagine that for us, in '71, this was a novelty, as the first Pizza Express in the UK had a few years before opened in Soho

We took the boat from Palermo to Tunis, where the pervasive intermingled aromas of incense, mint, spices, bread, fruit, coffee, leather and jasmine all confirmed our arrival in a very different culture. Dense, tightly packed buildings defined narrow lanes, shade combatted the extreme heat. The contemporary architecture, by contrast, was a lesson in the daftly inappropriate. A black glass office tower in the middle of a traffic roundabout screamed of the kind of unsustainable building neither Philip nor I wanted to be part of in our careers ahead.

We soon abandoned hitchhiking as a Tunisian driver deliberately steered at us and we only narrowly avoided injury by leaping into a roadside ditch. Travel by train made safer sense. El Djem, though little more than a truck stop, just happened to have the third largest colosseum of the Roman world. The overwhelming scale dominated the empty desert landscape with no other visible memory of its imperial history. The arcades, arches and columns of the ancient structure were sculpted by time and extreme weather. The temperature topped 43 degrees Celsius in the middle of the day. Makeshift cafes served sweet tea while the locals played cards and noisily clacked dominoes. They were tough, as weather-worn as the old stones of the colosseum, and laughed a lot. At night, half the small population slept on mats along the side of the street. Little besides cacti grew, the prickly fruit tasted of melon with acidic seeds. The barking of dogs started and ended the day.

After two slow trains and an antique bus we arrived at Matmata, a destination we had chosen for its two-thousand-year-old troglodyte settlement. The land became hilly, scattered balls of tumbleweed rolled in the breeze, clumps of palm trees decorated the hard-cracked ground and patches of wind-blown sand. We had reached 33° N latitude. It seemed both exhilarating and unsettling to have arrived in a place so different from leafy green Dulwich.

Matmata was once entirely underground, consisting of hundreds of hidden pit dwellings dug by the Berbers sometime after the Punic wars, 200 years before Christ. In 1971, it had basic stores around a central square, with a few visible dwellings and *marabouts* shrines dotted across the hillside. We set ourselves down and chatted in broken French with the owner of a shaded café with no running water. Playing dominoes, we befriended some bright-eyed youngsters. One, who seemed to know everyone, elected to be our guide around the unique underground village.

The 'pit dwellings' are large cylindrical holes dug into the ground which then have a series of caves carved into the soft earth. Several metres below the baked surface, the soil is more yielding to burrow into. There are often two levels with linking steps cut into the earthen wall. Caves are dug all around the cylinder: a two-storey circular courtyard. If two dwellings are close to each other, they are linked by a tunnel that is widened out to house animals away from the burning sun. Our young guide politely introduced us, without presumption, to lots of families. Each courtyard is home for one or two families with three or four generations all living together. Every carved room has a particular function: kitchen, living, sleeping, weaving, with stores for animals and winter food. A pinkish ochre wash to the walls of the cylinder binds the surface to limit dust and glare. The insides of the caves are whitewashed including part of the floor, which is covered with colourful rugs, woven straw matting, or bare from centuries of use. The compacted earth is polished to a dust free glaze. The kitchens have propane stoves with precisely arranged niches carved into the walls in the shape of jugs, bowls, pots, and jars.

The rooms, being 12 or 15ft below the surface, are refreshingly cool. Water, served from earthenware jars, is as cold as if from a fridge. Without the benefit of electricity, these pit dwellings were the most environmentally comfortable rooms that we experienced in the searing heat of Tunisia. The deep courtyard shape provided continuous shade throughout the day. The Berber residents were proud of their highly evolved homes.

Apparently Matmata had only come to the attention of the authorities in 1967 after a very rare flash flood. Five years after our visit, Matmata was chosen as the setting for the home of Luke Skywalker in the opening scenes of the first *Star Wars* film. The place was from another planet, another time, another world.[*]

After visiting numerous hospitable families in these remarkable dwellings, we climbed to the top of a nearby hill to watch the sun go down over the desert landscape. We looked out over the village of man-made craters dug into the earth.

[*] Some years later scenes for Monty Python's *Life of Brian* were filmed in Matmata. By then, a pit had been converted to a hotel and the local population were deserting their sustainable courtyard pit dwellings in preference for new air-conditioned concrete block shacks that are unlikely to last a small fraction of their predecessors' two-thousand-year lifespan. Time marches on and 'progress' may prove to be a questionable reality.

Above:
Marabout.
Watercolour by the Author
Right:
Marabout with Phil for scale

Above:
Berber pit family

Below:
Matmata pit dwellings, plan view:
The first time a measured plan
had been prepared

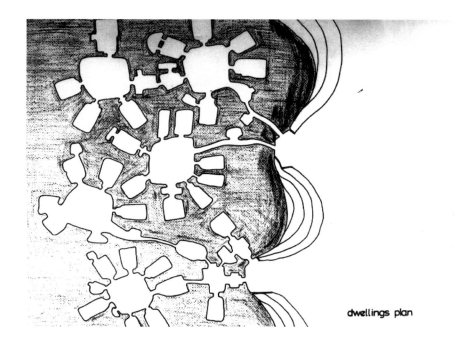

dwellings plan

43

The environmental logic of Matmata made the black glass tower in Tunis look as if modern man and his architecture had lost the plot.

Returning to the souk, we found most places shut except one small shop and a couple of cafes lit by paraffin lamps. Our simple supper was half a loaf of bread and two tins of sardines. The café owner gave us two thick straw mats to sleep on the paving outside his domain. The souk was watched over by a night guard. We felt completely safe as the Milky Way burnt spangled holes in the dark ceiling sky.

At 5 a.m., we were woken by Berber tribesmen and women setting out their stalls in the courtyard. We took tea with our café host, wandered to another hill to watch the sun rise at 6.30, then revisited some of the families that we had been welcomed by the day before. They were bemused by our pacing out approximate dimensions and preparing detailed sketches of their homes. This was to be part of my measured drawing college task. After all, the brief was to measure something never measured before and now I had found exactly what I had hoped for: ecologically sound vernacular homes that had passed the test of time.

On our wandering around the village, we had spotted a small shrine on high ground just above the cluster of craters. The base of this shrine was a buttressed square, rising to an octagon from which a dome sprang, the simplest version of the magnificent much larger mosques of Islam and cupolas of any creed. Extending from one side was a low rectangular storage room. We decided that this marabout would be ideal as a symbol of the life of the inhabitants as an addition to the dwellings for my measured drawing project. By 9 a.m. the heat was so intense that our only option was to retreat to the shade of the souk and chill out until the power of the sun receded. At three o'clock, we returned to the marabout and had just finished measuring the interior when a gaggle of colourfully dressed Berber women and 15 young children arrived and promptly proceeded with an outdoor class of arithmetic. This deeply symbolic female structure acted as a backdrop for their open-air school, while the side extension provided a store for educational equipment and drums. The afternoon class merged into a ceremony of drum music and a dancing procession around the village that lasted beyond the sunset.

After a supper of onions, tomatoes, pimentos, eggs and half a loaf of bread, we slept on our straw mats again, though somewhat less soundly after a shiny black scorpion scuttled out from under the shutter of the adjacent shop. The next day started at five o'clock again with both of us suffering very upset stomachs. Despite our discomfort, we marched off to the marabout to complete our measurement of the exterior. We finished our task just in time to catch the bus in scalding heat back to Gabes. The density of people, dust and torrid air was unbearable. One Berber woman was swaddling a baby girl who looked the dull green colour of death. Another woman began wailing as the bumping of the bus bounced her into labour. Her waters broke and the baby was born at the side of the road as we reached Gabes. We were glad to escape to the beach, release the tension of the bus ride and float silently in the sea for over an hour.

A visit to the Gabes *poste restante* found a blue airmail letter from Susie in England. It seems strange, now that we all have mobile phones, that this was how the postal service functioned 50 years ago and how people stayed connected in distant parts of the world.

The old wooden carriages of our next train to Metlaoui were like cowboy trains in wild west movies, only the ladder to the roof was missing. Our connection to take us to Tozeur was even simpler, sitting on a flatbed sideless wagon with our feet dangling towards the rail tracks as the steam engine dawdled southwards. It was the best possible way to marvel at a landscape such as we had never seen before. An immense flat desert descended from misty blue hills in the north and to the south, the borderland scrub of the Chott el Djerid, the largest of the Saharan salt lakes. As the sun began to set, the windblown sand turned into a fertile belt of palms: Tozeur, an oasis in the middle of nothingness. After the subtle monochrome tones of the desert, the contrast of sudden rich greens and bright oranges against a perfect blue sky was like seeing colour TV for the first time. Jumping from the planked deck of the antiquated freightwagon, we found a secluded spot on the edge of this desert haven and slept until woken by flies.

The day ahead was to prove an unforgettable and surreal experience. Walking through the beautiful, intricately woven, brick-patterned walls of the medina's narrow lanes, Philip recalled reading that Frank Lloyd Wright had visited to learn about the decorative possibility of brickwork. It felt good to be following in the footsteps of an architect hero. After a sweet milky coffee, we set off into the shade of the oasis, where sandy paths meandered through tall date palms bordered by cool irrigation rills. Our aim was to find the Chott, which lay, according to our detailed map, somewhere on the far side of this fertile paradise. Young boys herded goats and sheep passed us as we walked on, lost, for maybe an hour.

An old man, bent, withered, and almost blind, accompanied by his cheeky grandson, led us to his *jardin*. They opened a little straw hut and six more children appeared from nowhere, one carrying a rug for us to sit on. We were soon joined by the father of the children and the eldest son, Hassim. The liquid content of a large, round earthenware pot was poured into delicate bowls. This date palm sap has for centuries been tapped and fermented to produce a lethally strong alcohol. In his book *Fruits of the Earth* André Gide noted this concoction to be the most potent alcohol on earth. As we sat in a small circle in the shade of the straw shelter, shot after shot was poured. Hassim directed his younger brothers to bring fruit from the *jardin*. Figs, peaches, tomatoes, grapes and dates were piled on the rug, and we all feasted as more fermented date sap was imbibed. We contributed a loaf of bread, and I had some ciggies to share. Philip only smoked grass, Hassim smoked anything and passed a tiny *kief* pipe around the circle. The old man keeled over as if *rigor mortis* had hit him. Each of us that remained upright would periodically wobble and roll giggling onto our backs.

Somewhere around three o'clock, we set off towards the Chott. After cooling down by dipping our intoxicated heads in a shallow stream, we emerged from the palms to find two rows of simple shacks that the locals had optimistically named 'Paradise'. Beyond, we stumbled across open scrubland, not yet onto the saline surface of the Chott. Mirages of the sky ate into the earth, an out-of-focus illusion

Above:
The salt lake *Chott el Djerid*

Right:
Infinity in a floor

**Opposite
Top:**
Berber tent enclave, Tozeur

Middle:
Texture reduces glare:
A lesson to Frank Lloyd Wright

Bottom:
Oasis *Jardin at* Tozeur

46

of steely frozen water coming closer yet suspended in a distant haze. The path faded to nothing; silence resounded. With this immersion in spatial nowhere, time dissolved. There was just sand, salt, sky, sun and stillness. The crisp white crystalline crust of the salt lake crunched and sparkled in the sunlight, then cracked and sank below our feet. Beneath this unreliable surface skin, an unexpected layer of black, greasy mud and fetid oily water flowed into our footprints. Was the dried-up lake concealing slimy quicksand? We had come far enough. We stood motionless then carefully sat, anchored, as though we had arrived on another planet. A favourite sci-fi film, George Lucas's *THX 1138*, used a white infinity as a metaphor for an inescapable prison. Was this Nature or an unnatural apparition? Was the curvature of the earth a real horizon or imagined hallucination? Were we witnessing a majestic panorama or portentous future telling us to look inwards to our lives ahead? It was hard to grasp the emotions we felt being in this solemn and inhospitable landscape. How and why had we come to be here? A huge and bulbous red sun began falling towards its daily oblivion.

We began the long walk back towards the thin line of palm fronds that was 'Paradise'. Surely this was just another mirage. How long had we been walking? It felt like days or weeks, not just a few hours. Words from Dylan's *The Ballad Frankie Lee and Judas Priest* rang in both our heads. We sang out loud about how you should never be where you don't belong, laughing about how we shouldn't mistake Paradise for a home across the road, checking that we were still sane as our feet crunched on. Finally, back in Tozeur, we collapsed with mental, physical and experiential fatigue. Philip had a very bad stomach; our brains were spinning. It had been one of those rare days which marks some sort of turn in life; somehow too much to assimilate, even long afterwards.

We decided to move to the hills and recuperate across the Algerian border. Tebessa, an old Roman city on a high plain, was much cooler and there were even a few drops of welcome rain. We discovered a Roman bathhouse that was still functioning, and for a few dinars you could stay overnight. After the heat of the desert, it was invigorating to throw buckets of hot and cold water at each other, then dry off, lounging on oriental rugs and richly embroidered cushions. We slept in the same stone-vaulted room, lit by candles. The ancient construction was cleverly ventilated and comfortably cool.

On waking, Philip was seriously unwell. There was a small hospital near the bathhouse, so we set off early and sat waiting outside. After an hour, the doors were still firmly locked, and a watchful crowd was gathering. There were men and boys with amputated limbs, crutches and wooden legs; victims of the civil war not long ended. Women huddled together with small children and babies whose tiny stomachs were grossly distended with sickness and lack of nourishment. The need of others was evidently greater than ours, so we returned to spend a second recuperative day in the bathhouse.

We travelled on to Constantine, a gloomy, depressing concrete hole, with decaying bullet-damaged blocks of flats interspersed with mountains of used car tyres, repair shops and grim cafés. It was good to get away and even better, after a short hitch to Setif, to stop in a roadside tearoom and meet Ed, a Kiwi mechanic who had a *Deux Chevaux* Citroën that he'd picked up for $50 in Egypt. He invited us to join him all the way across the bumpy Northern plateau of the Sahara to the far side of Algeria, a very long hitch. The map showed occasional place names and road intersections. As we approached each one, we would speculate on what might appear. Mostly, it would be just another track appearing to go from nowhere to nowhere else. Some were marked only by a single telegraph pole with a dangling disconnected cable. Hours passed without change in the barren landscape. The intense heat forced itself through the open windows, a cloud of dust swirled behind us.

The terrain became more contoured as we drove towards the coast, rising through the Massif de l'Ouarsenis. Here the land was more fertile, with sweeping wheat fields and more colour in the scenery: rich red earth and pale terracotta, variations of grey and even olive green. Berber encampments arose, their dozens of expansive tents magnificent with broad stripes of earthy undyed tones of brown and grey, reflecting the forms and colours of the hills. Their flocks of sheep and goats appeared to be in the thousands, while hundreds of horses and camels explained their ability to migrate and trade across this vast landscape.

Reaching Mostaganem on the Mediterranean coast, we enjoyed a well-cooked French meal of steak and ratatouille. Two bottles of red wine, courtesy of generous

Ed, seemed an appropriate celebration. Ed took a room above the restaurant, while Philip and I headed off to the end of the beach. We liked sleeping under the stars, and it was free.

Eighty kilometres in the back of a truck brought us to Oran, a lively city which seemed a happy mixture of Arab and French, urbane and sophisticated after our experiences of the last weeks. As evening approached, we set off to find a place to sleep. What we hadn't realised was that we had stumbled into a major Algerian army base. Mile after mile of high barrack walls lined our route. Eventually we reached an open area of mortar-cratered ground and crept into one of the hollows, fully clothed in the cocoon of our sleeping bags. But as we were drifting asleep, an officer in full-dress uniform, peaked cap, medals, golden epaulettes and sword appeared on the ridge above us and shouted that we must leave. We were too exhausted to move. Now he unleashed his sword and began to mime a pirate-like attack by potential villains. Holding back laughter at this pantomime performance, we held out our passports for inspection. He seemed reassured and told us we could remain, on condition that we moved directly under the glare of his watchtower searchlight.

Over the border into Morocco the next day, we caught a grubby bus to Fes. This great medieval city was one of the first in the world to house over a million people. Its medina was bursting with every craft, food, produce and activity conceived by mankind. Most striking were the colourful rooftops with skeins of dripping dyed wool in the brightest colours of the spectrum, dangling from a cat's cradle of ropes stretched between tall poles. Set against the dense white cubist metropolis with the grey blue haze of the mountains beyond, the intensity of paint box dyes was unforgettable.

Our weary bodies told us to miss out on Marrakesh, so regrettably we turned northwards. At Moulay Idriss, the burial place of the first king of Morocco, we were fortunate to be allowed to visit the shrine with its impeccable geometric faience mosaics (it had not long been open to non-Muslims). The packed hill town structures were not dissimilar to the fortified Italian towns we had seen at the start of our journey. What had become evident was that historic built forms were determined by climate, landscape, defence and the efficient use of land. Society's present-day fear of the word 'density' had not caused historic city builders to waste the precious resource of land.

In Barcelona ten days later, we were met off the train by Philip's father Russell and my beloved Susie and driven at last to a comfortable rented villa with hot running water, a pool and comfy beds. Two long-haired dishevelled hippies slept like babies.

We were both unwell. Even though I had replaced my tattered canvas shoes with leather sandals in Morocco and had torn up my spare shirt to bandage the open sores on both my feet, they refused to heal. A fresh graze on my arm quickly turned septic. Hitching a week later to Paris with Susie, I started hallucinating in our tiny attic hotel room. She realised I was seriously ill. We flew home and she drove me to our family doctor in Dulwich village, but he failed to recognise, in this sickly tattered hippy, the clean-cut Davis boy he had often treated over the previous fifteen years and slammed his front door in our faces. We made it up the hill to the East Dulwich Hospital, where a receptionist explained that the emergency department had closed several years before. Luckily, a passing nurse saw that I was close to collapse and spinning a waiting wheelchair, caught me before I fell. A few minutes later, I was tucked up in the only available bed in a geriatric ward, where Susie waited all night at my bedside.

It wasn't until morning that a blood test confirmed that my infection had turned to gangrene in my left leg. The doctor prescribed intramuscular penicillin and morphine, unsure as to whether he should amputate my foot to stop the malignant poison spreading through my body. Luckily for me, he decided to wait and see if the penicillin took effect. Four times each day for 14 days a nurse would inject alternate buttocks with the viscous fluid, paralysing the whole of the attached leg. Morphine saved the day. By the third week, I was able to walk with the benefit of two intact feet. The worst was over, and the morphine dose was gradually reduced to avoid cold turkey.

Unable to return to the architecture course at Nottingham, I convalesced at home and eagerly drew up the measured drawing of the Matmata marabout and pit dwellings, which I put together with photographs, a watercolour painting, and a bold, meticulous, colourful Islamic geometric pattern cover.

On my delayed return to the university for the final year of Part 1, I submitted my A2 size document to Dr Norman Summers, head of architectural history. He had been deposed as acting head of department by the arrival of Professor John Tarn and was evidently bitter at his loss of status. One of the old school of university grandees, Dr Summers had not forgotten my involvement in the senate sit-in. When the Measured Drawing results were posted on the student notice board, I was incensed to read that I had an 'F' for fail. Dr Summers was political point-scoring. With continuous assessment as the basis of the course, I would have to repeat a year, which apart from the ignominy, meant I would not be eligible for a student grant or fees being paid. Passes, meanwhile, had been given to friends who had traced and represented objects measured and submitted multiple times before. This was 'not cricket' and seriously upset my sense of fair play.

I went to see Dr Summers in his study, but he was not present. Fortunately, my submission was. Removing it, I drove to Professor Tarn's house. He was home and welcomed me in. Without mentioning my Fail marking, I gave him a copy of the brief that stipulated the task to measure something 'never previously measured'. After he had read the brief, I presented him with my submission and asked if he would mark it as a response to the brief and told him that I would abide by his decision. Then I left. I imagine he had guessed what was going on. Next day, he called me to his office and congratulated me on the originality of the work and awarded the work an 'A'. I never spoke to Dr Summers again, nor he to me.

I left Nottingham at the end of an intense third year of study with a first degree in architecture and no regrets.

6   TWO HOUSES

My wife Susie (we married in October '72) was always very supportive about taking trips to seek out places and buildings that I wanted to learn from. One such excursion was to Glasgow, the city where Charles Rennie Mackintosh had flourished at the end of the 19th century and first decade of the twentieth. Susie and I set off on a pilgrimage to find as many of his buildings as possible, having marked them all on a map of the city. We took afternoon tea in the Willow Tea Rooms and spent the next whole day in the School of Art, riveted by the originality of design, materials, and every detail from staircase balustrades to pendant light fittings. Whilst the School of Art is impeccably rooted in its Scottish urban landscape, the influence of historically closed but newly opened Japan was obvious.

Having scoured Glasgow for Mackintosh's less-known projects, we set off in search of Hill House in Helensburgh, an hour northwest of the city at the mouth of Gare Loch on the river Clyde as it meets the sea. It was late afternoon as we drove down a wide boulevard towards the water, I screeched to a halt, unnerving Susie.

'What's the matter?'

'It's over there, to our right and back up the hill.'

'How can you tell? We've never been here before.'

'Trust me, I can sense it.'

Two minutes later we pulled up outside the ornamental gates of Hill House. An elderly gatekeeper approached us and introduced himself as Duncan. He told us the house was about to close but would be open the next day at noon. We asked him if knew anywhere we could stay the night.

'You can stay here if you like.'

We couldn't, he went on, sleep in Mr and Mrs Blackie's famous 'white bedroom', but we were welcome to stay in the room next to it. He would even bring us breakfast in bed with his homemade whisky marmalade.

It transpired that the house had recently been acquired by the Royal Incorporation of Architects in Scotland. Duncan, a retired borstal boarding house master, had delightedly taken the job as caretaker. He was even pruning the standard roses to the elegant shapes in the original stylised design of the Mackintosh drawings and placing the correct colour, pink-to-mauve blooms in the various rooms. He told us he found peace in the beauty of the house after his tough life with troubled boys. Susie and I explored the place thoroughly and imagined being house guests of Walter Blackie, the publisher who had been the original client.

When Mackintosh was commissioned, he went to stay with the family to learn how they lived. Then he designed the house around their lifestyle. The plan came first, the exterior forms were a subsequent expression of the plan. This is the right

Opposite:
Fallingwater:
Architecture in conversation with nature.
Photograph: Elisabeth Kendall

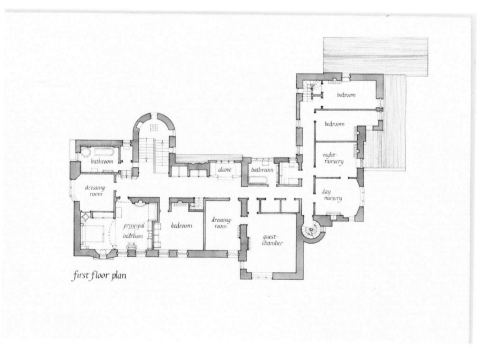

first floor plan

ground floor plan

Hill House, Helensburgh, Dumbartonshire
1902-1904, architect : C.R.Mackintosh

sequence in my opinion. So many buildings are designed starting from the outside and then have the internal plan forced to fit. This rarely works with houses or residential buildings. The plan is the part people live in and should come first. It's an iterative process, but if the plan doesn't work then it's unlikely to be an enjoyable place to live. Over the years, I've seen too many flat and house plans that just don't work for people or their lifestyle. You can't even furnish them logically. Mackintosh's design strategy for domestic buildings was a useful one to absorb.

Walter Blackie's study is the first room off the outer hall, placed there so that if he was meeting someone on business, it didn't intrude on the family. The living room has a winter end and a summer end. The summer end opens to the garden. The winter end has a fireplace and a wide bow window. Under the chest-high sill is a long, slender drawer for a telescope, just the right place to stand with a warming fire and watch for shipping passing in the windy distance.

The kitchen has simple, dark-green stained, wooden joinery base and wall cupboards; 70 years on it, could have been installed yesterday. The hall is an elegant sequence of simple spatial events. The first entry level connects to the study/library, cloakroom and to the side, a billiard room and gentleman's den. Then it contracts as four steps lift you to the main hall, accessing the living and dining rooms. At the narrowing point, four steps rise back towards the front door, then turn 90 degrees. The stair rises and turns within a turret to arrive at the first floor landing. Every inch had been designed in detail: the balustrade, the carpet, the light fittings.

The famous principal bedroom is a masterpiece. Generous but not huge, it has a series of defined uses within one room. The bed space is quite narrow, the ceiling above is vaulted and creates an intimate embracing alcove. A small bow window allows light into this space, whilst capturing a view of the sea from the bed. Shutters provide protection from the winter weather. The main body of the room has exquisitely decorated 'his and her' wardrobes with art nouveau motifs and inlaid enamel mosaic squares, separated by a ladderback chair. The nursing corner is a delightful high-backed banquette adjacent to the fireplace for warmth. Opposite this are the dressing table and nightstand. It is surely one of the finest, most elegant, yet specifically liveable principal bedrooms ever designed. It was a joy just to be there. Even if we couldn't sleep in this delightful space, it was a privilege to be in the next room.

We dined at a local hotel down by the nearby loch and returned in darkness to find Duncan had left a couple of drams of whisky for us on the hall table. Next morning, he arrived with a huge white-painted wooden breakfast tray with a pink rose on it, toast, his promised marmalade, boiled eggs, and a pot of leaf tea.

Some years later in '81 Susie and I made a tour of America, mostly staying with friends. A $99 TWA ticket flew us from New York to Cleveland to St Louis, Seattle, San Francisco, Los Angeles and back to New York. It was amazing value even then. Luke, our first born, was just under two years old, so he flew for free.

In Cleveland, Ohio, we stayed with Ralph, who was a photographer we'd met with Supertramp in L.A. He had never visited Frank Lloyd Wright's famous Fallingwater as it was more than a four-hour drive away. We talked him into making the trek. In the dense woodland southeast of Pittsburgh in Pennsylvania, Edgar and Liliane Kaufmann had owned a plot of land next to a waterfall. Their son had been working as an intern with Wright when his career was flagging in 1934. On a visit to see him, they met Wright and decided to commission a house in their favourite countryside setting.

In the early '80s, you parked easily and walked up through a woodland path. Enveloped in trees with leaves of all colours, one of the most imaginative of all private houses of the 20th century emerges. A series of oatmeal-coloured cantilevered planes glides out over the layers of grey rock that channel the succession of waterfalls that are Bear Run. The dramatic horizontal planes are held in place by a strong vertical core of stacked rough-cut grey sandstone sliced into by a three-storey gridded window with autumnal red-brown frames. On the inside, the staircase is a journey. At each half landing the view changes. Looking outwards, there is a rising perspective of the waterfall and woods beyond; looking inwards, the balustrade becomes a metal-framed bookcase set within wall surfaces of varied textures. It is more than just a staircase, the delight of movement within it is an example of architectural spatial genius. From the outside, the house is as captivating as the architectural picture books show it to be, somehow even more rooted in its natural setting than I had imagined. It is not a large house. It is perhaps the most spectacular country cottage in the world.

The plan is more abstract than Mackintosh's work and yet carries a similar clarity of plan organisation around family lifestyle. At entry level, there is one expansive living space, a kitchen, and a staff room. On the level above, there is a master bedroom and a guest bedroom. The top floor has a third bedroom and a study that is more of an eyrie. It is the extended floating terraces and thin planar brise-soleil that give the house such dramatic jutting presence, while connecting inside to outside.

The main ground floor living space (35 x 45ft) has a surprisingly low ceiling. The raw, rough-hewn stone floor flows from outside the entrance, unbroken, through the main room onto the two huge terraces. The ceiling and floor combine to give an embracing cave-like intimacy. The main living room is a series of spaces within a single room. There is built-in seating, a dining table, and writing desk. The hearth is formed from carved boulders, part of the original rock formation. Most remarkable is the glass pod raised above the floor that opens to give access to a suspended, open-tread stair leading down to the waterfall below.

Everywhere you look, the inside links to the outside, the rocks, water and trees. The limited palette of materials, and the abstraction of structure and spatial dividing walls is reminiscent of a late Ben Nicholson painting. *Falling Water* is the ultimate resolution of plan and exterior form. Comfortable to live in, it is a perfect reflection of lifestyle and a sculptural form that is in harmony with its romantic natural woodland setting.

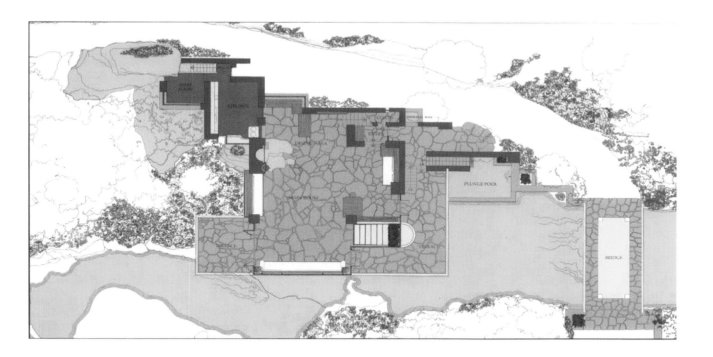

Above:
Falling Water site plan.
A plan as abstract painting
© Fallingwater.org

Mackintosh and Wright were inspirational for me, and have remained so, especially for these two remarkable houses. My architectural purpose has always been to design homes that are enjoyable to live in: the nuance of plan, the sequence and balance of spaces, small or large. The placement of windows is so essential for light and aspect. A door in the wrong place skews the layout of furniture; in the right place movement and use are enhanced. Both these sensitively designed houses use forms and materials that sit comfortably in their landscape. They each speak to their natural context.

These two great architects found influences in diverse cultures from around the world and integrated them into their work. They did this while creating buildings that are individual, connected to their setting and, like the best vernacular architecture, enhance man's intervention in nature. They resolve concept, vision, and detail in the search to design spaces that are a joy to live in, homes not just brilliant houses. In doing so, these buildings become timeless; they are architecture not fashion. Experiencing them at first hand offered profound lessons.

7 FORTY DAYS BY LADEN CAMEL

Susie and I had lent the little house in Kingston that we had bought for just over £11,000 to our friend Miranda, and now were nearing the end of a two-month journey around most of what had been ancient Persia. Before setting off, I had learnt 50 words of Farsi to help us during our trip. We had been traveling through spectacularly varied landscapes. Across Cappadocia and Eastern Turkey, passing Mount Ararat en route to Iran and the ever-distant, snow-capped Elburz Mountain range rising above both cultivated and arid high plateaus. We had visited majestic, complex cities with their baked and mud brick buildings merging and emerging from the mirage of desert sand and dust; we had revelled in towns built of one material, the desert clay, monochrome, interspersed with moments of outrageously vibrant *haft-rangi* (seven colours) ceramic cladding. These glazed-tile and mosaic-wrapped walls, minarets and domes emerge from the sandy city surface like gardens in the sky. The seven musical notes are represented by seven colours, that envelop entire sacred buildings, as if in vibrant ceramic sound.

Iran is home to some of the most highly evolved vernacular architecture that enabled comfortable settlement within one of the most extreme inhabited climates. Daily temperatures sometimes reached 54 degrees Celsius and higher. One dramatic and effective feature that provided comfort were the tall, decorated brick *badgir* (wind towers) with silhouetted slots to catch the prevailing wind. These filter, humidify and duct cool air around the rooms of the houses. For centuries, they have provided impressive, natural, renewable energy air conditioning. Courtyard dwellings, the predominant built form, provide shade, privacy and urban density. They are almost always enhanced with a crystal-clear pool of water to calm the spirit, humidify the dry air and irrigate the garden setting.

Water in Iran was supplied by a system of *qanats* (underground tunnels), each as much as 40 miles long, dug deep and gravity-fed from the ground-bearing aquifer close to the mountains, then channelled onwards to arable land thus creating the potential for settlements, towns and cities. These feats of irrigation engineering date from the seventh century BC and ultimately spread east to China and west to Morocco. They were excavated with such surveying precision that one would expect laser technology to have been requisite. Travelling around Iran was intense, full of wonderful experiences of people and places. Gardens were planted with roses, irises, oleander, jasmine and aromatic herbs and shaded by albizzia, mulberry, oak and cypress trees. We explored cities, towns and villages, and in the wide landscape saw nomadic tribesmen and women coaxing huge caravans of horses, camels, sheep and goats. We wandered round aromatic bazaars bursting with carpets, ceramics, spices, intricate metal and woodwork. These colourful bazaars were constant reminders

Opposite:
Gonbad-e Qabus.
A brick rocket, 61m tall,
built in 1006

Right:
Borujerdi House, Kashan.
Exemplary courtyard design for
climate control

of Iran's place on the Silk Road that has joined East and West through centuries. Everywhere the tapping and clattering of craftsmen at work resonates, the scent of spices and huge bundles of mint and coriander fill the air. Bubbling samovars distribute sweet tea in delicate *chai* glasses served on small round trays of polished patterned brass. The form of these bazaars with sales stalls at ground level then a room over and lit from above were to be carbon-copied at the Burlington Arcade in 19th century London. Some of the Persian bazaars stretch for miles. Iran is a country overflowing with poetry, discussion of the stars and hospitable intelligent people. The exquisite miniature paintings that depict all the romance and colour of Persian civilisation seemed ever present.

The only dark moments occurred when we discovered that we were under surveillance by SAVAK, the Shah's secret police, who were intent on restricting freedom of movement and visas for young 'radicals' such as we had befriended. There were occasions when I narrowly avoided arrest by uniformed officials. I naively photographed an ancient shrine within a military compound and was then swiftly surrounded and held at gun point. By sleight of hand I managed to give a blank film cassette to the indignant military policemen, while keeping the whole roll of exposed film in my other hand.

Our journey had taken us overland from Istanbul, through the lunar landscapes and cave dwellings of Cappadocia, alongside the River Euphrates where we learned to tickle trout with Bulgarian truck drivers. The only real problem on the way had been how attractive Susie was to several Turkish men whose technique was to feign friendship and try to get me drunk on *raki*, the locally distilled, potent *eau de vie*, so that they could then molest Susie. In one village café in the middle of nowhere, we had been eating and drinking with a bunch of welcoming locals. It had been a friendly and light-hearted evening. There were no rooms to stay at the café and no hotel nearby. Ali, who had been showing us photos of his wife and children, insisted that we return to his home with the promise of a comfortable bed and ensuite bathroom. Following him along an unlit lane, we eventually arrived at his house beyond the edge of the village. But when we entered it was devoid of the promised family. Declining more *raki* and his advances on Susie, we retired to the bedroom, locked it and wedged a chair under the door handle. Ali prowled in the hall asking to be let in. This went on for over an hour and became increasingly threatening. The best solution seemed to do a runner. Climbing through the bathroom window and escaping into the night, we walked till dawn.

By comparison, arrival in the Northwest of Iran proved delightful. Tabriz was genuinely friendly, and a refined cuisine was available to us even on our modest budget. For me, ever the architecture addict, there were vast domes under restoration to be entranced by. It was fascinating to see the inventive cantilevered formwork support systems and spiral herringbone brickwork that might have inspired Brunelleschi when he was building the Duomo in Florence. The brick dome of Hagia Sophia in Istanbul had been completed in AD 537 using brick and a thick mortar almost like modern concrete. Its span is 33 metres, but it is the shape of a shallow dish, not unlike the Pantheon in Rome.

Soltaniyeh in Northwest Iran, completed without buttresses in 1312, was the next largest brick dome in the world at the time. Standing in majestic isolation, it has a taller, egg-shaped profile that is akin to the Duomo. History records that

Left:
Mausoleum of Öljaitü, 1302-12:
Inspiration for Brunelleschi?

Brunelleschi disappeared from Florence for almost two years after winning the Duomo competition in 1418. The competition required a top to the already completed walls that had no buttresses. At the time, he was not alone in not knowing how his design could be built, but was secretively working on an engineering solution. My theory is that he travelled to Persia to learn from the master dome builders of his time. His radical solution to create the taller profile of the Duomo entailed using spiral stone *voussoirs* on the inner shell and herringbone brickwork for the outer dome, similar to Persian engineering which appears to defy gravity. He also invented or introduced into Europe a radically faster crane technology with a gearing and clutch mechanism that trebled the speed for lifting stone blocks to a height. Given the huge size of Soltaniyeh, speed would also have been a crucial factor, as the herringbone brick format requires nimble skill.

Next, we travelled southeast to Tehran to stay with David, an English professor, and his family. David kindly introduced us to some of his ex-students and Karim became our guide. The capital city was scarily fast with the most dangerous driving we had ever experienced. Every traffic light was like the starting grid for a saloon car grand prix with ten cars abreast. At major junctions, tall concrete plinths displayed the mangled wrecks of crashed cars as a warning against dangerous driving. They seemed to have little effect; every outing resembled a scene from *Mad Max*. Like all large cities, the place had its own specific energy, but it was hard to get under its skin. We got lucky with people to meet and places to stay before preparing for our main trek. Karim was a graduate from the University of Tehran, where he had been marked as a radical. He had studied Spanish and was a proficient classical guitarist. Passionately keen to visit Spain, he had frequently applied for and been refused a visa to travel there. One evening, he took us for dinner at an edge-of-city garden restaurant. On arrival, he explained the reason for his choice of remote venue. A cousin that he had not seen for years had arrived unannounced from Tabriz where we had last been. He was convinced that this cousin was an informer for the Shah's secret police, and that we and he were being followed. He poured out his heart about the suppression of dissidents and how he longed to travel beyond his homeland. The ultimate irony was that the eventual fall of the Shah would come at the hands of the conservative mullahs and disenfranchised nomads, not the progressive educated young adults.

We visited some friends of Karim, a Muslim family who lived in a Parisian format flat in Tehran, where the layout took no account of Muslim family structures and behaviour. The flat plan might have been fine for a French family but was simply wrong for most extended families in Iran. With just two bedrooms, one was used for all the women, the other for the men. What had been designed as a dining room had to be used by the married couple with no access to a bathroom. The only place to eat was on the floor in the hall. The importance of understanding, listening and designing appropriate solutions for differing cultural lifestyles was glaringly obvious.

After a week of meeting people and looking round the city, we set off northwards to Gorgan beside the inland Caspian Sea to visit the unique funeral tower at Gonbad-e Qabus. It is 61-metres tall, resembles a brick rocket and had survived countless earthquakes for over a 1,000 years. The Persians were the masters of building with brick and Gonbad-e Qabus is an exceptional edifice. We then travelled by bus eastwards along the Turkmenistan border to Mashhad, a shrine city which was rich with turquoise and travellers. Susie put her knowledge of gemology to good advantage, and we had fun bargaining and buying the most beautiful unmounted polished turquoise stones that either of us had ever seen. Mashhad was best known as the last stop before Afghanistan where most young hippies headed in search of the finest hash that money could buy. Unconventionally, we turned instead to the south and took the Old Silk Road across the two deserts of central Iran. Our historic map described the route as '40 days journey for laden camels'. Passing ruins of ancient forts and caravanserai, we crossed mile upon mile of sun-parched landscape until we reached Tabas, then a small watering point midway across the desert. The heat was extraordinary. The dusty street burnt through our shoes, and we skipped into a tiny café, the only source of shade to be had as the sun hung directly overhead. After 11 a.m. no one ventured outside. There were no buses, so we would have to wait for a truck at dawn the following morning. Stuck for the day, I asked in my best Farsi if we could rent a room for the night. Something got lost in translation. No rooms were available for the night, the café owner told us, though we could see that there were plenty of empty rooms. Unfazed, we decided to just rest; it was too hot to move or debate. At about 6 p.m., our host showed us up to the roof. There, along a series of brick barrel-vaulted roofs were a line of metal framed bedsteads; one straddling the summit of each vault. That's where one sleeps at night under the stars. In the morning, when we had first arrived, we should have asked for a room for the 'day'. At night, the interiors reradiate the stored heat of the day and are hotter than a sauna. Tabas is where the American helicopter hostage release venture would crash out some years later. I have often wondered what the locals we met would have made of that bizarre incursion into their remote landscape.

We woke early as the sun started to light the horizon. Soon after, two oil trucks arrived and agreed to take us to Yazd. We endured endless hours of bumping and roasting in a 1950s truck cab through the dessert, our mouths and noses full of the taste of diesel and the grit of wheel-blown sand. Eventually, our reward was the spectacle which began to emerge on the horizon through the shimmering heat haze. To traders in centuries past, taking the Silk Road between China and the Mediterranean, Yazd must have been a revelation, a substantial city rising out of the desert in the same colour as the earth, all monochrome sandy brick, except for the exaggerated tall, glazed-mosaic pinnacled city gates visible as markers from a distance through the wavering heat mirages. Within the city walls, clusters of minarets and domes pointed to the sky, a wash of faded daytime azure, at night a Prussian blue blanket as a backcloth to a brilliant ceiling of stars. In 1974, it seemed unchanged from the days of the camel trade, a living piece of archaeology. As a reincarnation of the past, still thriving in the 20th century, it was an architect's feast. The continuous baked-brick vaults that enclosed the linear bazaar and craft workshops roofed over and shaded the surface of the city. These were punctuated by arcaded courtyards

Opposite:
Magnificent minaret markers for travellers in the desert, Yazd

Left:
Tabas Courtyard

Middle left:
The Old Silk Road to Yazd

Below left:
The only way to travel

each with a refreshing pool of water mirroring the sky and deep green trees. On the rooftops, you could walk for hours across a moonscape of sculpted shapes and small glazed pyramids that let shafts of light into the occupied spaces below. In my enthusiasm to capture the domed roofscapes on film, I was chased unceremoniously by local policemen back to ground level Apparently, the joined-up rooftops were used by robbers at night.

Susie and I revelled in the brilliant colours of newly made, hand-knotted carpets, seeing their true vividness before they were deliberately faded for western taste. When they are not draped in bright sunlight to achieve export 'vintage' appearance, the rugs, kilims and fine loom carpets cover the lanes through the market and encourage continuous foot, bicycle and moped traffic. Susie and I developed a taste for the sweet tea, served from tall filigree-embossed samovars in gold decorated glasses. The aromas of sheaves of fresh coriander and mint filled the air. It could have been the setting for a movie like *Indiana Jones*, or even the bar at the end of the universe in *Star Wars*. It did seem like another time on another planet.

Opposite:
Baked brick vaults shade the linear bazaar, Yazd

Below:
Cool, colourful bazaar interior

We travelled onwards in unbearable heat to Isfahan, the Florence of the Near East, once one of the most beautiful and sophisticated cities on Earth. Isfahan was amongst the first cities to have a population of a million people. I had studied its form before travelling and found it totally absorbing whilst staying there. Years later, I would lecture on its structure as an exemplar of a successful city. London, New York, and many other great trading cities have essentially the same urban structure, but Isfahan was one of the first. By clustering trades together with all the requisite support services, they created critical mass and customer footfall. Looking at any successful city one finds these groupings: Harley Street for medical, The Inns of Court for barristers, Charing Cross Road for bookshops, Gerrard Street for Chinese food, Oxford and Bond Streets for fashion; the list goes on, in London and elsewhere. The more you look the more you see. In Isfahan, the sequences of spaces continue interlinked and flowing across miles of the city, whether they be for trade, manufacture, social interaction, educational, residential or sacred worship. They advance through covered and open

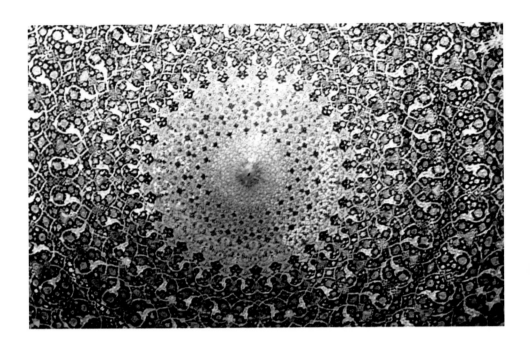

Right and below:
Mosque of Sheik Lutfullah:
Interior and exterior of Dome

lanes, magnificent domed halls, intimate and grandiose courts, simple earth brick or exuberantly coloured *faience* and tiled façades. The experience of spatial and human dialogue is overwhelming.

I have never encountered splendour of this kind before. Other interiors came into my mind as I stood there, to compare it with: Versailles, or the porcelain rooms at Schönbrunn, or the Doge's Palace, or St Peter's... All are rich; but none so rich. Their richness is three-dimensional; it is attended by all the effort of shadow; in the Mosque of Sheik Lutfullah, it is a richness of light and surface, of pattern and colour only. The architectural form is unimportant. It is not smothered as in rococo; it is simply the instrument of a spectacle, as earth is the instrument of a garden. (From *The Road to Oxiana* by Robert Byron).

After a week of immersion in this urban paradise, we headed south to Shiraz. At the time, it was a city of red wine, holiday makers from all around the Gulf, and palaces of sparkling-faceted mirror mosaics. It was fun and full of joy. Further north, in Nain, a small town that is famed for its delicate silk carpets, we watched dozens of old ladies and young female apprentices hand knotting classic designs, sitting cross-legged on the floor in front of antique wooden looms. Their masterpieces can take years to complete. It was a privilege to sit with them, take tea and observe their dexterity. We slept peacefully that night in a simple room above the workshops.

Qom is the holiest of Iranian shrine cities. We had not previously experienced the wrath of shrine guards. Iranians had welcomed us to visit their holy buildings, to

Left:
Masjid-i-Shah, Isfahan. 1612-1629: Haft Ranghi tiles enabled huge buildings to be enveloped in colour

rest and even listen in to readings from the Koran. Not so at Qom. As we neared the centre of the holy city, guards armed with golden maces shooed us aggressively out of sight of the huge, high-walled and gated mosque complex. Respectfully, we made our retreat. Turning the first corner, we got surprisingly lucky. A guest house did not seem to care that we were non-Muslim and showed us to a delightfully furnished room on the top floor. Opening the shutters, we had a perfect view over the high shrine walls to the array of *faience* and golden domes. We rested through the heat of the afternoon. As the sun was falling lower in the sky, I climbed to the roof of our retreat, to enjoy and photograph the cluster of domes sparkling and reflecting the orange glow of the sun. It was one of the most dramatic sights of man-built architecture that one can imagine. As a 14-year-old boy inspired by the tales of the *Arabian Nights*, I had a mental image of a Persian cityscape and painted it in the art room at Alleyn's. Now, I was witnessing it for real, admiring it not from within the sacred walls that excluded infidels but experiencing a high-level overview where I could observe the dramatic shapes of soaring minarets and spectacular domes with more glazed turquoise and golden tilework than anything of which my teenage self could have dreamt.

After Qom, it was time to head towards home. We were weary and a long way from Kingston-on-Thames.

Departing from Iran was like leaving colour behind. Even the sky had turned grey with a chill in the air. There was just one decrepit bus a day from the shabby little concrete frontier town of Maku to the Turkish border at Bazargan which left after lunch and arrived at the border post just before dark. Here, across low barren hills, coils of barbed wire stretched as far as the eye could see. To the Northwest, a wide plateau provided the setting for Mount Ararat, which rises like the Hokusai

Above:
The real thing: The Golden Dome
and minarets at Qom

paintings of Mount Fuji, a perfectly conical volcanic Vesuvius. The sky darkened and threatening clouds gathered, carrying a sense of foreboding.

As the Iranian guards completed their tediously detailed departure paperwork, the first rumbles of distant thunder echoed around the semi-derelict, brown brick buildings. Half the courtyard was Iran, the other half Turkey. More coils of barbed wire and a single boom gate separated the two nations. We were ushered into the yard along with a few other disgruntled travellers, the boom was raised, and we shuffled across to the Turkish side. Guards in high-level sentry boxes with mounted machine guns surveyed our plodding passage.

At the Turkish passport counter, we were subjected to an alarmingly political interrogation about the purpose of our visit. We stayed silent on having witnessed expansive fields of sunflowers turn to mile upon mile of military hardware stockpiled in readiness for transport south to the Mediterranean Sea. This was the autumn of

'74, a few short months after the Turkish invasion of Cyprus. James Callaghan, the UK Foreign Minister at the time, had made comments in favour of the Greeks. Unaware of political pronouncements, we did not realise that being British was less than ideal.

After this deliberately slow bureaucratic process, we were allowed into the main border building rooms and were keen to find somewhere quiet to chill out. The place was semi-derelict. The first floor was a series of empty, one-time dormitories. What we had learnt during the interrogation was that this region was regarded as Kurdish bandit country and no-one, but no-one, especially the Turks, would venture out at night to cross the 50 kilometres to Dogubayazit, the next town. We had no alternative but to while away the night and wait for the first transit vans to arrive at dawn.

At about 9 p.m. the border commandant invited Susie and me for a drink in a tiny office. It was so small that we had to leave our rucksacks outside his door. He seemed convivial. We were guarded in our responses but shared the inevitable shots of *raki*. Outside, the wind, rain, rumbling thunder and now incessant lightning shook the building as Mount Ararat made ready to receive Noah and his Ark. There were no white doves, just squawking black crows.

Half an hour passed, and I made an excuse to get some Iranian sweets from my bag. But when I looked there was only one bag, not two. Someone must have picked it up by mistake. There was nowhere to go, a closed border to Iran and Kurdish bandits on the road to Dogubayazit; the bag must be here somewhere. I walked anxiously into the counter area where the border guards were playing cards and drinking.

'Have you seen a faded blue rucksack?'

Ignoring me, they continued with their card game, swigging their hooch.

'Sorry to bother you, have you seen a bag?'

A 6ft 5in Turkish border guard wearing a uniform slung about with a gun belt walked slowly over to the counter, leant across, and shot a swift blow of his fist to my cheek.

It was like being struck by a truck! I could feel anger, fear, helplessness, and what-to-do-next spinning in my brain. Adrenalin surged through me. A flash of lightning momentarily lit the scene and the building rattled.

'No problem,' I said eventually. 'I'm sure it will turn up.'

I walked slowly back to the little office, acutely aware of our predicament.

On joining Susie and our host, I feigned jollity despite my throbbing cheek and was glad to sink another shot of *raki*. The apocalyptic storm raged across the plain, glimpsed through the office window as the shutters banged and swung in the wind. I had just begun to explain to the commandant the missing bag and that the guards had seemed unable to help when there was a knock on the door and a clean-shaven lieutenant in an immaculate uniform slid into the room. He spoke alarmingly good English. He read from a document in his hand.

'Mr Davis attacked one of the border guards,' he announced. 'This is a serious offence. My guard has filed a report, witnessed by his senior officer who was present at the time of the incident. You are to be arrested. The warrant will be completed in the morning.'

'I did no such thing!'

'This report states that you shouted at the guard and then hit him whilst he attempted to assist you.'

He placed handcuffs on my wrists.

'You will accompany me to my secure office. Your wife may stay with you. She will be free to depart in the morning.'

Susie and I were led through the tall steel gate into the floodlit courtyard where dense drops of rain signalled the arrival of autumn. The lieutenant pushed open a series of doors into another section of the building, locking each door as we passed through. We arrived in a grand office with comfortable sofas and rich deep red and blue oriental carpets. On a huge wooden desk with an inlaid leather top, there were fine crystal glasses and a full bottle of *raki*. The lieutenant suggested that we sit and relax, then poured three full measures.

'I'm afraid that your offence will carry a sentence of 6 to 9 months in jail in Erzurum.' He paused. 'Please relax tonight.'

As he ogled Susie, I slyly emptied my glass into the adjacent cactus plant pot.

'More *raki* please, let us drink together while we can,' I encouraged our gaoler.

He downed his drink and poured more. Susie held his attention with questions of how she should travel across the mountains to Erzurum now that the rains had come. I delivered another alcoholic dose to the cactus. This scary farce continued for an hour or so, though it seemed to last forever. Susie suggested that we get some sleep at which point the lieutenant passed out, drunk as a skunk.

We waited, watching in silence as his heavy breathing slowly turned into a loud snore. It was almost a pantomime performance. The keys were on the big desk. Slowly, I moved to it, lifted them without a sound and passed them to Susie. She unlocked the handcuffs from my already raw wrists. Silently, we crept to the door, unlocked it, moved into the adjoining room, tiptoed to the next door, turned the key and stepped into the courtyard. The rain had eased, the thunder had subsided and there was no sign of the sentry in the watchtower. Thankfully, the floodlights had been turned off and the courtyard was lit solely by moonlight, barely filtering through the night clouds, like some atmospheric '50s war movie. It was 4 a.m. We unbolted the steel gate and eased into the vehicle tunnel which would take us out of the border complex and onto the road to Dogubayazit. Fearful of imminent recapture, with one rucksack between us now, Susie and I set off on foot in the dark. It didn't matter that it was Kurdish bandit country. We figured the bandits would still be asleep. We had only an hour or two to get as far from the frontier as possible. The chance of consular assistance was as remote as this place: the wrong side of the Turkish eastern mountains. We had escaped the frontier, but we still had a long way to go to get to Istanbul.

A few years later, sitting hands clasped in a cinema watching John Hurt suffer the degradation of a Turkish gaol in *Midnight Express*, we both realised how our lives might have changed had we not escaped that night on the Bazargan frontier.

8   THE CRACK THAT LETS THE LIGHT IN

If a journey begins with a single step, so an architect's design begins with a single line. Just as yards multiply to become miles at the start of a journey, so lines on blank paper may emerge as no more than a walk to the bus or with application expand into a great adventure: each line a journeyman's best attempt, or a path of discovery to design a masterpiece.

Is this first line a wall separating space, inside from outside? What is a break in that line? An opening, a doorway connecting two sides of the line. Or is it a window, the source of light framing a view, the crack that lets the light in, sunlight and warmth to bring comfort to life? What has determined the placing of the first line, the second, the third? It takes a multitude of lines to conceive, depict and define the space that may become a place. The sculptor feels the rock before him to see the David within. The writer listens to the daydream words that join, one after another, to tell of an idea, a poem or a story that inspires the imagination from the first to the last line. The musician uses the colour of sound; single notes become a chord, a melody, rhythm, emboldened by instruments and orchestration to burst on our ears as soul-enriching music. The coda, a summation to hold the complexity of the whole, resounds beyond the conclusion. Drawing in two dimensions, seeing in three dimensions, builds space on paper. A good line, a bad line, a better line, a worse line, through trial and error, gradually become the best lines. Line-on-line of sketching, creating a Giacometti complexity of texture, is followed by a release of abstract clarity. One decision after another is taken to determine scale, balance, proportion, and relationships. Lines drawn that become shapes, materials, colours, forms, light and shade, textures and the space that becomes place. Is this line to be the floor on which the occupants will stand? How will it be bounded by walls, windows and doors? How will it connect to other rooms and to the natural world outside its confines? How will it connect vertically? The stair, will it be a means to an end or a statement, an experience? The introduction to the third dimension, will it form a spatial whole? Releasing and connecting two dimensions into three.

What will the sense of arrival to these lines feel like? Will it welcome the visitor with open arms, or will it define a barrier saying, 'keep out,' exclusivity over inclusivity? Will it excite, invite, surprise, and say 'stay' or be metaphorically locked and bolted?

Will these spaces provide welcoming shelter with comfort, shade, warmth, light, aspect and delight? Will they be for domestic life, work or play, generating care, culture or entertainment? Will they be for conversation, government discourse, judgement, democracy or authority? In what social context will this place of lines find itself within a wider climate and landscape? Will it contribute to that context

Opposite:
Moonrise:
Watercolour by the author

77

and what meaning will it assume? Factory or farmhouse, mansion or workhouse, resort or prison, all hold nuance of interpretation. Temple, church, mosque or synagogue, whichever way they face, each reflect the beliefs and symbols of their worshippers and non-believers.

The first purpose of building was for shelter, then places for meetings, for civil organisation or sacred edifices. Stone circles were used to record and understand the movement of the sun, moon and stars, enabling measurement of the passing seasons and the year in time. They became both symbolic and sacred connections beyond daily life. Pyramids still confound us with their astronomical and geometric precision, creating a gateway to the afterlife for Pharaohs, the ultimate of sacred symbols. More everyday buildings hold equally profound symbols in human life. The bazaar, souk or street market anywhere in the world is a symbol of community as well as trade. In France, every village, town or city has a *Halle* (market hall), a covered meeting place where people gather to exchange or sell local produce. The market is a symbol of the community, of regional identity and the national passion for food. It probably scores equally with the *Mairie* (Town Hall) as a symbol of the citizens' Republic.

If a building reflects the society in which it stands, it is even more determined by its landscape and climate. Rivers, lakes and harbours share one reason for settlement: life-sustaining water. Water is the element that also enabled the transport of heavy goods and distant trade. Hills and cliffs provide military or defensive security. The sun brings warmth and light: the vernacular builder and architect cognisant of its angle of variance through the seasons utilises it to generate energy-efficient comfort, the geometry of sunlight through time. Wide projecting eaves provide shade in the summer, whilst in winter the lower angle of the sun draws in light and heat to warm the building fabric. Then there is the wind, its prevailing direction impacting orientation. Rain or the lack of it determines the choice of materials and the shape of weatherproof covering. Snow brings its own specific requirements for material insulation, pitch and load-bearing capacity of roof. Before mass transportation, the local availability of natural materials such as trees for structural frames, clay for bricks and tiles, stone as varied as limestone, slate and flint, all determined the form and appearance of architecture. So many great cities have cohesion because of the singularity of their primary material. Bath has its warm honey stone, Florence or Albi have fiery orange clay tile roofs, Yazd has its sun-baked sand bricks, continuous domed roofs and wind catchers. As transport advanced, so came different materials, methods of construction, greater diversity, and often less cohesion.

When does a post become a column? Once upon a time, a man building a shelter for family or livestock erected a post, then several more posts and beams cut from trees to form the structure of his building. Was this the first true vernacular? A stone column may fulfil the same task as a supporting structural post, but it is more a symbol of power. The stone has been quarried, a specialist skill. It has been cut and fashioned with expertise and transported at cost. Throughout the centuries and across cultures, the column has become a symbol of power and wealth and hence an expression of social division.

As buildings and settlements advanced beyond personal purpose, specialist builders, stonemasons, bricklayers, carpenters, tilers, roofers, all became necessary skilled craftsmen. The master builder evolved with the need to understand the trade crafts, materials and geometry. The invention of a profession evolved, and they called the trained professional 'architect'. Do architects design buildings or symbols? Are their creations fulfilling a useful purpose, or have they become mere product, investments, units for people to sleep or work in: the meagre product of the big 'house bashers' with whom the architect has become complicit? The choice partly belongs in the hand and mind of the architect; the balance tips over with regulation, cost, and the degree of engagement of the client, or, if you are uncommonly fortunate, the vision and culture of the patron. Regulation impacts architecture for better and for worse. Escape from fire is fundamental and it is tragic when rules are broken, standards fall short and too often it takes a disaster to shake out complacency. Adversely, the ubiquitous monotony of most Hong Kong residential towers comes from one regulation. Gross floor areas are strictly defined but bay windows are excluded from the floor area calculation; there are HK towers that appear entirely constructed of boring bay windows, monotonously stacked from rocky foundation to the hazy sky above. There are countless other examples of how regulation can impact on form. To break rules, you need to learn them inside out or have very full insurance cover. My personal strategy has been to consider context as best I can, to aim for buildings that are in conversation with their neighbours, to consider the setting where a new or reinvented existing building stands with civility and contributes to the life, activity and experience of those who use it or just walk past. I like to think of this as the act of placemaking, where the relationship of one building to its neighbour and the space between the buildings is the priority, rather than the architectural statement of ego. I never did do icons. Maybe I don't have the imagination, or was too polite and didn't want my buildings to shout at their neighbours. It takes a different courage to design a background building. Place is when the space between buildings becomes the subject, and the object building becomes subordinate as a backdrop to human activity. The line between a masterpiece of architecture and a masterpiece of place is a hard one to draw. A symphony does not require the voice of a *diva* to fulfil its beauty.

9 THE GENTLE SOUND OF FALLING WATER

During the long hot summer of '76, my final year of architecture college, I spent days, nights, weeks on college work. My major design project was an arts and education building set in Yazd, on the edge of the two great deserts of Iran. The aim was to contemporise the historic vernacular that created comfortable living in that most extreme of climates. I envisaged courtyards with humidifying, reflecting pools of water, wind towers to catch the breeze, perforated mashrabiya (decorative wooden shade screens) to filter the brilliant penetrating sunlight and cloisters to give shade. I was pleased with my detailed fine-line pencil and sepia ink hand drawings which I had printed on large textured sheets of watercolour paper. They captured the atmosphere of the place.

Alongside this drawn design project, I had written a major tome, entitled *Second-hand Civilisation*, a four-inch-thick, handbound thesis on the history, evolution and traditional crafts of Iran, one-time Persia. I had had to relearn my history of Europe in the light of all that had happened between the fall of the Roman Empire and the Renaissance. Mum had proudly typed the text for me, and I had added copious photographs and sketches from my travels with Susie around Iran in '74.

At last, all submissions had been made. I was 25, and the prospect of no more exams lifted my spirits. It was time to relax and party in the sunshine.

My car was out of action, but Roland Castro had offered to take me and Susie to the South Coast for the day. Roland was my friend Miranda's father, a health fanatic and vegetarian in his early '60s, who had founded Time Off, an innovative travel company specialising in weekend city breaks around Europe. He was slight, always in pressed jeans, white trainers and a freshly laundered shirt. Originally from Egypt, his family had immigrated to England in the late '50s. He had moved from the exclusive Woodhall Estate in Dulwich after his divorce and had acquired a lease on the whole of one side of a mews in Belgravia. 1–3 Chester Close was a motley amalgam of a vintage car garage, the car showroom where the notorious Bank of America robbery had been plotted, a series of isolated office rooms, two flats above, and at the end of the mews, No.3, a pristine, white-painted early 19th century cottage with an enchanting courtyard, where Roland himself lived.

No.3 was immaculate, a perfect reflection of Roland. It had a central front door and one richly furnished room to either side. Everything was white except for the exquisite artefacts from Roland's travels. The courtyard was an oasis of calm, scented by white climbing roses, wisteria and honeysuckle. Herbs flowed over the paving edges by the back door to the kitchen. Roland always entered via the kitchen door, and this was where he prepared simple Middle Eastern vegetarian nibbles. He seemed to exist on delicious, spiced dips and vegetable *crudités*.

In '76, numbers 1-3 Chester Close had just 15 years remaining on the lease from the Grosvenor Estate: too long to leave as it was in a largely dilapidated state and too short to warrant substantial investment. Roland had previously appointed two separate firms of architects to devise plans for the redevelopment of his half of the mews. He had not liked the designs they came up with, and both Westminster City Council planning department and Grosvenor Estate had greeted them with a resounding 'No'.

On the beach at Climping that Sunday in July, Susie had prepared a sumptuous picnic and Roland had brought along a coolbox full of champagne. With Miranda and her boyfriend Andrew, we celebrated the end of 20 years of studying in uncommonly hot sunshine, with white sand between our toes, and the English sea warmer than I had ever known.

We all drank our fill of champagne and even Roland had more than his usual fastidious 'only a glass or two'. It was on the way home that quite unexpectedly, Roland began to talk more openly about his aspirations for Chester Close.

'Now you've finished studying architecture why don't you have a go at designing a scheme for the mews? You couldn't do any worse than these other buggers that I've appointed and sacked.'

I could hardly believe he was seriously asking me.

'I'd like light and airy offices for Time Off,' he went on, outlining his ideas for his company, 'with opening windows and no-one sitting more than 20ft from fresh air, definitely no air conditioning, real fresh air. I want to retain my house and courtyard and whatever else I need to have to make it happen. I've already told you that Westminster and Grosvenor don't even want to pick up the phone to discuss any form of development.'

'What do you really want to achieve with Chester Close?' I asked, as we arrived back at our tiny home in Kingston.

'A thing of beauty is a joy forever,' he replied, as we squeezed out of his little MGB sports car. Then: 'Are you busy tomorrow afternoon?'

Job No.1, my first proper project. It was hard to imagine how to begin; this was the real world, not just college theory. Last week I had been a student and suddenly I had a serious first commission. It was my first break. Now I had to deliver and meet the challenge. I was confident in myself but also aware that I didn't really know what I was doing. I was still in short trousers, a naïve 25 year old, my only experience to date being disparate spells of intermediate work experience.

I arrived at Roland's office at 3 p.m. sharp. I knew he was pedantic about punctuality. He talked more about his brief for Time Off's offices, and I was shown around the various ramshackle buildings. The flats were in desperate disrepair and the areas of corrugated iron and flat roofs were dangerous to walk on. I clambered over all that I dared and photographed not only the existing structures, but the many boundary houses and gardens that overlooked the site. Subsequently, I had to deal with 27 party wall awards. At that time, I barely had a clue what those were and certainly no idea of the complexities involved. Fortunately, Roland already had extensive survey drawings of the existing buildings, so that was one good starting point.

Above:
Chester Close: Prior to demolition
Multi-shot collage used by
architectural students before David
Hockney popularised the technique

Roland explained the realities of dealing with the Grosvenor Estate, the freeholder and wealthiest historic landowner in London. In contrast to Roland's up-to-date, informal though exacting standards in life and business, the Estate was old school, extremely formal and staid. It was unlikely to be easy on an inexperienced youngster like myself.

On leaving our meeting, I wandered around Belgravia, the most coherent conservation area in London. It had all been built to Thomas Cubitt's masterplan between the end of the Napoleonic wars and 1846, its grid of white stucco terraces crowned by the grand set pieces of Eaton and Belgrave Squares. Eaton Square is long and linear with a wide road through the centre and more private side lanes, and Belgrave is almost square with a huge central garden and ambassadorial-scale residences and embassies around the perimeter.

At each cross street, the scale steps down, then again, and then to the mews behind that serviced the grand houses with stables, hay lofts and now, shiny polished motor cars. The architecture is exceptionally consistent in its palette of materials: yellow London stock brick, white stucco with coursed banding, white painted vertically sliding sash windows and Welsh slate roofs behind parapets. Railings at pavement edge and first floor balconies are always black. The clever part is the variety created by minor details such as the arched window heads, front porticoes, parapet embellishment and especially the balcony metalwork. What particularly struck me were the smaller standalone houses that turned the corners from one terrace to the next and to each side of the entrances to the many mews. In these, I saw the appropriate scale and inspiration for Chester Close. I studied and photographed every example on my exploratory walkabout.

Armed with my site survey and neighbourhood observations, I began sketching ideas with a mix of offices and houses or flats. Aligning uses side-by-side, I just couldn't make it work. Roland wanted the offices to be open plan and on one level. By retaining the courtyard to no. 3 and creating another at the entrance, then a third at the back of the ground floor, I achieved the appropriate square footage as well as the objective of close access to fresh air. But the offices and courtyards covered the whole of the ground level of the site, so any other accommodation would have to be on top.

The difficult problem was how to place residential accommodation at first floor and above when the complex boundary was surrounded by houses and compact gardens. I knew that overlooking and rights of light would be problematic in planning, with inevitable objections from the neighbouring properties. There was good aspect over the mews to the east and some space to the west created by the proposed rear courtyard to the offices. By treating the office flat roof as a podium, I could create another courtyard at first floor for the new houses or flats to look onto. A gentle winding stair rising from the entrance courtyard could give access to the podium. I had a preoccupation with steps being easier to climb if each landing was below eye level. This was something I had learnt from studying the tower houses of the Yemen – a nine-storey house must have a stair that is easy to climb or descend if it is to function effectively.*

As all this took shape, an awkward recess was formed beneath the upper section of the stair. The romantic in me came to the fore and I sketched a small grotto waterfall and pool at the base within this otherwise unusable space. I liked the idea of a waterfall in Belgravia, and Roland loved the concept of the gentle sound of falling water as a background to the open windows of his offices.

Before the days of computerised Rights of Light 3D modelling, I constructed a crude series of diagrams and began carving out the potential volume that might be achievable without infringement on the adjoining owners' right to sunlight. There were so many complex sketches emerging that I decided to build a large model out of white card. It wasn't good enough, so I built another that included all the surrounding buildings.

By this time in '77, I had teamed up with Alan Bayne, a fellow student from Kingston Polytechnic, where I had studied for my RIBA Part 2. He was one of the best draughtsmen at college and, like me, addicted to work. He was tall, good

---

* Regrettably, I never managed to visit the Yemen, though its spectacular buildings had been part of my extensive interest and study of the region.

84

Left:
The gentle sound of falling water:
Chester Close watercolour sketch

looking, with his moments of relaxation spent in the gym listening to Motown music. Alan had not yet quit his day job, so worked non-stop and would join me after hours. Then in '78, we moved our workspace from the spare bedroom of our house in Avenue Road to the rent-free, unheated car showroom that was part of the Chester Close site. In reality, it was a long thin garage with draughty, double glass doors that allowed an alarming inch of rain to flood in when the wind was in the wrong direction. But the SW1 address looked good on our first 'Davis & Bayne' headed notepaper. It was a beneficial piece of start-up branding, as long as we avoided inviting prospective clients to our new makeshift office.

Gradually, a design scheme emerged with five houses and two flats, on first and second floors. One house abutting an adjoining tall blank wall had the potential to rise to a third floor. The design was taking shape and I enjoyed the task of planning the inside of the various dwellings. My key focus was on placing windows to maximise potential daylight and outward views, and then building the internal layouts around light and aspect. The key was designing and refining the inside to make the living spaces as useable, light, balanced and enjoyable as the footprint would allow. Each house had a generous glazed lantern skylight above the stair to draw light into the centre of the plan; designing from the inside to the outside, as I had learnt from Charles Rennie Mackintosh. It is of course an iterative process, inside to outside and back again, but I wanted to design great homes for people to enjoy living in. I started with optimising the interior spaces rather than an image of the outside.

The detailed plans emerged over several months and we built yet another revised model with the new layouts within the framework of the surrounding buildings. The next task was to interpret the ideas gleaned from the small corner houses that I had photographed around Belgravia and to adapt the materials and proportions to create attractive contextual elevations. As these emerged, we attached them to the blank white model.

At each stage of the evolving design, I would meet with Roland who was enthusiastic and encouraging and kindly paid our fee accounts promptly. Somehow, I managed to arrange a series of informal meetings with two young Westminster planning officers, Paul Velluet and John Dyke. I was aware that they had been extremely negative about previous proposals for the site. It seemed best to ask them what they wanted to see happen at 1-3 Chester Close. Their overriding priority was for residential use. They would accept re-provision of the offices and, importantly, wanted the design to relate to the historic context of Cubitt's Belgravia. Velluet, the conservation officer, even advised on the specific brick that he wanted to be

Right:
A message from Roland Castro: The most generous and optimistic of clients

"We are such stuff as dreams are made on".

Roland Castro
Director

2a Chester Close
Chester Street
London SW1X 7BQ

01-235 8070

TIME OFF LTD

used. I took their comments to heart and quickly realised that I had to get them on side. After all, this was my earliest encounter with the planning system.

My baptismal meeting at the Grosvenor Estate was as daunting as Roland had intimated it would be. Their offices in Mayfair were a series of linked listed buildings redolent of history and the Duke of Westminster's ancestry. The waiting area was a dark panelled hall hung with family portraits, furnished with antiques and elegant table lamps. I felt like a schoolboy, out of place, waiting for a scary headmaster.

At that time, the London landed estates did little or no development themselves, preferring to grant 'building agreements' and then new leases to developers or occupiers on completion of a project. But an era of change was imminent. Grosvenor were considering whether to develop their substantial landholdings themselves. This evolution of strategy was dispiritingly slow to an impatient young architect.

After numerous meetings, Grosvenor agreed to support the planning application for Chester Close. This was a big step forward, but they were taking their time in considering terms for how to proceed in the event of planning permission and conservation area consent.

In September '78 Westminster granted the consents and we thought we were on the way. We celebrated in Roland's kitchen with plentiful champagne and the inevitable spicy nibbles. The next day a bottle of vintage champagne was delivered with a card attached.

As Grosvenor deliberated, I was called to a meeting with their longstanding advising residential estate agent, Michael Minting, of George Trollope & Sons. Michael and I did not click. Having presented our scheme to him, Michael gave it a very low valuation, and that spelt the end of the scheme in Grosvenor's eyes. The idea of the dwellings above offices, a mixed-use scheme, was surprisingly radical at the time, although commonplace today.

'I can't sell flats above shops,' he declared. I could feel the carpet being pulled from under my feet.

Dejected, I left Grosvenor's offices and walked slowly from Mayfair to Chester Close, determined not to give up, repeatedly muttering to myself 'Perseverance will bring success,' my favourite hexagram from the I Ching.

Sitting with Roland, I asked, 'What would a wise man do?'

I answered myself, 'Pause for thought.'

A solution came, which was obvious really: we needed to get a second valuation. I was still in short trousers for my first real-world project.

I met with Belgravia-based agents John D. Wood and talked them through the scheme and asked them to prepare a sales valuation on behalf of Roland. A week later, they came up with a figure 40% higher than the Minting valuation. This had to change the game. I rang Eric Gittins, my liaison surveyor at Grosvenor, telling him that I had some additional information to discuss. At our meeting, Eric was not sure how to respond. George Trollope & Sons had been Grosvenor's sole external advising agents for years. However, he could see that I was determined to take the scheme forward. He would have to take the new valuation to a higher authority. I was walking on thin ice. The Estate Surveyor, Stanley Coggan, was not impressed.

'Who does this young man think he is, challenging one of the Estate's most long-standing and experienced consultant advisors?'

Nonetheless, the new valuation was fed into the appraisal process and the negotiations moved slowly forwards. Although the Estate Surveyor continued to treat me almost contemptuously, it is perhaps more than coincidental that on all subsequent schemes, valuations were sought from two agents, not just one. Time dragged on and we weren't sure that Grosvenor would proceed.

Right:
The Grosvenor team:
Nick Loup left, Colin Redman centre, author and Henry Thompson right

Below right:
Grosvenor payment to D&B when works were on site, many times my annual mortgage

To push things forward, Roland appointed a very bright and charismatic surveyor, Peter Farrington, to lead the financial negotiations between himself and Grosvenor. The deal that we struck was that Grosvenor would develop the project, and grant Roland a new long lease on his house, No. 3, and a ten-year rental lease on the offices for Time Off Ltd. Grosvenor would take the proceeds of the house sales. The clever part of the deal was based on a drastically reducing office rent if the house sales achieved certain levels. Peter and I were confident that the sales would achieve the highest levels and that Roland's Time Off rent would be next to nothing for ten years. As Peter and I skipped towards Berkeley Square after the final meeting, we passed a brand new scarlet red Ferrari.

'Roland should buy us each one of those cars for the deal we've just done,' said Peter.

Back in Roland's kitchen, we killed a few more bottles of champagne.

As the project moved forward, Colin Redman took the overseeing role for Grosvenor with a supporting surveyor, Nick Loup, who was even younger than me. The consultant team prepared construction and tender information and Fairclough won the contract. Works on site progressed with the kind of headaches I would come to know all too well in later work. There were plentiful amusing moments of building-site banter. As it was my first site with a tower crane, I was challenged to climb up to the cab at the top, a breach of every health and safety regulation in the book. I can understand why. Climbing the ladder inside the hoop frame attached to the steel lattice tower as it swayed in the breeze tested my nerves to the limit. Looking down on the site below from the top was one of the scariest moments I had ever known. Climbing into the cab brought relief for a minute; then I was gripped by the fear of climbing back through the trap door in the floor and retracing my steps down the ladder to ground. I did it once and never again. It was a rite of passage for me and my relationship with the men on site. I was more than grateful when rake-thin Eric, the ever welcoming and whistling, close-to-retirement 'tea boy' brought me a relaxing cuppa after my descent.

A few months before practical completion the major electrical and plumbing sub-contractor went bust; this was more nightmare than headache. There was a vast amount of carpentry partition work to advance while the services installation was effectively on hold. I asked the 'chippy' team, all Asian men, if they would work Saturdays to prepare as much as possible so that the electrics and plumbing work could advance unencumbered once we had solved the services installation problem. The next Saturday all the carpenters arrived at 7.30 a.m. to hit key areas. They were surprised to see me there too, and even more so when I picked up a broom and cleared debris to assist their progress. A bond was forged between us, and great progress was made that day and subsequent Saturdays. Through extensive discussion with the Estate, the main contractor and the services foremen, we negotiated the direct employment of the electricians and plumbers, and within 14 days their work was resumed. They were relieved not to be unemployed and were able to work more efficiently as a result of the chippies' Saturday task force. A potential disaster had been averted.

Right:
Chester Close presentation
watercolour and the end result

As the works neared completion and the cobbles were being re-laid on the mews surface, two local policemen wandered by. 'We don't remember it being like this,' they observed, 'but it's not new, is it?'

I was pleased to hear that it seemed to fit its historic Belgravia context.

At the grand opening, I presented four framed watercolours that we had used to illustrate the design for the planning application to key members of the team. Whenever I had arrived on site, whistling Eric would welcome me with a mug of tea. He also introduced me to the undervalued skill of manhole 'benching' of which I would never see better. The happiest moment of the event was to surprise him with one of the paintings and to see him being applauded by the assembled dignitaries. We shook hands sharing respectful smiles, these days it would have been a warm hug.

Soon after this, I was asked to take Gerald, the Duke of Westminster, around the scheme. As we finished our tour, he lit a cigarette and observed,

'You haven't wasted many square inches of my land, have you.'

The finished scheme sold well and exceeded the sales target figures, thus achieving the lowest rental deal for Roland. In 1984, the City of Westminster held a special architectural award to celebrate the 350th anniversary of its foundation. The Queen Elizabeth Conference Centre on Parliament Square won the large project prize, and our Chester Close scheme won the small project award. Lifetime friendships were cemented with Colin Redman and Nick Loup, and would lead on to us working together on multiple projects in London and later in Hong Kong and Tokyo too.

Ten years later, after D & B had fallen apart, and I had just taken the plunge to restart my career as Paul Davis + Partners, I got a phone call out of the blue. 'You don't know me,' said this gentleman caller. 'Roland Castro gave me your phone number. My wife and I have lived in number 5 for the last ten years. I want to say thank you for putting so much care into the design of the house that we have greatly enjoyed living in. We are so glad we bought it.'

I was in tears. It was such a kind and timely gesture. His generous words confirmed my purpose and belief in being an architect.

Left:
Recognition

This plaque was awarded in recognition of an outstanding contribution to Westminster's Heritage during The City of Westminster's Quatercentenary Year

10 ROCK N' ROLL

Gus Thomson, of our light show gang, had made friends with Supertramp and crew whilst building mixing consoles at Midas in the mid '70s. Their base was just behind the Capital Radio tower on Euston Road in a courtyard of workshops where they built the best recording and PA equipment for touring bands. Supertramp band members and crew always turned up when they were in town. They invited Gus to join their team and he left for Los Angeles in the summer of '76. Gus had introduced me to some of the band and crew on a couple of their visits and Susie and I had been invited to concerts with back-stage passes.

In the spring of '78, not long after Davis & Bayne had submitted the Chester Close application, the phone rang. It was Gus calling from Los Angeles. Would I like to fly over to L.A. to design a stage set for the next Supertramp tour? The band were writing and recording songs that would become the album *Breakfast in America*. Their studio, workshops and offices were in downtown Burbank. I could bring Susie and stay with John Helliwell (sax and frontman), his wife Christine and little son Charles in their new house in Topanga Canyon. The deal included flights, a convertible Ford Mustang hire car and I would be paid $1000 a week! This didn't just seem like rock n' roll! This WAS Rock n' Roll!!

So, Susie and I flew off to sunny Los Angeles, while Alan held the fort in London. Topanga Canyon was like being in a perpetual Joni Mitchell song. We saw Joe Cocker live at the Country Club. We went to the premier screening of Scorsese's *The Last Waltz* in the Sunset Boulevard cinema with the first Dolby sound. Not surprisingly, John had a great home sound system and as he was without near neighbours he would broadcast to the hills at night, whilst watching the stars from a hot tub on top of the canyon.

Downtown in the rehearsal studio in sunny Burbank, I was given a workspace to design and start model building. The stage risers were to be a series of interlocking hexagons coloured in tones of grey triangles to create a three-dimensional illusion, like one of my favourite Escher drawings. That was the easy bit. The lighting rig was to reflect the stage as a series of interlocking triangulated hexagonal trusses. I built a cocktail stick model of the whole rig and mounted it over a model of the stage.

So far so good. Some full-size components were needed to show how the rig could be put together. Many of the technical crew were Brits and frequented the English pub, where the creative and technical boffins who had made the models, scenery and cameras for *Star Wars* also went for an English pint. Both crews played football (soccer) together and were friends. Off we went in Gus's mate Tony's ageing white convertible Cadillac to the Lucas Films workshop. Kindly and quickly, the *Star Wars* technicians fabricated exquisite components for my prototype rig. The model

Opposite:
St Ann's Court detail
Photograph © Clive Helm?

Above:
Man and Mustang, shirt sewn by Susie
Below left:
Darts on the verandah with John Helliwell
Below:
Susie in Topanga sunshine

makers, scene builders and special effects guys were keen to show me the things they had created. It was inspirational to see all the models, backdrops and camera technology and be shown how they filmed the first *Star Wars* episode. I was a huge fan of the movie, so this was a real backstage treat. In any event, I wanted to thank the guys for all they had done.

'Who can I say thank you to for helping me out so swiftly?' I asked.

'Thank George,' came the response.

Next thing I know, I'm sitting taking tea with George Lucas in his office, talking about *Star Wars,* and its predecessor *THX 1138*, a favourite of mine, with the prison of white infinity I had remembered in the Chott el Djerid. The film had bombed at the box office and Lucas and Spielberg had lost money and credibility over it, so much so that George had had to fund *Star Wars* personally. It was a nice irony, since if he'd had studio funding, he might not have made such a great film (and series), nor such a huge personal fortune.

'And by the way, George, I stayed in Matmata for a week in '71 and made drawings of the pit dwellings and the pretty little *marabout* on top of the hill. It was a great setting for the opening of a space movie, it did feel like another planet.'

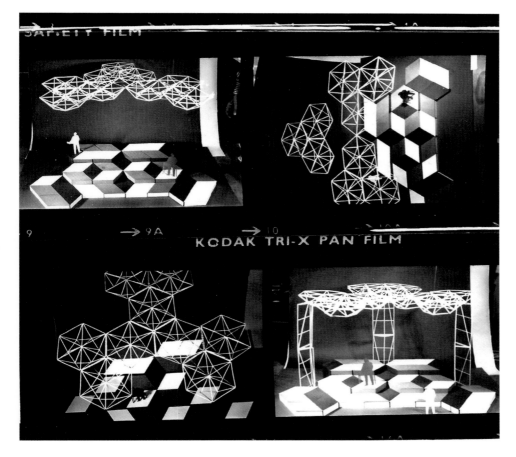

Left:
Escher-like model of stage set:
My obsession with pattern and
geometry proved to be a
step too far

Lucas hadn't met anyone else who had been there independently, let alone measured and drawn it. One wonderful thing about travelling to remote places is that it creates bonds with unexpected people in unexpected situations. Who knows when? Thank you, George, it was a memorable cup of tea! My eldest son Luke, who was born nine months later, has always adored the *Star Wars* movies and DJ'd under the name of 'Red 5' as a grown up.

Our friend Miranda's wedding was taking place on Midsummer's Day. I barely knew her fiancé Simon and, in any case, it was a weekday. 'You are allowed to take one day off,' Susie said. 'It'll be fun, and you'll catch up with old friends.'

So somewhat reluctantly I drove us to Simon's parents' small but elegantly manicured country estate in Buckinghamshire. His parents were living in the Tudor-style main house, Miranda and Simon in the cottage in the grounds. After the service in the gardens, we wandered across to the reception in a marquee on the lawn next to the house.

It was a beautiful sunny day and I had started to relax at last. It was good to see so many old friends eight years on from leaving school. We were all leading new lives. Phil Targett-Adams, the tall, shy, short-sighted guitarist from teenage parties, had now adopted the stage name Manzanera and was part of Roxy Music.

'Hi Paulus,' he said, making a beeline for me. 'I was hoping you might be here. How's it going?' I told him about my work, and we chatted about Roxy's break-up and the chance of them getting back together. Then: 'I've bought an Art Deco house in Surrey,' he said, 'and I've started building a studio in the wreck of the Old Coach House. It's all going horribly wrong. Would you like to take a look?'

Our meeting the following Monday was to lead to a long sequence of serendipitous projects and relationships. Thank you, Miranda, Phil, and Midsummer's Day. And thanks, Susie, for making me go.

St Ann's Hill was fortunately only a half-hour drive from my house in Kingston. Rusting plate steel gates at the top of a narrow tree-shaded lane concealed an enormous circular concrete and glass house, the most significant work of Raymond McGrath, designed and built in the late 1930s. It had replaced the derelict 18th century country house built by Charles James Fox, the prominent Whig statesman. Adjacent was the shell of a derelict coach house. Works had begun to stabilise the walls and inside the shell a mountain of rubble was piled high.

Phil was in loose partnership with Lol Creme and Kevin Godley, who had recently split from 10cc. A surveyor had been appointed to design the studio on a percentage fee. As the estimated build costs were escalating, so the surveyor's fees went up and up. It didn't make sense to Phil and his managers. Considering this, an early question to me was how would I propose putting together a budget for the works and hence a fee? At that time, the convention was to base fees on a percentage of construction costs, so it was easy to understand why the question had been asked. The solution was simple but often hard to achieve. We agreed to estimate the budget, design to it, and have a fixed lump sum fee. It formed our working basis for years to come.

Above:
St. Ann's Hill in 1938

With that tricky conversation out of the way, Phil and I talked about what he wanted artistically. 'There isn't a studio that I particularly like anywhere in the world,' he told me. 'Why don't we take the best bits from all of them and create something amazing and new?'

His reasoning was simple. The recording process and technology had changed but studios had not. The days of engineers in a small control room recording a band in a series of single 'takes' in a large studio with separating screens were over. The advent of multi-track recording had led to a process of recording one instrument after another, creating multi-layered recordings and listening back in the control room as the tracks were built over time, sometimes quickly, sometimes over days and weeks, months and years.

'Why not have a much larger control room and less studio space?' was my innocent suggestion.

'Exactly,' he agreed. 'Let's go and have a look at Strawberry Mastering. It's the best new final mixing room, 10cc built it. It's in Victoria, then we can see if we can base the size of the control room on that.'

Next, we set off to Tittenhurst Park near Ascot to see the studio that John Lennon had built in the 72-acre grounds of the mansion. The studio wasn't memorable but being in the house and gardens was. Sitting on the floor in the expansive, resonant, unfurnished, all-white salon with the legendary white grand piano where Lennon was filmed playing *Imagine* brought a long moment of still

97

contemplation. Ringo had bought the estate from John in 1973 and I was amused to observe that the white plug sockets still had 'John - Yoko' etched into their surface. Wandering in the gardens, Phil and I mused on ideas for the studio and rested in the shade of two blue 'weeping' Atlas cedars. I recalled the line from George Harrison's song *Beware of Darkness* on his *All Things Must Pass* boxed solo album in my collection at home. It proved to be a day of inspiration and reflection in the Buckinghamshire countryside.

Phil arranged for us to visit various studios in London to learn first hand what he did and didn't like, and then we went to New York. On the top floor of an old warehouse building on the lower West Side, we visited the Power Station, which was regarded as the best studio in the world at the time. Nile Rodgers was working there with Chic. The famous engineer Bob Clearmountain was recording Springsteen, the Rolling Stones and others. They had done some simple experiments with absorbing panels in the studio and had a unique echo chamber installed in a resonant seven-storey steel and concrete escape stair with microphones at every landing. In part that is why those recordings had such a great sound. NYC wasn't all work. One late night Phil and I headed downtown south of Canal Street, a no-go zone where the Mudd Club could only just be found on the corner of an unlit alley. The club was notorious as a collision of the New York art scene. Inside the raw interior was enlivened by two of the coolest and fastest Vietnamese cocktail mixers. Sitting with John Cale of the Velvet Underground made the dangerous outing worth the hangover.

Chris Turner, the harmonica player who was an experimental musician of exceptional talent, had been living with us at our little house in Kingston. He practised his various wind and brass instruments in our bathroom, a most resonant and brightly reflective room with hard '50s glazed tiles. Going to places with Chris, I noted how he listened to and felt different spaces for their acoustic character. Architects and designers generally note and feel the sense of light, colour, texture and materials of a space, often without the same depth of feeling for the acoustic environment they are in, or are creating. This lesson in sound awareness was to become an important and useful tool to me in studio design (and should in my opinion be given more emphasis during the training of all architects and designers).

Roxy Music had regrouped and were recording tracks that would become the album *Manifesto*. I went to their working sessions frequently. Besides being fun, this allowed me first-hand insight into the changing processes involved. Intimately crammed into a small control room at Basing Street studios in Notting Hill Gate, I watched and listened, whilst Phil, Andy Mackay, Paul Thompson and Bryan Ferry laid down layer upon layer of individual instruments and vocals.

Back then, when designing variable lighting for a space, we were using multiple circuits and dimmers to create varied and flexible atmospheres; different moods, if you like. There was no computer or app-based programmable scene setting lighting as is commonplace today. What the studio design needed was to achieve different acoustic atmospheres, changeable sound environments to suit different instruments, and to be able to 'tune' the rooms. The problem was that components that 'move' in the building industry are generally expensive or bespoke and hence even more costly to incorporate within a limited budget.

One Sunday morning, I was driving to Notting Hill to observe yet another Roxy session. En route, I drove past Earl's Court where huge billboards announced the last day of the Boat Show. Eureka! I suddenly realised that boats have all manner of simple, inexpensive components that move, clasp, unclasp, slide, pivot and more. This was worth being late for.

Earl's Court was displaying another realm of design and I was mesmerised as I wandered round the huge hall. The scale of the enormous boats inside the building was mind-blowing, especially dramatic in their dislocated waterless context; elegant, smooth, fluid shapes that came in such playful colours. It would have been too easy to wander for hours in this gigantic world of aquatic design. But that day I had a studio to think about.

The experimental pragmatist in me sought out the many specialist chandlers in the perimeter stands. They had pulleys, clam cleats, coloured ropes, yacht spars, and an amazing array of inexpensive solutions to enable a flexible, moving inner skin for the studio and control room spaces that we were in the early stages of designing. After a couple of hours of immersion in this, to me, new world, I had discovered a portfolio of components ready made to create a flexible acoustic design. I arrived at the recording session in buoyant spirits, my mind spinning with ideas.

As I sat squeezed at the back of the cramped control room, I decided to design the biggest, most comfortable control room that had ever been conceived. It had to be possible to achieve this aim with imagination, sensitivity to the acoustic performance of materials and smart control of geometry to limit reflecting sound waves. I was armed with catalogues of moving yachting parts. It had to be achievable. We just had to be brave enough.

Phil's managers, who were concerned at his level of potential investment, appointed a known studio acoustician to keep an eye and ear on what we were to come up with.

'It won't work,' he said bluntly, at our first meeting.

We ignored him, and happily so did Phil.

As our design drawings emerged, the studio was to have two of the original arched windows looking westwards over the arboretum to catch the afternoon light and setting sun. The presence of natural daylight and countryside views is a rarity, since most studios have neither daylight nor views, and hence no connection to the world, weather or even time of day.

The studio was to be about 25 x 40ft (8 x 12m), not big, but big enough if we could alter the reverberation time simply and quickly to suit different instruments. The proposal was to build a dense concrete block shell on isolated foundations within the repaired brickwork envelope of the old Coach House, to ensure structural sound isolation. The block walls would have a series of piers to stiffen them and carry the load of the heavy ceiling insulated with sand. Each of the piers would become a hub for adapting and 'trimming' the acoustics, and for direct input electronic interface with the control room. Under the heavy isolating ceiling, a second acoustic ceiling was made of a series of seven-metre yacht spars hung across the room on pulleys and coloured ropes secured on the piers with clam cleats. Natural un-dyed canvas was draped from the luff grooves and billowed like wind-filled sails between each of the five horizontal masts. By raising and lowering the masts, the acoustic volume and atmosphere of the studio could be changed in minutes.

Between the piers, canvas panels created a decorative skin. Behind these panels were concealed the magic ingredient. It was the simplest example of inexpensive acoustic control: two layers of rockwool with a thin layer of roofing felt sandwiched together by two 2in x 1in (50 x 25mm) battens hung from pulleys at the edge of the ceiling. They were raised or lowered by colour-coded ropes on the face of the pier. The theory was that as these 'absorbers' of differing sizes hung freely, when sound hit them it caused them to swing gently, soaking up pure sound energy and converting it to kinetic energy. By raising or lowering the 'absorbers' and trimming their sizes we were able to 'tune' the room and subsequently make areas of the studio more live or more neutral.

We devised other moveable features, each with individual coloured rope controls. At each pier, a series of red, green, yellow, blue and black vertical parallel cords were secured in black clam cleats. The cords were the only decoration of the plain, fair-faced, white-painted blockwork. Importantly, we hoped that these ropes would provide a simple human interface for musicians to experiment and play with. Being legible, tactile and playful, they came to be used as we predicted. The studio was to have an industrial feeling to its finishes, robust and practical.

We wanted the control room to feel more comfortable, almost cocoon-like. It should be contemporary and cool in style, materials and colour - definitely not like the American studios of the time that were more in ranch style with shag pile carpets and random stone up the walls. Completely isolated foundations were essential because of even higher noise sensitivity levels. The planning permission had restricted noise break-out to 43db which was equivalent to the rustling of leaves. The room was to be eight metres wide and 11 metres long on two levels. The front lower area housed the first ever Trident series 80 mixing console with full sight view via the triple-layered glass window wall into the studio. Behind the mixing desk, carpeted steps led up to the listening, playing and hanging-out area. Direct input hubs on raised plinths built onto the steps allowed instruments to be plugged from the control room direct to amplifiers in the studio, recorded and simultaneously listened back to in the control room.

The control room walls were lined in simple slub silk panels on broomstick battens held in small black plastic rowlock stirrups which cost about 5p each. These concealed suspended 'absorber' panels that we could easily trim with a Stanley knife to fine tune frequency absorption. The ceiling was a more complex affair. It was to be faceted and hung with no one face parallel to another to break up frequency reflections and avoid standing waves. Some facets were clad with cedar boarding, others had stretched muslin on removable frames. These acoustically open facets allowed the passage of high sound energy into the cavernous ceiling void where an array of different sized (different frequency) absorbers hung from a grid of scaffold

Left:
Finished Control Room with
Trident desk
© Clive Helm

Below:
Studio 1:20 scale model

poles. The idea was that we could readily hang more or fewer absorbers in the ceiling void to tune the sound curve and achieve the acoustic atmosphere in the room that we were targeted with.

Later, on completion of the build, when we compared the sound curve with that of Eric Stewart of 10cc's studio at Strawberry Mastering, it was nigh-on identical.

Before agreeing the plans with Phil, Lol and Kevin, who were at this stage to be joint owners, we encapsulated our ideas in a series of large-scale hand drawings and sketches which we worked on over several weeks. Towards the end of preparing our presentation material, my partner Alan and I worked non-stop for three days and nights and built a 1:20 scale model with all the finishes, just like a giant doll's house. We set off, exhausted, to discuss our ideas with them at Lol's contemporary house in the woods of the Surrey Hills. On arrival, Alan and I set out the drawings together with the model and then both promptly fell asleep. An hour later, we awoke to much laughter; they could see how hard we'd been working, preparing the presentation.

'We like how it looks,' they said. 'Can you explain how it works?'

We took them through it and then asked how they would know if the studio was a success.

'If the first album goes platinum!' they replied.

We built Gallery Studio for Phil as we had designed it at the outset. The first album Roxy recorded there was *Flesh + Blood*. It went platinum. Paul Weller, Robert Wyatt, Dire Straits, OMD, Cliff Richard, The Moody Blues, Duran Duran, and Siouxie and the Banshees were some of the people who subsequently wrote and recorded there. Lots more platinum albums. Job done, I thought.

Alan and I went on to design and advise on studios in New York, Paris, Oslo and London. The principles of adaptable acoustics and use of yachting components allowed many elements of prefabrication which enabled manufacture in England and hence rapid on-site construction overseas. The Oslo studio was built in just two weeks as a result of prefabrication in the UK prior to shipping.

Opposite:
Studio with adaptable acoustic
Photograph © Clive Helm

11 THE FLYING HANDBAG

Supertramp toured the world with *Breakfast in America* in '79 but the set design I'd had fun working on in '78 didn't happen. I had been too wrapped up in my complex geometries and had failed to understand enough of the practical realities of touring and the inherent conservatism of the business.

While I had been designing Phil's studio at St Ann's Hill, Roxy Music had reunited and were recording *Manifesto* at Basing Street Studios in Notting Hill. I'd been intimately involved with the band, observing how they made their music, listening to their conversations, and through that had built a close knowledge of how they worked and what the music meant to them. These observations and interactions had inspired my ideas for their radical studio design. Phil and I had become closest of friends, but I still wasn't expecting what he said to me as the album was going into its final mix.

'You know what the music is about, you've done great light shows, why don't you design the set for the *Manifesto* tour?'

I was more than excited to get a second chance at rock n' roll set design. The brief was simple. The set had to transport in the least possible space, be installed in the least possible time (PA and lighting come first), work faultlessly at every gig and be capable of being lit to great dramatic effect. Oh, and by the way, it had to be done on the smallest possible budget. The band wanted to have a curtain for the set to open behind. I was fascinated by light and shade and by reflected colour; bouncing coloured light from one surface to another, and how pure coloured light is reflected and absorbed onto an adjacent surface lit with another colour. I had an idea.

I would construct the biggest ever, 6m high, silver-slatted Venetian blinds. They were to be 7ft (2.1m) wide and have broad four-inch (100mm) slats. When retracted, Venetian blinds compress into almost no space. Their housing could be the flight case (as the large robust black rock n' roll storage boxes on wheels are called), and with carbine hooks each case could fasten directly onto the lighting rig. When it was lowered and the blades were closed, it would look like a 6m silver wall. Then when the blades were turned to open, gradually the wall would become a transparent, cage-like structure. There could be light from top and bottom, front and back, and the possibilities of reflected light could be endless. You just had to plug in the flight cases and power up. The stage set could be installed from the underside of any lighting rig in no time.

Hunter Douglas were launching new ranges of venetian blinds, and they made electric ones. The motors that raised and lowered the blinds had the right speed setting for the effect that I wanted, but the tilt motors were too fast. I wanted the blade tilt movement to be imperceptible. I described what I wanted, and Hunter Douglas had special slower tilt drive motors made up in Germany.

They had, as a new standard, 100mm satin silver aluminium blades. These would be perfect for my purpose as they were lightweight and light reflective. Hunter Douglas fabricated 11 of these largest-ever, colossal scale venetian blinds each 2.1m wide with a 6m drop. Flight cases were made up and wheeled dollies each taking three blinds were fabricated for rolling from truck to stage. The crew appreciated how quickly the flight cases could be hitched to the lighting rig and the set lit even better than I'd hoped for.

Roxy built the instrumental opening of the playlist around the design. After the support act finished, three pairs of blinds were lowered to the stage and closed, creating a gigantic silver wall; a curtain to finish the set-up behind. Five more blinds formed the back of stage and were lowered behind the drummer and side wings. The band came on behind the silver wall and started to play, invisible to the audience. Bryan, Andy and Phil were each back lit from the floor. As the blinds started to open, 6m shadows of their characteristic silhouettes emerged on the front row blinds. Gradually, the wall became open yet cage-like. Then the centre pair lifted, Bryan Ferry centre stage became visible and framed, then in turn Phil Manzanera appeared and played a guitar break, followed by Andy Mackay with a burst of saxophone. The whole sequence took several minutes of instrumental build up. As the music progressed, the blinds would slowly rise, fall even more slowly and gradually tilt one way or another. As the blades changed the angle of tilt and were lit from different sides, and the light bounced between the slats, the brazen Cinemoid colours diffused into subtly blended, but still bright shades of colour. Further impact and effects were achieved between the layers and angles of the front and back rows of blinds. A very simple idea had solved a clear but demanding brief. The blinds toured the world.

Roxy Music were a cult band amongst the London design community, you could clock that easily by the clothes the audience wore at their gigs. Within weeks of the sell-out concerts at Earl's Court, shop window displays along the King's Road in Chelsea were decked with Hunter Douglas silver and coloured blinds. The sales director told me that their turnover went up ten-fold that year.

A while later Roxy were preparing for a tour of European open-air festivals. Bryan had the neat idea of creating a portable concert bowl. Great idea, but how the hell!!??

An even lower budget was proposed, and it had to be made up quickly. Could I come up with an idea?

What I decided on was windsurfer masts, structured to be like the ribs of a fan. They were flexible and surprisingly cheap. I sourced 16 masts, each 5.5m long, that fortuitously fitted neatly inside scaffold tubes. Henry Thompson and I fabricated an axle arrangement like the springing point of a fan, with one tube for each mast. Then we used stainless steel wires to tension the masts to form a shell shape. So far so good.

How should the shell be covered to resemble a concert bowl? If we draped it in a single skin of fabric, it would function as a giant parachute or half a balloon. In the open air with even a slight breeze, it would take off into the air. But it needed a skin to take lighting and look like a concert bowl is supposed to. We tried various materials and failed. Boating technology solved the problem again. Long strips of rip-stock sail cloth were tied and twisted at each rib, thereby allowing air to pass through but also giving a textured surface, and as they were white and translucent, they allowed coloured light to blend and take on varying depths of hue when lit from different angles, front and back.

The first outdoor festival gig was in Lisbon. It was a hot, sunny, still afternoon for rehearsals. The set did look like a 11m diameter concert bowl, but we had to wait for the full effect until the sun set and the night sky darkened. Roxy started playing at about 9.30 p.m. Twenty minutes into their set the breeze started to blow, gently at first, but growing in force. The concert bowl began to sway, then to lift. Hell, I thought, it's going to take off. Mark Fenwick, Roxy's manager, aka Spark Manic, lived up to his name and wanted us to let it close back into its folded shape – oblivion, nothing. Henry (my erstwhile co-designer) and I moved to sit on the back boom, in the spirit of 'fat boys up' which is sailing terminology for when a yacht is keeling over too far. Then many of the road crew joined us to hold the 'flying handbag', as it was rapidly christened, firmly onto the stage. At the time it was horribly tense and stressful, thinking back it must have looked hilarious.

The next night at Faro, we concocted a scaffolding method to hold the set and stage tight to each other. Fortunately, the wind was never so strong that the stage lifted into the air like a 11m diameter parachute or half a hot-air balloon.

In the early '80s, Susie and I shared cottages in Cornwall with Phil Manzanera, his wife Sharon and all our kids for family holidays. On one occasion, we met up with Justin Hayward and his family. He was as relaxed and laid back as the Moody Blues music he created and very friendly. When our car broke down late one evening in the middle of nowhere, he came out and rescued us, an exceedingly kind gesture.

We talked about light shows in the '60s and '70s, plus he had seen the sets I had designed for Roxy Music. The Moody Blues were to be on a tour along the East Coast of America in the autumn of '83, and he asked if I'd like to design a set for their tour later that year. They wanted something cosmic and spacey that would orbit above the stage.

In the spring, I met up with Justin and some of the band, and it became a design project. Henry Thompson and I devised a series of flying saucers, satellites and orbiting planets. With the model makers at RVPB, we worked out how they could be built, rotated, flown from the lighting rig and transported. We drew up our idea and priced it. It would take ten weeks to build. We showed it to the band, they liked it, then they all went off on their summer holidays without any confirmation of the commission. We heard no more until into September. Then I got the call.

'We'd like to go ahead with the set. Can you be at technical rehearsals in Lititz, Pennsylvania in the second week of October?'

I should have said no. We needed ten weeks to build and freight, and we only had five. Naively, I said yes.

The model makers said they could do it as another big project was on hold.

Top:
Roxy Music on stage
with venetian blind
set
Above:
Set model with
Duplo Roxy
Right:
Sound & light
rehearsals

Right and lower right:
Roxy Music in Lisbon with
the *Flying Handbag*
portable concert bowl

Above top to bottom:
Stages of construction

There was a problem getting all the motors that we needed in the UK. We were assured that the lighting outfit from LA could source them and bring them to the technical rehearsals. It was proposed that I install them in Lititz. There would be a workshop and all I'd need.

Lititz, Lancaster County, is in the middle of Amish country. The Amish reluctance to accept modern technology, together with a belief in simple traditional ways of living and farming, makes for exceptionally beautiful countryside. On the outskirts of Lititz is a huge hangar-like building set up for bands' technical rehearsals before they tour the big East Coast stadium venues.

When I arrived on the Monday morning, the PA was there and getting set up for testing. I unpacked the stage set flight cases and assembled three large space objects and found some hanging points to suspend them from. So far so good. What I needed was the motors from LA. The lighting rig and crew didn't arrive until the Wednesday afternoon, three days late. When they did turn up the motors were a box full of second-hand bits, none of which worked. There was no point in expressing my anger and frustration, the lighting crew had enough to do and were in any case laid back LA flakes, totally unconcerned with my stress.

It was fortunate, as it turned out, that we were in Amish country. I came across the most wonderful hardware store ever. I could hardly believe my luck. It had everything that you could make absolutely anything from. Rummaging through wooden boxes, racks of tools and shelves laden with components, I spent an enjoyable morning in hardware heaven and emerged with all the bits and pieces that I needed to fix and install the motor drives. Amish home-baked cookies and carrot cake served with a pot of leaf tea and a smile set me up for my return to the hangar. Courtesy of my new box of Amish hardware components, I had reconstructed each of the malfunctioning motors and connected them into the structures by three o'clock the next morning. On the Friday night the rig was in place, and once the lighting plot was completed, it could be lowered, and the spacey set structures could be hung in place. Strangely, there was no sign of the band to see how it was going and play some music to check it all out.

'When are the Moody Blues coming?' I asked. No-one knew.

Saturday passed, Sunday too. All the gear was packed into the flight cases for trucking to Hartford, Connecticut and the first indoor stadium gig on Monday night. By early afternoon the rig was up, the PA in place and the cosmic set was orbiting as planned. At last, the band appeared, and a rudimentary sound check was done. That night, their poor performance showed up a dreadful lack of rehearsal. Unfortunately for the Moody Blues, on the previous Friday and Saturday the Grateful Dead had played the same arena. 'The Dead' had been touring continuously for years and, more than simply well-rehearsed, their performance had blown the audience and press away. Next morning, we were on to Worcester, Massachusetts, the band all very grumpy after being slated in the music papers. That night was better, but still not what it could or should have been. At least the Dead weren't coming to the same town until the end of that week. Wednesday, we moved on to Buffalo, New York State and the atmosphere was a long way off cosmic. Blame filled the air. Thursday

This page:
Moody Blues set in action on
the US East Coast tour

was a night off and I got to see the Dead gig myself. *American Beauty* had been a favourite album of mine in my university days, and it was a treat to see such a joyful party-like performance.

Once my part in the Moody Blues set was running as it should, its operation could be handed over to the lighting crew. I said my goodbyes and took a plane home from Boston. I felt enough was enough. I was glad to have seen a little slice of Amish country, but the episode was a disappointment, since Justin was such a friendly, generous, and talented musician.

A couple of years later, Peter Weir's moving film thriller *Witness* was released. Set in Amish country, it contains one of my favourite movie scenes about the potential worth and meaning of architecture. When the young Amish couple are to be married, their wedding gift from the community is a barn. The whole village congregate to erect the huge structural timber frames. The barn comes to life and a celebratory picnic is held. The barn brings the gift of a livelihood to the couple at the start of their new life together. The extended scene is the perfect metaphor to illustrate the value of architecture and community.

Back in London, Roxy Music's managers had set up a development company as an investment vehicle for the band's royalties. D&B advised on a series of acquisitions and design projects near the river in Old Chelsea. One of these was Alexander Fleming's house (the inventor of penicillin had lived there). On completion, the first apartment was purchased by one of the Rolling Stones, more Chelsea rock n' roll.

Roxy's management offices, EG Music, were on the upper floors above three shops in a white stucco building opposite the Markham Arms pub in the middle of hip '60s King's Road. We were working on designs for Bryan Ferry's country house, Andy Mackay's Georgian townhouse overlooking Clapham Common, as well as St. Ann's Court for Phil and his wife, Sharon. Mark Fenwick had a large house near Wimbledon Common where we redesigned the ground floor living spaces. Sam Alder, the band's Manx-born finance manager had a house on Wellington Square with a sprawling mews that we adapted over a series of phases. He had an accountant's prudent approach to the 'availability of money over time'. He and I got on well, especially after I had arrived on the dot of time for a 10 a.m. meeting following a heavy overnight snowfall that brought London to an inevitable standstill. I had set off from Surbiton very early, but had to abandon my car near Wandsworth Bridge and trudge the last two miles to make the meeting. Sam only had to walk a hundred metres from the far end of Wellington Square. Mark arrived an hour late full of his nightmare journey even though he had come half the distance I had. Sam did not fail to note my professional determination.

I was in and out of the EG offices like a jack-in-a-box with so many projects on the go. On one occasion after a rare lunch with the band members, I arrived for a meeting with Sam. I was wearing a smart jacket, freshly laundered white open collared shirt, pressed blue jeans and polished brogues.

'Did you have a good lunch?' Sam enquired brusquely.

Before I could reply, he continued, 'You are the band's professional advisor and as such, I expect you to present yourself in a suit and tie.'

I was accustomed to adopting formal business attire for Grosvenor Estate meetings, but this aspect of music business conservatism struck a weird chord. Maybe he wanted to keep me away from the frequent wrangles between the three central Roxy characters.

Sam was also treasurer of the Nordoff-Robbins music therapy foundation on whose behalf he had acquired a small run-down light industrial building in Kentish Town. He asked me if I would be interested in designing the world's first dedicated music therapy centre. The brief was to provide a series of sound-isolated therapy and observation rooms as well as teaching space for new therapists, administration offices for the charity, and staff accommodation. The proposition seemed of great interest, but I had no idea what music therapy entailed. I asked if I could observe a few sessions so I could start to understand how they worked and what was needed for the teaching spaces.

Sybil Beresford-Peirse was the formidable director of the charity's work and cause. I arrived at the makeshift accommodation in part of Whitelands College in Roehampton, and after a short explanation of the nature of the therapy sessions, was led to one of the observation rooms. I sat quietly behind a one-way mirror in the shared wall to the therapy room. That morning, I saw four individual therapy sessions with children aged between nine and fourteen. Each child had serious but varying degrees of mental and physical disability. The therapists used musical instruments and songs to engage them. At the start, each individual displayed a mixture of anxiety and expectation. As time advanced, their attention grew, their involvement in drumming and singing brought about change. The making of music transformed their whole demeanour, their eyes sparkled, smiles reshaped their faces, their damaged bodies danced with the rhythms of self-made music. Each of the sessions brought a flow of tears to my eyes; a dreadful sadness for each child's disability but tears of hope for the sense of healing and evident joy that the music brought into their lives. Then there were other tears of admiration for the patient perseverance of the therapists' devotion.

Soon after this experience, I was invited to a charity luncheon to raise funds for the works to convert the building in Kentish Town. The attendees were a Who's Who of the music business. Sam would circulate from one table to the next between courses. Before dessert was served, he returned and sat down next to me.

'Paul, you have a project, we can get started on building the first Nordoff-Robbins music therapy centre in the UK. I won't say who, but I've just been given a cheque for one million pounds.'

12 WILD BOYS

When Roxy Music were promoting *Jealous Guy* in Munich in '82, Duran Duran were in the city at the same time. Roxy were their heroes and when they met at a club one night, they were quizzing Phil on who should help engineer their next album. Should it be Rhett Davies or Bob Clearmountain? Phil suggested they should try someone new, young and experimental. They should meet Ian Little, a friend of mine from art college who had been caretaking at Phil's studio and had enthusiastically learnt first to be a tape-op and then swiftly a sound engineer.

Duran Duran recorded *Is There Something I Should Know?* at Gallery with Ian Little soon after. They all got on well, loved the studio, and Ian was then off to the south of France to work with them on what became the album *Seven and the Ragged Tiger*.

The band members spent a lot of time with Phil while recording at Gallery. Phil's 1930s house was right next door and he had shown them the work I had been doing restoring and remodelling it.

As Duran's success was exploding, they each wanted to buy houses in London and were looking for someone they could trust to advise them. Simon Le Bon (vocals) was first to call, the rest of the band followed soon after. I must confess that I had to buy their album, *Rio*, so that I knew each band member's name.

Simon and Yasmin's first home was a former boathouse on Apollo Place, tucked behind Cheyne Walk, next to the river in Chelsea, only yards away from where I had first stayed with Peter and Gillian as a teenager. It had a tiny, secret entrance that opened up into a large double height space. Alan and I worked up the designs with a series of levels including an eccentric master bathroom on a raised level, reached by steps, and overlooking the main bedroom. Alan designed most of the funky, post-modern furniture.

While the designs for the house were progressing, the boys were recording in Paris. Simon invited me and Susie over for a long weekend to stay in their apartment and go over the plans. He kindly agreed to meet us at Charles de Gaulle airport and even though our plane was delayed a couple of hours, he waited for us and drove us into the city. Although running late, Simon took time with young fans to sign autographs. He took special time with one young girl who he remembered had a sister who was unwell.

Later that evening, Simon and I returned to their high-ceilinged rented flat for supper with Yasmin and Susie. Simon was most excited to show us his boyish skill at flying his remote-control helicopter around the flat, telling us that the only reason for renting the unusual space was the exceptionally high ceilings so that he could play with his latest toy.

When Simon and Yasmin first moved into Apollo Place, Viv Lythgoe, the builder, and I needed to make a final snagging visit. Viv was nervous about asking how early we might arrive.

On the phone Yasmin had said,

'Your working day starts at 8 a.m. doesn't it? Come then, if you like, I'll be up to see you.'

Most celebrity clients are much less considerate of builders' working hours. Viv and I arrived on the dot of eight. Yasmin, a radiant natural beauty, answered the door in faded blue jeans and denim shirt with rolled up sleeves, looking like she meant business.

'How do you like your tea?'

Standing proudly in her new kitchen and filling a bucket of hot soapy water, she chatted about how much she and Simon were enjoying being together in their first home.

'Didn't we do a thorough enough clean?' Viv asked.

'Yes, you did fine, but it's my first home and I want to get to know it and make it even shinier. I'm doing the bathroom first. You guys give me a shout when you want more tea.'

Nick Rhodes (keyboards) was the most fastidious of the group, always immaculately dressed in the latest fashion; his slight frame topped with a mop of dyed white hair, he looked like a prettier version of Andy Warhol. Undoubtedly the artist of the band, he and I developed the deepest level of discussion over his new home and a shared passion for Art Deco design and artefacts. He bought a run-down, end-of-terrace corner house on Gilston Road at the south end of The Boltons, a prime location in Chelsea. Nick wanted an Art Deco party palace for his first home

Right:
Simon & Yasmin's sitting room
at Apollo Place

with Julie-Anne, his fiancée. That's what we delivered. Alan and I were lucky to have Adrian Jones and Henry Thompson working with us at the time. They were the authors of impeccable drawings with outstanding vision and detail. The house at Gilston Road was a triumph and, once finished, was probably the most valuable two-bedroom house in London.

We based the entrance hall floor on an extract from a Kandinsky expressionist painting made in coloured inlaid scagliola. Piano keys were the inspiration for the dining room, which was entirely black and white with meticulously curved ivory-coloured cabinet work and a bespoke black lacquer oval table. For the drawing room, Nick found a half-moon Strohmenger 1930s baby grand piano in maple veneer, one of the few specially built for the Cunard liners. An Edgar-William Brandt *Temptation* serpent *torchère* would stand to the side of a Ruhlmann-inspired one-off fireplace, which Adrian had sketched and detailed. The room was almost a perfect square, so within that geometry, we were able to set a circular recessed ceiling like the one Nick had admired floating above the St Ann's Court drawing room. That's where he would also have seen Phil's Strohmenger, another of the prettiest pianos ever made.

Above:
Phil's *Strohmenger*
at St Ann's Hill
Photograph © Clive Helm

The whole of the first floor was given over to the master bedroom suite. A key element of it was a vast walk-in closet entered via an octagonal plinth with mirrored panels that folded out to enable a 360-degree vision of the fashionista clients' chosen outfits. The *pièce de résistance* was the lower ground floor, the party place. We designed a spectacular stair as the point of arrival. This had been the subject of unending phone calls to Adrian and me from Nick in different parts of the world. Whether he was in a spectacular hotel or had just watched a classic Hollywood movie, the new stair was a big priority. Descending from the back of the ground floor hall, the swooping 'Bette Davis' stair was pure silver-screen fantasy. It was designed with sensuously curved treads and a finely wrought Art Deco inspired balustrade and handrail, providing a glamorous scene setting for Nick and Julie-Anne's star-studded parties.

The first party met '80s rock n' roll expectations. I spent most of the evening in the kitchen with actor Christopher Walken. I found him just as intense as he was in his role in *The Deer Hunter*. He had a sense of the weird, was complex but

Above:
Nick Rhodes and Susie:
Matching smiles

charismatic, and had eyes that could see through stone. I can't remember how or when Susie and I got home.

Roger Taylor (drums) was the least demonstrative of the band members, quiet and seemingly self-contained; he didn't revel in the attention of pop-stardom. He bought a white stucco Regency villa in Little Venice, near Maida Vale. We set about designing an understated, cool conversion for him and his fiancée, Giovanna. I wanted to design a bespoke joinery kitchen for them. Ever since seeing Mackintosh's Hill House kitchen, I had a thing about the cost of branded cupboards compared to hand-crafted English joinery. But they were determined to have a Smallbone kitchen. I'd said we could design a better one and for less money, but they wanted the brand name. When it came to completion, the Smallbone installation was so poor and out-of-true that I had to instruct its removal and complete re-installation. I felt for them as the refit delayed finishing, but they liked the end result. After all, it was their home, their choice and their money.

John Taylor (bass guitar) was bouncingly energetic, with legendary, chiselled good looks. He found a perfectly renovated house in one of the most desirable Kensington Mews, which was suitably tucked away. He asked me to take a look and I advised him to buy it as it suited him admirably without the need for building works. He bought the house and moved in without the agonies of delivering a building project.

Andy Taylor (lead guitar) was seemingly the dark horse of the band, the outsider with a gritty Geordie sense of humour. We got on well and he talked about creating a New York loft in London.

Alan and I, meanwhile, had moved our office to the Royal Victoria Patriotic Building (RVPB) in '81. The RVPB is a huge, French-inspired, Victorian Gothic listed building complex next to Wandsworth Common, on a low hill just south of the Thames. Originally built for orphans of victims from the Crimean War, it had fallen into neglected disrepair. Not knowing what to do with it, Wandsworth Council sold it to Covent Garden entrepreneur and wine bar owner Paul Tutton for £1. It needed imagination to transform it and a seven-figure sum to deal with the dilapidation repairs.

Paul had set about clearing out the ground floor spaces to become studio offices and preparing the upper floors as shells ready for residential conversion. Alan and I struck a deal with him to fit out the first office studio space on a low rent so that he could use it as a marketing suite for future lettings. The huge building wrapped around two formal courtyards and another big workshop yard. A drama school occupied the main hall and a series of other large spaces. A restaurant and bar set up in the courtyard next to our office. At the time, access to the RVPB was through an estate of social housing tower blocks off the wide dual carriageway that heads south from Wandsworth Bridge. This meant that despite being easily able to spot its towering scale, it was almost impossible for new visitors to find their way in. It does seem strange that such a hugely visible edifice could simultaneously remain a secret. The restaurant and bar became popular with young members of the Royal Family until some fool let the press know that Princess Diana liked to escape there. The paparazzi showed up and blew it.

The RVPB complex became a lively centre full of creative energy. The workshops housed model makers, furniture builders, a top film prosthetics artist and up above, the flats housed writers, a doctor, musicians, studio owners and a juggler, tightrope walker amongst other interesting personalities. We showed Andy around the northwest wing and helped him negotiate the purchase of five shell spaces including two of the dramatic tall turrets which had phenomenal views over London. The Thompson Twins bought two shells next door and their glamorous friend Debbie Harry was occasionally spotted in the bar.

Flat 27 had amazing potential to deliver a playful rock n' roll loft and Andy was up for it. We had great fun designing it and when Andy was back from tour, I used to enjoy popping upstairs from our studio for a cup of tea and other '80s diversions. The high Gothic-arched volumes were a young architect's dream to play with. I inserted mezzanine galleries, a Jacuzzi bathroom in one of the towers and a meditation observatory in the other. The model makers made a huge raw aluminium laser-cut map of the world with tiny LED lights marking the cities where the biggest Duran Duran gigs had been. We hung it in the sitting area under the mezzanine gallery. When the lights were turned on, we indulged in a very '80s rock n' roll celebration.

In the spring of '83 Andy rang from New York.

'We're doing a big charity gig for Mencap at Aston Villa on 23 July. We want a stage set that looks like a Roman temple. We want you to design it for us. Can you do it in time?'

Henry Thompson, who had worked on Chester Close and the Roxy Flying Handbag, and I put our thinking caps on. The stage should be a simple set of risers, like wide steps, leading up to a row of five or six Roman columns as high as the lighting rig, 25ft (7.6m) tall, to form a temple façade. So how could we build a temporary columnar temple façade and move it? The supplemental brief was that they might take the set on a world tour.

How about making them as inflatables? We decided that there should be six columns each about 1m in diameter and 7m tall. For transportation, our idea came from a jack-in-a-box. Each column would have a plinth cum flight-case with the capital as the lid; that way, the lid could be clipped to the rig and lifted prior to inflation. We sourced inflatable fabrics and found a pale cream textured cloth that would look like stone from a distance. The columns would appear authentic as the backdrop to the stage when lit externally from the sides. What else could we do to light the columns? What if we could light them from inside? If we made the plinths a bit taller, then we could mount a stage light in each base under a sheet of plexiglass and the columns could be lit from inside to create a completely different effect. The collapsed column fabric would then sit above the plexiglass with the capital forming

Right:
Andy Taylor's Gothic loft
at the RVPB

the lid of the box. The plexiglass would have to have an airtight seal. The upper half of the plinth would have a tube to connect to the inflation fan.

Now all we needed was someone who could build something between the base of Nelson's Column and a giant jack-in-a-box in next to no time, not just one but six. Andrew Aldridge, a close friend, and Peter, his erstwhile joiner foreman, had the will, skill and sense of humour to fulfil the task.

'How soon?' Andrew jested.

I found out later that they were sorting things out on the phone till three in the morning. Anything is possible with a little help from your friends; without them, forget it.

Henry and I headed up to Birmingham to set up the stage: six giant jack-in-a-boxes that we hoped would inflate and turn into an imposing Roman temple backdrop for the Duranie charity gig for Mencap. With help from the road crew everything was positioned, the column capitals connected to the lighting rig; up went the rear rig truss and with it the limp, empty, inflatable tubes. One by one, Henry and I connected the giant air blower, a sort of over-sized hair dryer, and once filled with air, the tubes turned into surprisingly convincing stone columns. Dress rehearsals on the Friday evening before the gig went well. With everyone happy, the columns were deflated and lowered back into their boxes. We all headed back to the hotel for a few beers.

Next morning, we went back to Aston Villa football stadium to fine tune and make ready for the gig. We were confident that it looked good and would light effectively. Complacency is always a dangerous feeling; it stops you getting out of bed as early as you should. Mounting the back of the stage, we found that one of the internal plinth lights had been left on overnight and burnt a hole in the Plexiglass and the column's inflatable material, a very big, scorched hole. We needed the biggest puncture repair kit imaginable, and we did not have much time. A chauffeur-driven car appeared, and we raced around Birmingham. The city was the home of Dunlop tyres, so it had to be possible. Several tyre fitters did not have what we needed, it seemed inner tube repairs were a thing of the past. At the last minute, we found

Below:
Dress Rehearsal:
Inflatable columns in place

a plastics warehouse on an industrial estate that had plexiglass and a range of promising adhesives. Fortunately, we had brought some spare inflatable fabric with us. The driver raced us back to the football stadium. We dismantled the box, installed a new square of plexiglass, re-made the silicone seal, then cut around the burnt-out half-metre square section and applied copious, multiple tubes of repair glue to stick on the new piece. As we were running out of time, we borrowed two hair dryers from the costume department to speed up the drying time. It wouldn't have looked good if the repair failed and one column suddenly, or even gradually, deflated like a giant limp dick.

Only minutes before the gates opened and 18,000 fans rushed in, the sixth column was re-inflated, and the stage was set. Henry and I had a couple of well-earned beers and, still anxious, wandered through the crowd, climbed to the top of the mixing tower, and watched Robert Palmer powerfully open the show. The first half of the Duran performance was still in daylight and the columns were only lit from the outside. They did look like the robust stone columns of a Roman temple as per the initial brief. In the second half, the internal lights transformed the image of the columns into something playfully cosmetic and very different. But we had done it, and the gig went well.

Above and below:
Columns lit from inside, and the view
from the control tower

When I'd left Paris after the recording sessions in October, Nick Rhodes had said that they'd be back in London to celebrate New Year, and they'd love Susie and me to join the party. I didn't get another call until about 7 p.m. on New Year's Eve. It was Nick.

'We're mortified,' he said in his Brummie accent. 'We're sitting in the bar in the Savoy and just realised none of us has called you. Can you get here? We're heading off to Stringfellow's for a private party.'

Susie had already decided that we'd been forgotten. She was grumpy and had just gone up to check on Luke and baby Jessica, heading for a very early night.

'It's OK Nick, we'll never get a babysitter on New Year's Eve at short notice. Anyway, we're out in Surbiton, don't worry, you guys have a great night.'

'Leave it with me, I'll call you back in a few minutes.'

Ten minutes later the phone rang again.

'The Savoy nanny is in the limo on her way to you. Better get dressed to party. Sorry to rush you.'

Susie and I glammed up at double speed.

The nanny arrived and the chauffeur held open the door to the classic Daimler limo. Between the two back seats was a tray of caviar with all the traditional accoutrements and an ice bucket with a bottle of Dom Perignon and two crystal flutes. The Daimler glided up the A3 and through the New Year's Eve throng around Trafalgar Square, coming to rest in St Martin's Lane with a huge crowd of Duranie fans packing the wide pavement outside the venue. As we drew up, a team of bouncers parted the sea of young girls. Simon skipped out to greet us and Susie and I were whisked into the notorious nightclub. We had a great night, and I was particularly chuffed when Robert Palmer (Mr Cool) asked me where I'd got my cream silk suit made.

'Thailand.'

'I must go there again.'

In the early hours, the Daimler re-appeared and delivered us safely home to our kids.

13 DREAM OR BRAND?

By the mid '80s, Susie and I had three kids, Luke born in '79, Jessica in '82 and Henry in '87. Life was all I had wanted it to be, and we had moved to a family house with a generous garden on the hill above Surbiton. Things were going well for Davis & Bayne (D&B), it was time to fulfil another dream. Several small specialist car manufacturers were building affordable replicas of the 289 and 427 AC Cobra. The originals had become expensive historic collectors' items. BRA manufactured the prettier 289 that had raced at Le Mans in 1963. The director of BRA was selling his own car. I took the train to Doncaster on a wet February morning. The car was as refined as I had hoped. I set off back home to Surbiton as night fell. Rain dripped on my legs and my feet roasted from the heat of the V8 engine. The wide Dunlop tyres slid and searched for grip as I pressed the accelerator pedal. I mused on how daft my acquisition seemed to be. I needed to learn how to drive the beast. Brands Hatch circuit had a racing driving school, so I signed up to the course to qualify for my National Class B competition licence.

I joined the Cobra club and met like-minded nostalgic petrol heads making race day outings to UK circuits and team outings to Le Mans. My off-duty uniform was a Levi's denim jacket with a weighty badge collection from gigs, favourite cars, cartoon characters and Apollo space missions (an idea borrowed from Peter Blake's Pop Art *Self-portrait with Badges*). Club members would meet up at our Wandsworth office before setting off for the Friday night King's Road cruise. One friend, Colin, arrived early to find me dressed in a smart work suit. He joked that he didn't recognise me. I quickly changed into my more identifiable off-duty uniform and realised that the Cobra had become part of my persona, my dream had become part of my brand; suit or denim jacket an identity uniform. It was fun to cruise the King's Road with friends and all manner of automobile exotica.

In 2002, Peter Blake held his 70th birthday party at the Chelsea Arts Club. I dressed for the occasion in jeans, baseball boots, red polo shirt and badged Levi's jacket. Peter got the joke and with a fat black felt pen signed my denim homage. It hasn't seen the washing machine since. Paul McCartney arrived as a friendly gesture to the artist of the seminal *Sgt. Pepper's Lonely Hearts Club Band* album cover. As I ordered a round of drinks at the bar, McCartney complimented me on my badge collection and signed Blake artwork. I was pleased to tell him that I had designed his drummer's house.

When the Cobra first parked outside our office, it attracted many inquisitive admirers, one of whom worked at a neighbouring successful graphic design firm. Marks & Spencer were one of their major clients. The big brand clothing chain wanted to move into selling food and commissioned the graphics firm to come up

Opposite:
My everyday work car borrowed for Sock Shop marketing

Above:
Boy racing his dream

with the imaging and branding for M&S Food. There was too much 3D presentation work for the graphics office to handle and they invited D&B to assist.

We had regular, generally early evening, meetings with George from the M&S in-house architecture and design division. George liked to come after work because there was a bar adjacent to our office. Also, he lived only a few hundred yards from my home in Surbiton and he could cadge a ride home with me in the Cobra.

On one such evening, we had been discussing ideas for the main external logo lettering and its illumination. We hadn't managed to solve it over a pint or two, but driving home in the dark, I noticed the green halo lighting around the bezels of the speedo and rev counter.

'Hey, George, look at the instruments on the Cobra dashboard.'

'Yes, we are exceeding the speed limit,' George replied, missing the point.

'No, look at how effective the dials are in the dark, what about green halo lighting for the main store and the same type face but with a light blue halo for M&S Food?'

He liked the idea, we mocked it up and it was adopted.

Next we worked up further interior images for the new food stores as a handbook of the various elements from signage to merchandising cabinets and typical layouts.

The success of this work led on to developing new ideas for some of the main store departments across the UK. At the time, M&S were expanding across Europe and soon we were appointed to prepare whole new store layouts.

The next advance was for M&S out-of-town stores. These were usually part of large schemes promoted by either Tesco or Sainsbury's. The outcome had been that the M&S stores looked rather like the little brother to either of these two big chain supermarkets in materials and forms. George commissioned us to come up with ideas for a more identifiable image for M&S out-of-town stores. He wanted something more classical and less 'orange-tile-roofy'. It was the era of post-modernism and perhaps predictably and naively, we drew a series of options with pedimented entrances. These were surprisingly well received back at the M&S HQ in Baker Street, and we were asked to draw up a series of versions for new stores that were being discussed with the Big Two. Once these had been agreed, we were instructed to prepare a handbook for other architects to use as further schemes moved forwards.

Our workload with M&S was becoming a major commitment. Unfortunately, George was either under-resourced or just badly organized. Often his paperwork for confirming work instructions was muddled, late or had repeat order numbers. This made extracting payments from the M&S accounts department problematic and slow. We sorted this with him, and things got better for a year. D&B acquired two £20,000 computer workstations, which were state of the art at the time and a big investment for us. We bought these to cope with planning and visualizing the increasing number of stores across Europe.

George would regularly call on a Monday afternoon saying that he would drop in the following evening with the next scheme to design. Often, he would turn up on Friday evening and want the drawings for 8 a.m. the following Monday. This meant we had to initiate an M&S weekend shift. Since the fees were time based, we just had to get on with it. The trouble was that only four of our staff could operate the complex software efficiently, so they took most of the burden.

As the '80s wore on, the accounts department payments became slower and later. Our terms of payment had been agreed on 28–day settlement. M&S had slipped to over 90 days and our monthly billing was sometimes £60 to £70,000 pounds. Our accounts manager kept chasing with no result. She suggested that we might get a more positive response if I called in person. When I eventually got through and went over the £84,000 of payments that were overdue by three months, I was told, 'If you knock off 10%, the balance can be paid next week.'

'I'll see you in hell,' was my reactive response and put the phone down.

I called George and told him that we were suspending all work for M&S until we got paid. Two hours later George arrived in the office and the money arrived the same week without a discount deduction. But, over the following months their instructions gradually declined to nothing. We had to conclude that either they were investing less in new stores or they were commissioning others who accepted their arrogant attitude towards the supply chain. As the recession hit in the late '80s, we could have done with the work, but at the same time, with salaries and overheads to meet each month, cash flow was crucial, and I refused to be messed around.

Left:
An early M&S out-of-town store

14 THE BATTLE OF HANS STREET

Stuart Corbyn had worked in Amsterdam for eight years up to the early '80s and on his return took over a recruitment agency for surveyors. In '85, the Cadogan Estate were looking to appoint a new chief executive and Stuart was given the instruction to find somebody.

'This one's for me,' he thought.

He applied, got the job, and sold the recruitment agency. At least, that's the popular version of what is said to have happened, though Stuart always insists that this isn't entirely correct.

Stuart joined the Cadogan Estate in January '86. At that time, in common with many of the London Estates, Cadogan had been continuing the role of passive landlord, an estate management approach it had followed for almost 300 years. It sold sites on long, typically 99-year leases to developers rather than actively developing properties itself. This had recently happened along almost the entire length of the south terrace of Cadogan Place. Simultaneous large scale reconstruction by different uncoordinated developers had caused disruption and anger amongst local residents. At the same time, complaints were being made to Cadogan about the actions, or lack of them, of certain head-lessees. The outcome was that Cadogan were lambasted for not exerting sufficient control over the developers and their contractors, and over some less than proactive head-lessees.*

Stuart had new and different ideas about the Estate developing in its own right as well as establishing a direct relationship with occupational lessees in place of intermediate landlords. This was to be on a very different form of lease that was closer to those he had worked with in the Netherlands. In addition to buying in headleases and adjacent freeholds when opportunities arose, he was on the lookout for architects active in the area. Our work for Grosvenor was only next door. The Leasehold Reform Act of 1967 and the second Act in 1974 empowered domestic leaseholders to purchase the freehold ownership of houses. This had impacted on the London Estates who were forced to sell much of their residential holdings. Stuart could see that through enfranchisement of their residential buildings, the Estate would become capital-rich whilst losing that part of its portfolio.

His plan was to invest in Sloane Street, Sloane Square, and the King's Road, using the capital receipts that were the resultant outcome of these Acts. These were causing the enforced sale of residential properties across the Estate including prime

---

* In many instances, the Estate had sold their direct interest to head-lessees who then sub-let to tenants. Part of Stuart's strategy was to buy back the head-leases to re-establish management control and form direct relationships with the tenants.

areas around Cadogan Square. Commercial properties did not fall under these Acts. The Leasehold Reform Act of 1993 brought apartments within enfranchisement, and this added to the impact on Cadogan. Many of their large Chelsea properties had been converted to flats and hence this Act would, over time, further reduce the size of the estate and reinforce Stuart's strategy.

'The Estate will be a shopping-street manager in the future,' he said in one of our many conversations.

Andrew Braddon, one of Stuart's friends from Amsterdam, was marketing director for Fairclough Construction, who had completed our early scheme for Grosvenor and Roland Castro at Chester Close in '84. Andrew was and is a most genial character and was keen to introduce me to Stuart. He arranged a lunch at the Greenhouse restaurant in Mayfair before it won its Michelin stars. The first time, embarrassingly, I forgot all about the invitation. I was lucky to get a second chance. What I do remember is that they were the best triple-cooked chunky chips I'd ever eaten. Stuart asked me to meet Andrew Oades, his chief building surveyor, the following week.

Our first commission, or 'starter for 10', was to refurbish the common areas of 190/192 Sloane Street. This was a '60s office building, subsequently given protected status in '95, because of its early use of lightweight metal and glass external cladding, otherwise known as 'curtain walling'. The tenants (floor by floor) were disgruntled because of historic poor management and the Estate were keen to see improvements. Cadogan had recently bought out a joint venture partner and taken responsibility for the management of the building. Our job, a good test, was to design and carry out the works whilst the office tenants remained in occupation. The key to keeping them happy was to explain what we were going to do and when we would do it, and then stick to it. It was mostly about straightforward communication and ensuring the site was cleaned up at the end of each day. It wasn't rocket science.

The building became the subject of an interesting regulatory paradox. It was listed for its early use of an external curtain wall. However, office interiors, suspended ceilings, etc, were all designed to be refitted every 20 years or so. As we will soon see, it is a criminal offence to remove fixed items from the interior of a listed building without consent. How's that for a contradictory piece of very confusing bureaucracy?

As this first Cadogan project neared completion, a private client asked me to remodel five floors of a house on Cadogan Square. I arranged to meet Stuart to check whether acting for an individual leaseholder would be a conflict of interest whilst working on behalf of the Estate.

'What number on Cadogan Square?' asked Stuart.

'Number 24,' I answered.

'That's the one with the kitchen at the front of the raised ground floor,' commented Stuart in an instant.

Stuart advised that since we had restored numerous private houses and apartments whilst working for Grosvenor, acting on No. 24 would not be a problem for him. At that time, Stuart had been at the densely built 96-acre Cadogan Estate for not much more than a year. As I left the meeting, I vowed to get to know those acres better than anyone other than Stuart. I walked the area a lot and observed carefully. It paid off.

Our next project was No. 1 Hans Street. This was one of the original Henry Holland houses dating from the 1790s, which had been part of a terrace on the west side of Sloane Street and was now Grade II listed. When its 99-year lease had ended in the 1890s, its neighbour to the north had been demolished to create Hans Street, a narrow lane linking to the newly formed Hans Place. At that time, No.1 had been radically and individualistically altered by Arts and Crafts architect, Fairfax Wade. The entrance was moved to the newly exposed side elevation and the most drastic change was to import and reconfigure a 17th century staircase from a building being demolished in the City of London. A possible early example of architectural salvage? So, here was a listed building with elements from three centuries that needed reinvention at the end of the 20th century.

As a young architect with a practice in my own name, I was more than excited to be appointed to restore an individual historic building on Sloane Street. In the mid-'80s, the street was best known for Sloane Rangers and Princess Diana's shopping trips to The General Trading Company. In fact, it had become a second-tier fashion-label street with mostly out-dated retail accommodation and poor-quality walk-up flats or offices above. It is hard to believe how neglected many of the buildings were, in such a famously expensive area of London. Active management and major investment had been lacking at Cadogan before Stuart's tenure.

My first inspection of No. 1 was a surprise. Having forced the front door open, I discovered piles of mildew-ridden junk mail and was hit by the overwhelming musty odour of fungal dry rot. There were six floors to explore, and each was full of intrigue and danger. Mountains of now worthless gambling chips, a broken roulette wheel, brocade curtains and worn plush carpets told of its abandoned, once glamorous night-time use as a casino. It had stood empty and unused for five years. On the upper levels many of the floorboards were rotten and I needed to tread carefully to avoid falling through to the ceiling of the room below. I ventured by torchlight down to the basement where ceilings and walls dripped dank water into stagnant slimy puddles. I should have worn wellington boots, not polished black brogues. The putrid smell of saturated plaster filled my nostrils and made breathing unpleasant. The back rooms on the principal levels were west facing and had been extended by Wade with an expansive bow-shaped wall and two tall sash windows. These were intrinsically dignified spaces but were in a sorry state of neglect. The best feature was undoubtedly the imported 17th century oak staircase. Its treads wound up and around the corners in sweeping double-centred curves, while the barley-twist balusters were topped by a robust carved handrail. It must have come from a far grander house.

The first thing to do was to organise a clean out of the detritus and then carry out our own measured survey of the whole structure. The best way to get to know an old building intimately is to sketch and measure each element and then, at the drawing board, carefully record its story to paper and memory. That way, even though it takes several days, you feel and learn its character and evolution. You begin to know and understand your architectural canvas. The Grand Tour had been the means for generations of would-be architects to travel to Italy and Greece to study, draw and hence learn the elements of classical architecture. If one couldn't afford to visit Europe, then the British Museum was the place to learn the language of classical proportion and detail through measuring and drawing.

Armed with our drawn survey of No. 1, we began preparing design options. The first key consideration revolved around retention of the stair whilst meeting fire separation regulations at each floor level. This we achieved by a glazed oak screen linking front and rear rooms. The principal rooms would largely look after themselves if we could carefully weave in modern services and air conditioning. Reconstruction of the basement was essential and by extending further under the rear courtyard we would be able to introduce a substantial skylight and create a large, state-of-the art conference room. This would help the balance of accommodation that would be essential to create a desirable, albeit small, headquarters office building. A major challenge was to squeeze a lift shaft into the tight plan without compromising the stair. This was nonetheless essential to achieve a workable six storey building.

We prepared a detailed set of planning and listed building application drawings and began negotiations with the planners from English Heritage and the Royal Borough of Kensington and Chelsea (RBK&C). Our design was mostly acceptable with minor refinements and supplemental detail, but not the stair. The balustrade handrail was too low for building regulation compliance and the depth of the sweeps of the stair treads too variable. English Heritage would not consent to adapting the stair to comply, and non-compliance would mean the converted building would be unusable. It was stalemate. Round and around we went with frustrating meetings, arguing and no one listening to each other. It felt like the conservation officers were determined to thwart our progress as a young practice. We had to find a solution or lose our best new client. We hit on the rarely used option of a 'Building Regulation Appeal'. This was the only time I ever had to revert to this exceptional process in 40 years of practice.* Common sense prevailed, and we were granted consent on the simple premise that the 17th century staircase had been adapted when moved from the City in the 19th century, so it could reasonably be adapted again for beneficial use in the 20th century. Our win on this was not yet over, although conservation officers of RBK&C and English Heritage clearly regarded the determination as a defeat.

The debate had caused considerable delay and Mr. Oades at the Estate expressed mixed feelings of sympathy and dissatisfaction. However, with the staircase issue resolved, all consents were in hand, and we could proceed to construction.

---

* Planning approval refusals often resort to planning appeals because of the subjective and political nature of the process. Building regulations are an objective set of rules that can be negotiated and agreed in most instances. Here, the debate between objective rules and subjective opinion clashed.

Left:
1 Hans Street:
After the battle

133

Once on site, the extent of excavation to solve the basement damp, underpinning for settlement and the new lift shaft coupled with the decay of floor and roof structures proved exceedingly complex, with major works at every level within a tight space. The precious staircase was at risk, even with fastidious protection and the expense of an enveloping scaffold and temporary roof. The job of restoration required expert joinery skills in the protective environment of a well-equipped and clean workshop. The whole staircase needed to be taken apart piece by piece to adapt and restore it. On site was not an appropriate location. Peter of Andrew Aldridge's company in Sussex was the best joiner I knew. He and his two assistants arrived at Hans Place and began carefully inscribing every piece with a coded Roman numeral system as they dismantled and bubble wrapped each oak segment for transport to his workshop.

But after only a couple of hours of diligent work, conservation officers from the Royal Borough and English Heritage strolled into the hallway unannounced.

'You are aware,' they said, 'that removal of a fixed element of fabric from a listed building is a criminal offence. Consent has not been granted for the removal of the staircase from this building. Works must be suspended immediately.'

I can't repeat the words that went through my mind as I struggled to maintain my cool. Were we in the midst of the conservation officers' revenge?

I explained that my intention, and that of the Cadogan Estate and contractor, was simply to restore the staircase in the most appropriate environment, which was clearly not on a building site.

'I'm sure,' I added, through gritted teeth, 'that all of us want to avoid the process of criminal prosecution and court action over the restoration of a staircase.'

'We suggest,' they replied, 'that you write to us at the Royal Borough and English Heritage with a comprehensive report explaining why you consider that the staircase should be removed from this listed building contrary to the governing legislation. Until then, if you wish to avoid prosecution, the stair must remain in its present location.'

They left before I had time to bang my head through a plasterboard wall, which I did after the door had closed behind them. The assembled company of builders stood in silent disbelief over the conversation of the proceeding 20 minutes. After some sympathetic pats on the back and a strong coffee, I returned to our office with a racing heartbeat. Conscious of the implications of further delay, I sat down as though in after-school detention to write what became a 12-page report to explain in extensive detail the blindingly obvious.

Whilst writing, it occurred to me that the schooldays tables had turned. Who was teacher and who was pupil? Why should I be the one in detention teaching the detainee what they should well know? I submitted the report by hand the following day. Two weeks later consent was granted to remove the stair. Peter returned and painstakingly dismantled it piece by piece and delivered it to his workshop in Sussex. The outcome was inevitable, though it caused more delay on site and hence increased cost.

I was proud of the finished building. The reconfigured stair looked as though it had always been there. The new oak-panelled lift complemented the style of the historic interior and linked all six floors without impact on the principal rooms. The new sky-lit conference room in the enlarged basement added to the rich variety of spaces and the glazed oak fire-screens provided essential regulatory compliance in an elegant, unobtrusive way.

The smell of fungal damp was now replaced by fresh paint, aromatic French polish and newly stretched woollen carpets. At sign-off, my English Heritage combatant did admit that the leadwork on the reconstructed roof and the internal joinery were amongst the best he had seen. There was no apology for the grief and delay he and the borough conservation officer had wilfully inflicted without accountability. Nor had we seen the last of each other.

Underneath the floorboards between new structural timbers and the redundant, retained joists of the third floor we left a cryptic note for posterity describing the absurdly bureaucratic saga of our late 20th century restoration.

I was deeply concerned that the delays and increased costs would damage our chances of further commissions from Cadogan and Mr. Oades, who was still somewhat unpredictable in my mind. Perhaps our dogged determination and perseverance won out. We were strangely fortunate in the misfortune of another competing firm of architects. They had designed the first façade retention scheme on Sloane Street which was not well resolved, and we had to do better. At that time, there was a lot more to be done along that tired street.

The various terrace blocks dating from the late 19th century were made up of shops only five or six metres wide with cellular rooms on the floors above. Each had their own individual entrances with a poorly lit corridor about a metre wide leading to a dogleg staircase rising five or six storeys with no lift. These factors, coupled with half-metre-thick party walls and another dividing wall separating shop from corridor, made them inefficient, unattractive and undesirable. Most of these terraces were in designated Conservation Areas and hence could not be demolished to achieve improved lettability. They presented handsome brick, stone and terracotta façades but needed repair. How could the Estate create better, wider shops to improve rental income and form more useable offices on the upper floors when the buildings had statutory protection?

We talked over possible solutions with Stuart.

At 37 to 42 Sloane Street, our first such opportunity arose. The leases had terminated on six adjacent buildings which had become vacant with 36 metres (120ft) of frontage. Why not retain the façade, hold it up, demolish everything behind and lose all those wasted gloomy slices of corridor and thick, party walls? This approach would create more desirable, wider shops with useable basements and increase the valuable zone 'A' frontage by over 25%. This would also have the potential to introduce one attractive office entrance with lifts and concierge linking the upper levels with wide, open lateral office space across all six buildings. Could this be just what the office market was looking for in Chelsea where it adjoins Knightsbridge?

There was just one big problem. Almost all of the six buildings had shops at ground level with a mix of offices and a flat or two on the upper floors. Since these different uses shared a single staircase, they failed to comply with current fire regulations and mostly had been subject to poor quality post-war adaptations. Despite this non-compliance, RBK&C had a strict policy preventing the loss of residential units or habitable square feet. Although the flats at 37-42 Sloane Street were effectively unsafe and on a noisy main street, the quantum of residential space had to be retained. The solution came through 'planning use swaps'. The benefit of this was that the Estate owned other buildings in quieter locations that had office use, or again, a mix of flats and offices. In common with the other London landed estates, the potential for positive planning and place-making existed through their extensive land ownership and long-term stewardship.

Throughout the 1980s, the Grosvenor Estate had a similar problem with planning use swaps in Mayfair that we had worked on. During the bombing raids of the City of London in World War II, Westminster had granted a huge number of Temporary Office Permissions within residential buildings away from the focus of Luftwaffe attacks. Many were listed and all were in conservation areas and hence adaptions were restricted. Over time, these buildings had evolved with a similar mix of commercial and residential uses that Cadogan had in Sloane Street. In Mayfair, this was the cause of long-term debate between Westminster City Council and Grosvenor. It had become a major planning exercise since the many temporary office consents were all passing their expiry dates and the building uses had to be harmonised with planning and regulation compliance. This was a battle at the time and only partially solved years later by Colin Redman and Hugh Bullock, an exceptional planning consultant, effectively negotiating the informal concept of a 'use bank'. The idea being that because the landed estates owned multiple buildings, each could be assessed for its appropriate uses and then the quantum of square footage for each use be 'deposited' into a use class 'bank'. This was a logical approach and resulted in a rational ability for the Estates to plan for a viable mix of uses across Westminster in historically important buildings.

We proposed a similar approach to RBK&C, but they would not adopt the 'use deposit bank' idea even if it had to be in residential credit with no overdraft for office space. So, for Nos. 37-42, we scheduled the number of flats, their areas, and assessed the amenity of each to start to deal with the planning policy issue. Next, Stuart had to consider what other nearby buildings on the Estate had office use but could be suitable for residential conversion. We prepared sketch schemes for each of these buildings to calculate the number of units and total square footage of residential space that we could gain in each one. These became known as 'donor' buildings which we would compare with the amount of residential space at Nos. 37-42 lost through conversion to offices. This process we rapidly christened the 'Jigsaw'. The use swap balancing act provided the residential benefits required by RBK&C and we submitted a series of linked planning applications for several buildings including Nos. 37-42.

We had learnt some lessons from the battle at Hans Street. The solution suited the planners. It retained and restored the façade, thereby preserving the character of the conservation area. The Estate achieved a group of buildings transformed in terms of quality of space, efficiency and value. We even gained consent for an extra floor level, above which all the plant space was concealed within the roof section. This invisible plant solution became an exemplar with the planners and helped enhance our relationship with certain officers over the following years. Façade retention is a slow and costly process but ultimately worthwhile in such high value locations, though frowned upon in many architectural circles as 'façadism'.

Ultimately the 'Jigsaw' strategy worked extremely well. Stuart adopted it with us across dozens of buildings on Sloane Street, Sloane Square, the King's Road, and the surrounding streets of Chelsea. In the long term, this approach provided much-enhanced dwellings in quieter locations across the whole Estate, hugely improving its considerable residential lettings portfolio. Sloane Street was transformed into a world-class retail location and the King's Road was reinvigorated, especially following the acquisition and development of the Duke of York's Territorial Army Headquarters. More surprising and less obvious was the transformation of Sloane Street as an attractive office location, thereby adding to the overall mix of daily activity, footfall, and value of the whole Cadogan Estate portfolio. The addition of cultural venues over time would further add to the sense of place and re-energise Chelsea as one of London's best places to live, work and play. This was both smart estate management and creative placemaking.

We proceeded quickly through construction information and tendering procedures and started on site at Nos. 37–42. The erection of the massive steel frame structure to hold up the façade above the pedestrian pavement was a challenge. The northern section of Sloane Street was closed for a whole weekend whilst a gigantic mobile crane swung the steel frames into place. Once this temporary structure was set and the façade secured to it, demolition of the old structure commenced. The noble requirement to recycle as much material as possible did mean that the on-site demolition sequence took much longer than programmed. Reclaimed bricks were carefully cleaned, stacked and wrapped on pallets, whilst timber was de-nailed, sized and strapped before removal. I frequently climbed to the top of the retention structure high above Sloane Street. Each time, it was scary, exhilarating and frustrating to watch the original fabric slowly dissolve as recycling governed the pace. It was dangerous work and had to be done carefully in due sequence. Demolition was, and always is, a risky business.

As the new shell was advancing, Stuart requested a presentation from us to review the interior finishes for the offices. In most development circumstances, this leads to a 'value engineering' exercise; construction-speak for cost cutting. We laid out all the fittings, brochures and illustrative interior drawings on our expansive conference table and Trevor, the burly, bearded quantity surveyor, was there to explain the cost allowances for each element. Stuart liked what he

saw. Then, ever unpredictable, he asked: 'What would you change if you had another quarter of a million to spend on the finishes?'

We probably looked dumbstruck.

'You do lots of houses around here for wealthy private clients,' he explained. 'These are the people that I want to rent the offices. If they live nearby, wouldn't they prefer not to have to commute to another part of London to work? I want them to recognise the finishes in these offices as though they had chosen them, like their own homes. If they have Dornbracht taps at home, why wouldn't they want them at their place of business?'

So, we upped the specification on the office finishes as he suggested. The new business tenants of the completed building all resided locally as had been hoped for. The space let quickly and exceeded the agents' rental expectations. Sloane Street had started to become a better office location. This was something we would build on in future projects.

We had designed the ground and basement level retail space to be as flexible as possible. Alan and I had worked on numerous retail fitouts for end users and had been appalled at how little consideration had been given in new retail developments to the costs and options for the fit-out by prospective shop tenants. This learning was useful to employ on our first major retail shell. The Estate and advising agents assumed that there would most likely be five individual shops, each wanting to fit out differently. Assumption can be the 'mother of all cock-ups,' (Gerald Grosvenor,

The Duke of Westminster), or certainly can be proved mistaken. When the retail shell was ready for early handover, Armani approached the Estate wanting to take all five units at basement and ground levels plus the whole of the first floor as well. Could we accommodate the additional requirements for air conditioning this huge store? This was not easy, as retail air conditioning requires much more plant space than offices because of the necessary high lighting levels. But this was a challenge that had to be risen to. We were over the moon that Armani's advisors had told the Estate that 'It was the best and most considered retail shell they had ever seen.' This was equally good news for the Estate and for our future of work with them. It may seem simple, but it is disappointing that many major developers and architects fail to adequately consider the end user that they intend to sell or let to.

Armani took the whole space to create the first huge flagship store on Sloane Street. The street was on the up.

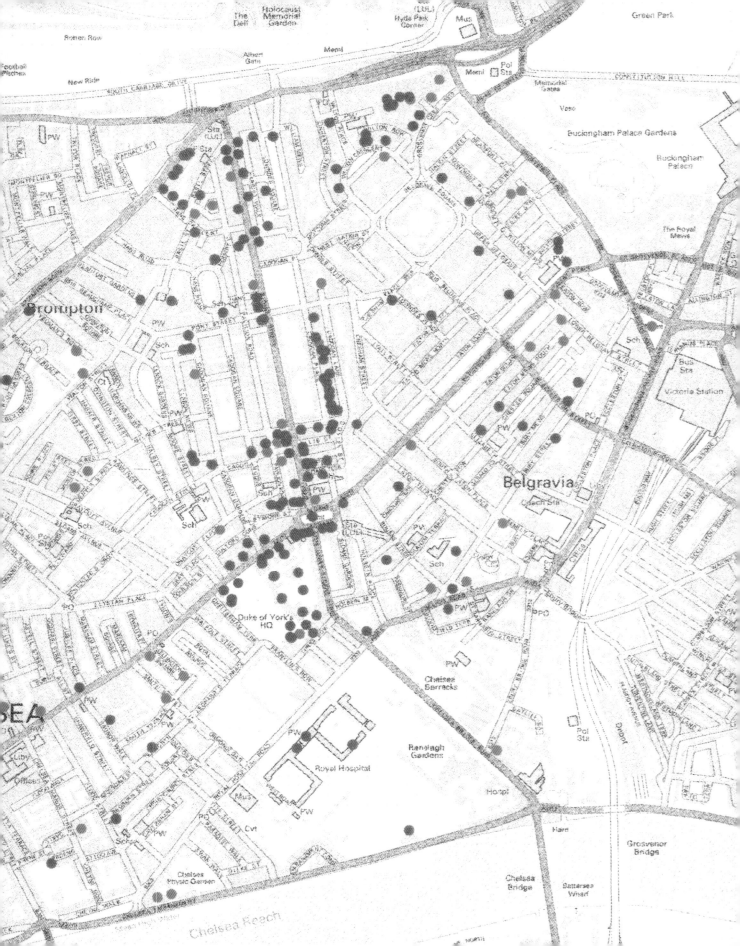

15 ALL THINGS MUST PASS

Perhaps the '80s were too much fun. It was an era of indulgent consumerism encouraged by Thatcher and her policies. A decade that ended with economic collapse and hiking interest rates. The architectural profession was particularly badly hit, and workloads collapsed as projects were put on hold. By '93, under- and unemployment in the profession had reached over 60%.

'What do you call an architect with a job?'

'Taxi!' went the answer.

But it was not a laughing matter. Davis & Bayne were not immune. Our bank, NatWest, were continually pulling the rug from under us. The bank held charges on our houses and the Chapel offices. If we'd had the funds, we would have sued them for advertising how they gave 'support to small businesses'.

I had a theory that even if projects were few and far between, there was always some work to be won. If you 'got out there' and were top of the list, then maybe you'd get the call. We did have Nos.37–42 Sloane Street on site with Cadogan, some small Belgravia residential schemes on behalf of Grosvenor and a major private house on Wilton Crescent. These provided some cash flow, but not enough. My 'getting out there' worked for a couple of years and had staved off the inevitable. Sadly in '92 we had to shed staff and by the end of '93 we had gone from 38 to 17 people. We always met salary bills for staff, but for many months Alan and I could not pay ourselves. It was harrowing making bright, committed young staff redundant. It hurt to let people go, but the bank was banging at the door. The stress dug deep, and the buck stopped with us.

Financial pressures exacerbate differences of input, work creation and personal opinions. Alan and I fell out. Without agreement on how to split the practice, I served notice to Alan under the Partnership Act of 1890, a last-ditch option. Conversations with the remaining senior staff were held to determine the proposed structure of a different business, Paul Davis + Partners (PD+P). The professional divorce was acrimonious and stressful, so much so that I was hospitalised with an olecranon bursitis, a sudden swelling the size of a duck egg on my elbow. The partnership break came on 30 April '94 without written agreements with our few remaining clients. We couldn't agree a split of work or clients. 37–42 Sloane Street was 70% complete, that is 30% incomplete, and there was an onerous responsibility to complete the appointment.

It was crucial that key clients gave personal and commercial support. Colin Redman of Grosvenor Estates offered me the Old School House in Ebury Street as a new workspace at an affordable rent. Although in need of a bit of care and attention, it was a fantastic barn of a building and only a few hundred yards from

Opposite:
Early PDP marketing plan
Projects and Studies in SW1 & SW3
Prolific in the area

Right:
Chapel Studio looking shipshape

Below:
166-172 Sloane Street, dramatic
double-height office space
© Adam Parker

Sloane Square. This was on 'patch' for our Grosvenor residential projects and only a five-minute walk from the Cadogan offices. On the May Day Bank Holiday of '94, 16 of us with family and friends moved across the river from Wandsworth to Belgravia. Alan remained in our offices in the RVPB Chapel, but I still had to meet half of the debt interest. Although most of the clients transferred the active projects to PD+P, the new practice could not afford a transfer of 'goodwill' since that would have triggered a tax liability. The task of setting up a new business with old debt and no new capital was tough.

But it's never too late for new beginnings.

I had agreed to meet Andrew Oades and Stuart's number two, David Clinch, later that week to formally agree the handover of 37-42 Sloane Street to our new business entity. Anxious and not fully knowing how they would respond, I prattled on about invoicing under the old practice up to 30 April for the completed stages and then finishing the project under the original terms with the new company. They let me go on, then looked at each other and began a double act.

'We know you will, and we agree,' said David.

'It's been a tough time, and we have a surprise for you,' Andrew added.

'We wanted you to have a major new project in the first week of Paul Davis and Partners,' David said.

'We have the survey drawings of 166-172 Sloane Street opposite 37-42, on the other side of the road,' Andrew added, handing over a long roll of paper prints.

'You can look at them later, now we are taking you to lunch,' David concluded.

We all started to laugh. I felt a warm and humble awareness of just how special professional relationships can be.

The exciting thing about 166-172 Sloane Street was that it wasn't included within the conservation area boundary. Hence it was not protected, could be demolished and was a great opportunity to design a substantial new building. We worked up ideas for a dramatic new building that would contribute and relate to its context and began discussions with RBK&C. Two weeks later, without any consultation, the Royal Borough suddenly moved the conservation area boundary to include our site, presumably as a reaction to our proposals. This was the same group of buildings that had been excluded from five previous reviews of the boundary. It was back to the drawing board.

The existing buildings at 166-172 had a series of different late 19th century gables facing the street with very low floor-to-ceiling heights on the upper two floors. One of the key challenges of designing a new building behind a retained façade is to align the new floor levels to relate in section to the original fenestration, at the same time making the windows feel right on the inside. At 166-172, we solved the problem of only 7ft 6in (2.28m) ceiling heights on the upper two levels by raising the rear section of the building and setting back the top level from the façade, thereby creating a dramatic double-height space across the whole frontage. The neat irony of this is that when so many completely new office buildings produce efficient but soulless workplaces, working behind retained façades can create far more interesting and enjoyable places in which to work: simply put, better architecture to be inside.

By '96, the Chapel was sold. It was a great feeling to sit in the Lombard Street head office of the NatWest Bank, repay the debt with a single cheque, and tell our account manager and his assistants, bluntly, what I thought of their actions through our hard times. Moving banks is tough when you're down, it's easy when you're on the up. Trouble is, they know and exploit it. *Déjà vu* from '78.

Twenty years of growth, challenges, achievements, battles and further recessions had just begun. It was great to have the Old School House, which proved capable of adaption and extension to accommodate growth to 100 people without having to move the business. It was exceptionally efficient for us to be within a short walk of most of our projects and enabled active site experience training for young staff. This proximity meant we could provide an unusually hands-on service to projects, site teams and clients. These were important factors in building and achieving so much in just two London boroughs, Westminster and Kensington and Chelsea. During the next 20 years we carried out somewhere in the region of 300 projects. It was better to be busy than to count.

This story was almost stopped in its tracks when a second conservation war broke out over a private house project in Kensington. At the north end of Holland Park are a pair of parallel roads separated by a mews and lined with stucco-fronted five-storey villas so close as to almost resemble terraces. Built through the late 1860s and 1870s, the villas have been home to the super-wealthy from the Maharaja of Lahore to Richard Branson and Simon Cowell. Our clients, Tim and Bettina, were less well known and had bought a wreck towards the top of the hill. It had been clumsily converted to flats in the 1950s and most recently occupied as a squat. A massive rusting metal fire escape wound its tentacled levels across the rear elevation interwoven with dripping black drainpipes. The back garden was concealed in unkempt vegetation and sloped up steeply to the park boundary. Inside, a 'fletton' brick lift-shaft cut through significant rooms like a toddler's car crash from a time when historic houses were unregulated.

Tim was an unlikely millionaire with a sharply focused brain and unbothered by appearances, his worn white shirt collars and shredded cuffs having minds of their own. Bettina also knew her own mind and was good at expressing it in the second of her numerous languages. They were an eccentric pair, demanding and fun. We would meet early-evening in a nearby rented flat to discuss how to most sensitively reinvent the once handsome house to meet their dreams. They had appointed Hugh Henry of Mlinaric, Henry and Zervudachi (MHZ) as interior designer to work alongside us. MHZ's work has included historic houses for the National Trust, the National Gallery, Royal Opera House and the Victoria & Albert Museum as well as British Embassies in Paris and Washington. Their private client list demands such discretion as to be beyond mention in this story. Needless to say, they know their history of houses. Hugh Henry is a gently spoken Scot, generally dressed in grey tweed, with a delicate humour and intimidating intuition; he was a delight to work with.

The original plan of the house had a broad hallway running from the front door to glazed French doors opening to a south-facing terrace and garden. The

lower ground floor borrowed daylight from generous light wells to all four corners. Each plot was a substantial 23m wide and the rear garden over 45m long. Many of these grand double-fronted villas had swimming pools under their back gardens. All its forerunners had resulted in having steps up to a raised terrace. This resulted in a spoilt view from the ground floor rooms and a lack of level access. Some even had projecting skylights in the middle of the terrace. These unsatisfactory designs destroyed the connection between the glorious high-ceilinged principal rooms and garden for the sake of underground luxury. Bettina and Tim enjoyed swimming and were keen to implement this shared dream. He wisely set the challenge of a cap on the pool budget. If we could design and deliver a 20-metre basement pool for under a specific number of thousands then he would go for it; if not, forget it. I was determined to solve the challenge and to have a level-access terrace as well as provide sufficient daylight to be able to swim without artificial lighting.

The first stage of the equation required a truly inventive and practical structural engineer. Bill Taylor was part of the consultant team used by Colin Redman at Grosvenor and our recommendation to appoint him was accepted. Convention would have been to drive steel or cast concrete piles to retain the surrounding ground pressure and then construct a waterproof layer within, but these procedures would cost far more than Tim's prescribed budget. Bill and I spent a stimulating and enjoyable evening exploring options over dinner. By studying the contour details, Bill determined that there was just sufficient width to dig the huge hole with battered (that is, sloping,) sides and hence build a much simpler and more cost-effective underground box. This approach would also avoid the expense and delay of party wall awards. The two light wells adjacent to the back of the house could provide daylight to both sides of the pool entrance end. The challenging question was how to entice daylight down from the steep garden slope to the far end of the pool surface more than seven metres below. We devised a pergola shade structure

Above:
The 'A Team' Saturday site visit:
Dad with Luke, Jessica and Henry

with a waterfall grotto as a backdrop. Behind the grotto, in the manner of a Baroque church, we hid a skylight to flood daylight onto the end of the pool. That all came out well and the pool was built within budget.

In the meantime, Hugh Henry and I worked together to refine the plan of the house with minimal intervention to suit the needs and aspirations of its new owners. Hugh was as obsessive about the exactitude of the plan as I was.

'Let's you and I get the plan right first. Once that's perfected, I can play houses with Bettina on the decoration,' he said, most memorably.

Beyond his masterful knowledge of the history of architecture and its decoration, Hugh researched the specifics of the Holland Park villas from original balustrade paint colours to lanterns, floor finishes, curtaining, etc. We submitted the detailed planning and Listed Building consent applications, then tendered the works. We negotiated with the District Surveyor for the removal of the eyesore fire escape by the provision of discreetly concealed emergency lighting within era-correct traditional lanterns at each landing and many more such delicate details. As part of the Listed Building submission, I'd had to write a minor treatise on the history of fletton* brickwork to prove that the lift shaft could not be part of the 1860s 'original fabric', a preoccupation of conservation officers. Works on site with an experienced contractor proceeded well despite the scale of the hole for the pool. On Saturday mornings, the 'A Team', my three children, would enjoy visits with their dad to explore 'the palace with a pool under the garden'.

As completion neared and our clients prepared to move in, the site manager rang unexpectedly at tea time one afternoon. He had bad news. The borough conservation and enforcement officers had just paid a visit to the house and ordered that all works cease immediately. The builders, the architect and client were to be prosecuted for 39 criminal breaches of the Listed Building consent. A formal writ was to be delivered. In the meantime, he had to lock up the site and leave.

'What on earth are the 39 breaches?'

'They wouldn't say. Apparently, it will all be itemised in the writ.'

Shaken, I knew the first thing I had to do was phone the clients to inform

*Fletton brick is made from South Oxfordshire clay which has an uncommonly high carbon content. This makes firing possible without the use of coal to heat the kiln for baking. Hence, it was used extensively after World War II when many materials were rationed. It is a hard, dense brick with a characterless, slightly shiny surface and an inelegant pinkish colour, best used where it can't be seen, in locations such as internal lift shafts.

them. It was not going to be an easy call to make. If that wasn't bad enough, a criminal conviction meant disqualification from practising as an architect and the end of our promising new practice. When the writ arrived, it was full of surprises. Amongst our criminal misdemeanours was the addition of window boxes to the rear elevation, a specific late request of Bettina's that had seemed reasonable. It still seems absurd to me that bureaucratic consent and public servant time should be required to place window boxes on the back of a private house. The stair balustrade colour that Hugh had researched and specified was not 'white gloss'. White gloss paint did not exist in 1870. Our offence was that we hadn't submitted the selected colour for approval. Really? The inclusion of small emergency escape lights on the landing after removal of the ugly external fire-escape, which had received consent, was another criminal offence. The greater implication of this and other building regulation items was that it would be necessary to have a completely specified and negotiated electrical, mechanical installation and decoration schedule for inclusion with the listed building submission. This would be impractical for any listed building application. However, this was a criminal prosecution and had to be taken seriously. We began preparing our responses to the 39 'crimes', one by one. Stress hit me hard. I felt alone, anxious and out of my depth. I needed a higher level of authority to advise me. In desperation, I telephoned Jane Sharman, then head of English Heritage in London, a charming woman with the air of an old-school academic, whom I'd met several times when speaking at conservation conferences.

'I was wondering if you might call,' she said. She knew that Kensington & Chelsea planners were having a blitz on listed houses being returned to their original single-family use. We were, she said, just one of those caught in their trap. Was there anything she could do to help?

I asked her if there was any chance she might come out and inspect the almost completed works.

Two days later, hours in advance, I arrived to lay out photographs taken before the works together with the approved planning drawings on a cluster of trestle tables. I could feel myself physically shaking, pacing the back terrace, lighting one cigarette after another. Jane arrived on the dot of five o'clock. She studied the information thoroughly and then suggested that she walk the house by herself so as not to be influenced. She had her own copy of the list of offences. I sat like a distressed schoolboy outside the headmaster's study for what seemed an age, grateful but nervous. Eventually, I heard her delicate footsteps descending the stair.

'Paul,' she said, 'you should be given an award for all the care and intelligent detail you've invested in bringing this house back to life. I have inspected and considered the list of breaches. In my opinion this is an exemplary restoration.'

She proposed writing to RBK&C advising them that if they proceeded with this prosecution, English Heritage would be representing me against them.

I was grinning with relief. 'I wish I'd called for your advice sooner.'

'You should have done. This case against you is monstrous.'

After receiving Jane's letter, RBK&C withdrew the case. I could sleep without the fear of criminal prosecution.

Pont Street

Sloane Street

King's Road

16 CLIENT OR PATRON?

By the mid '90s, Paul Davis + Partners (PD+P) was growing rapidly with major new projects for the Cadogan and Grosvenor Estates. We were working on the reconstruction of most of Grosvenor Crescent Mews, plus an acre of complex, high-density, new-build prime housing southeast of Sloane Square, not to mention Ringo Starr's country house (which has its own tale to tell). Although we had grown back up to 45 staff, we were still not big enough for the major Cadogan project on the northwest side of Sloane Square next to the Peter Jones department store, which would have a close to £50 million construction cost.

Stuart Corbyn came to discuss the project with me one evening and ask who I would recommend for such an important corner of Chelsea and the Estate. Sir Michael Hopkins had recently completed Bracken House in The City and Glyndebourne Opera House. He seemed the architect most capable of creating an important contextual new building that would enhance its setting on the Square. Stuart duly appointed Sir Michael and briefed him on wanting a great contemporary building that would take its lead from the rich architectural era of the late 19th century: the red brick, sandstone and terracotta Arts and Crafts vocabulary of the Estate. This style is known as 'Cadogan Dutch' because of the flamboyant gables reminiscent of Amsterdam townhouses.

Hopkins's first presentation to the Estate, which apparently looked like a toned-down white concrete American Embassy, was a great disappointment to Stuart. He asked him to take a closer look at the area, but then a second proposal, a rather mundane brick composition, fell on equally stony ground. Time had moved on and in less than two years PD+P had grown rapidly in numbers and confidence. The Estate needed to have a viable development scheme to achieve vacant possession of the run-down corner mansion block. Also, after our experience with the Royal Borough moving Conservation Area boundaries, we all knew that it would be fruitless to pursue anything other than retention of the façades. Stuart needed a scheme to submit for planning in order to achieve vacant possession and it had to be done quickly. This would be no easy task, since the relevant cluster was in fact five different buildings, each with different fenestration patterns and floor levels. The added complexity was that the Circle and District tube line crossed the site diagonally within the basement: not under the basement, within the basement. There was also a major gas main right under the corner where the retention structure would need to be the most substantial. Fortunately, we had introduced Adams Kara Taylor (AKT) to the Estate. They were amongst the leading structural engineers in London, regularly solving the most avant-garde design problems of the 'starchitect' community.

Opposite:
New life in the old Griffin

The scheme had many other complexities to resolve. It also included the adjacent block on Symons Street and Pavilion Road. Here the corner had to be rebuilt as a habitable bridge where the tube line passed under the site. To eliminate the noise of the steel train wheels passing through the tube tunnel, the new structures had to stand on huge 'GERB' anti-vibration spring mountings imported from Germany. These effectively dealt with vibration noise but also meant that the new concrete frame had the potential for differential movement of over 60mm from the original façade. When the building was demolished, there would be a danger of the tunnel and hence tube lines lifting because of the reduction in weight holding it down and subterranean water pressure pushing it up. AKT devised a computer monitoring system with Imperial College to check that there was no more than 3mm of track movement. This was ultimately agreed with Transport for London (TfL) and installed on a succession of nights starting at 3 a.m. in the brief time window when tube trains cease running.

General Trading Company (GTC) was famous at the time for being a favourite of Princess Diana and emulative Sloane Rangers. It was fashionable, but a characterful muddle inside with non-compliant access. In discussion with them, we designed a new shop around their brief and budget just around the corner on a pedestrianised Pavilion Road, opposite the Peter Jones store. This would be a still prominent and more affordable location for their shop. When it came to the planning committee hearing, the GTC planning barrister made vociferous objection to the application and was aggressively critical of the planning officer's handling of it, so much so that the committee clearly took exception to his attitude. Consent was granted unanimously for our scheme that night and we were on course to build our largest project so far.

While we were advancing the work, Stuart came to see me early one evening. He raised an eyebrow at the camping Z-bed I was sleeping on in the corner of my office, working so hard that I didn't even allow myself to go home in the week. He was appreciative of how rapidly we were moving the scheme forward but was fully aware that we'd had to take on more people to meet the demands of the programme. Yes, about 15 to 18, I confirmed, with attendant desks, drawing boards and computers.

'Expanding so fast is giving you a cash flow problem, isn't it?'

'We'll get through it.'

'I've a suggestion to make. If you bill the Estate every two weeks, and we pay it within one week, might that solve any cash flow issues the practice may be facing?'

What was unstated, as I thanked him and poured us both another large glass of red wine, was that we were on the same side and most importantly that we trusted each other. We were each understanding of what we needed and the support we could give each other. Was this good business? Patron rather than client? Whatever, it was uncommonly civilised. If only there was more of that in business and in life.

The very next week, Stuart offered me an empty flat for a nominal rent at the top of The Old Fire Station on Pavilion Road. This was to be included in our scheme for the site and would help me to feel the detail of the location. It

15 Sloane Square

Above:
Atrium
Below:
Daylit entrance lobby

Above:
Bridging the tube tunnel

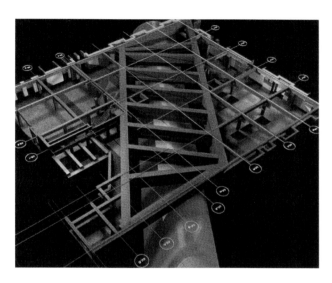

Above:
AKT Structural Diagram
Below:
Glass beam detail

Right:
The start of a pedestrianised
Pavilion Road ready to extend
northwards

Below:
Sloane Street becomes linked to
Symons Street and King's Road
with new retail
Photos © Adam Parker

was wonderful to have a proper bed to sleep on, though staying in town all week took its toll on my relationship with Susie, adding to a sense of isolation that was in retrospect entirely self-inflicted.

Notwithstanding having to retain the façades, or perhaps because of that, the offices were an exciting interior space with a central top-lit atrium supported by the longest structural glass beams in Europe at the time. The atrium and stair-top skylights were inspired by James Turell's famous 'sky cube' at his solo exhibition at the Hayward Gallery in '93, where white walls opened to an unrestricted view of the sky, bringing the changing patterns of clouds and light almost within the sculpture. One part that I was especially proud of was the office entrance. The design problem to solve was that with a tall ground floor and a mezzanine level, there were two floors to climb through before the offices started. Having a preoccupation with the importance of light, I wanted to be able to see natural light from the first point of arrival inside the entrance doors, not just a gloomy, internal lift lobby. The design we came up with was a sculptural journey with a part-stone, part-glass stair and a bridge wrapping around another sloping vertical plane of stone. It worked. As you enter the front door, daylight from the atrium is visible and further reflected by the polished black granite flooring. It may be an old trick, but polished black stone reflects light almost as well as a mirror. Dave Hoggard, a young associate at the time, detailed the whole composition with Cartier watch-like precision.

The Symons Street block was quite different. It had smaller retail units at ground and basement levels creating a raised first floor podium across the whole site. We formed a large open-landscaped courtyard at first floor level with a mix of multi-level flats in a horseshoe shape around the perimeter. The use of the courtyard as an urban form was something learnt from my travels in different cultures and climates. This principle for creating private space within a city environment remains constant wherever it may be. The residential courtyard became a quiet landscaped oasis, right next to the bustle and noise of Sloane Square.

Sir Robert McAlpine were the main contractors on the principal commercial building and did an amazing job. The brilliant engineer Hanif Kara of AKT used to give an illustrated talk on this, the most complex façade retention scheme carried out in London. The construction of the frame that spanned the tube tunnel less than a metre above the crown was a feat of engineering and construction skill. Equally remarkable were the quality and detail of the finished scheme.

The whole project was completed in a series of four phases. It included the buildings wrapping from Sloane Street around the northwest corner onto a pedestrianised Pavilion Road and the Symons Street retail and residential three-sided block. Once complete, we had successfully linked the retail from Sloane Street along the top of the Square to Symons Street, Peter Jones and the King's Road; an important connection for retail footfall and active frontages. It would set the scene for the subsequent potential to extend small-scale independent shops along Pavilion Road with a connection to Sloane Street.

Once again it proved my old mantra, that getting the architecture right paves the way for others to move in and create active living and working environments.

17 SIR CHRISTOPHER WREN WAS HERE

Sir Christopher Wren was one of Britain's most remarkable renaissance men. Prior to his intellect being drawn to the topic of architecture in his early 30s, he had studied Latin, philosophy, mathematics, anatomy, surveying, mechanics, optics, and meteorology. He had been Professor of Astronomy at Gresham College and subsequently, Savilian Professor of Astronomy at Oxford. He was one of the founder members of the Royal Society. In 1665, he had been asked to consider the renovation of the neglected St. Paul's Cathedral in the City of London and visited the Paris of Louis XIV to learn more about his new area of study. He returned to London in 1666 only days before the Great Fire consumed most of the City. Out of disaster came opportunity. Right place, right time, Wren's return was like the cavalry coming to the rescue and he seized the moment. Within days, he had proposed an urban plan for reconstruction. This was rejected but the Restoration King Charles II did appoint him to design a new cathedral. Over the ensuing decades, Wren would also be responsible for the reconstruction of 51 city churches. His symbolic masterpiece, St. Paul's, was completed 36 years after his first iterative drawings and models.

During my days as a student at Nottingham, Susie was working at Mappin & Webb, the silversmiths and jewellers adjacent to Bank Junction (the listed neo-Gothic building was soon to be controversially demolished to make way for No1 Poultry). I frequently took an early train to St. Pancras to arrive well before Susie's working day finished. I would walk the four miles across town observing the structure, forms, streets and squares, eras of buildings, materials, thresholds and roofscapes. My destination, St. Stephen Walbrook, was only yards from Mappin & Webb. For an hour or more, I would sit and contemplate, explore from every angle, sketch and absorb Wren's most intimate ecclesiastical space. The genius of how light is captured at every corner despite the constraints of the hemmed-in site was a profound lesson in the potential of geometry. Indented corners gather clear white light that defines the texture and understated decorative details of the coffered dome surface. The tall dark oak dado panelling connects wall to floor. This stark contrast of tone defines and exaggerates the slenderness of the multiple white stone columns. It is one of the most intimately uplifting of spiritual spaces. It is a masterwork of clear conceptual vision, understanding of geometry and structure, invocation of light, restrained palette of materials, understated decoration and inviting human scale. The vertical view into the dome is surely one of the world's most beautiful ceilings, as close as man can draw the celestial sky above our world. It was and is pure poetry of space.

By 1669, Wren had been appointed 'Surveyor of the King's Works'. Charles had been in exile in Paris during the Parliamentarian era and given sanctuary by his cousin, Louis XIV. On 24 May 1670, Louis's ordinance inaugurated the construction

Above:
The dome of St Stephen Walbrook
© Miscellany
Alamy stock photo

of the *Hôtel des Invalides* for the respite care of elderly, injured or infirm soldiers who had served the Crown. Charles II was impressed by his cousin's gesture of respect and in December 1681 appointed Wren to design the Royal Hospital for the same purpose on an expansive site on the banks of the river Thames at Chelsea. By the time of this major secular commission, the climate of architectural opinion in England was calling for a more pragmatic purpose-related style. Wren's magnificent new building acknowledged the call for something more English. Its formal courtyards vary in scale, and it is built in a dark brown brick with red brick details. The only use of Portland stone is at the central porticos and south cloister that connect and provide covered protection between the two 'Long Ward' wings, to the Great Hall and Chapel via the Octagon. The Long Wards have for 300 years provided the sleeping accommodation for the in-pensioners. These identical wings have wide circulation spaces with tall windows that encourage dwelling time and enable relaxed conversation. The sleeping spaces are within carved oak carrels by the greatest English wood carver, Grinling Gibbons. Another pragmatic Englishness of the design is that the ground, first and second floors break classical rules of fenestration scale by having the same proportion windows at each level.

The use and function at each level is the same and hence the same lofty ceiling heights, luxury of daylight and fresh air are provided for the benefit of the occupants. This appears entirely logical but broke radically from systems of classical renaissance proportion where windows scale down below and above the *Piano Nobile*: an early example of form following function? The profoundest tribute to the Royal Hospital is that it has been in the same secular use for over 300 years.

Skip forward to 1997 and PD+P's work across Chelsea and Westminster had become prolific and well known, especially for the number of listed building and Conservation Area consents and revitalised buildings. The practice was active across the community scene and supportive of local charities and fund raising. We organised a series of functions in the Royal Hospital State Apartments. Where better to celebrate with project teams and cement the profound friendships whose foundations are strengthened through the process of building? As a result of these occasions, we got to know Major General Jonathan Hall, who had recently taken the role of Lieutenant Governor. Jonnie was the most genial gentleman, who after a distinguished military career still exuded energy and an organisational capacity *par excellence*. We were appointed to upgrade the residential quarters in Light Horse Court for the chaplain, doctor and matron.

The new occupants were pleased with the transformation. Next, we were asked to consider options for sorting out the mess of prefabricated workshops hidden behind the Sir John Soane stables. This moved more slowly. In the meantime, we were granted the privileged commission to carry out a full but light-touch restoration of the Wren Chapel and Great Hall and the Octagon that links these two great spaces and provides the ceremonial entrance. To work on such important historic spaces was a joyous honour. Our project architects, Simon Gazzard and Grace Catenaccio, rose to the challenge.

The grounds of the Royal Hospital are well known as the location for the Chelsea Flower Show, an essential source of revenue for the upkeep of the Hospital. But regularly each year, the huge articulated trucks that deliver the marquees via the embankment gates would collide with and demolish one or more of the handsome stone gate posts. These are of course, original Wren gate posts and listed Grade I. The collisions were accidents but nonetheless, criminal offences for demolition without consent. The Governors rightly wanted to avoid the perennial cost and issue of the posts' reinstatement. One of Simon Gazzard's acts of extreme perseverance and pure determination was to draw and negotiate the consent to widen the opening between the Grade I gate posts to avoid their annual demolition.

The conversion and renovation of the old laundry and boiler house buildings together with a small new building as a music and band room enhanced a non-event courtyard and has been well used by the in-pensioners. It has been re-named Prince of Wales Yard.

As health and safety regulations for buildings providing care for the elderly had become more stringent, the Long Ward accommodation for the 300 in-pensioners no longer complied. An expensive nightmare of adaptation of the acres of Grinling Gibbons carved joinery carrels had to be undertaken. I was pleased not to be considered for this epic exercise in the adaptation of historic fabric. The Royal Hospital had held a big fund-raising campaign for the new infirmary building. Whilst that had been successful, it had pushed the limit of donors' generosity. Stuart Corbyn had been appointed as a commissioner in 2007 and we talked about how a very substantial sum could be raised through maximising the land use of the buildings and grounds. Were there any uses such as a home for the Royal Horticultural Society in Ranelagh Gardens along the eastern boundary? It would activate the parkland and be on site for the annual flower show. Were there any quasi-commercial uses that could provide community integration with the popular elderly residents without damage to the historic site? Could we find a valuable use for the large car park area on the west side behind the National Army Museum? Then there was Gordon House in the southwest corner which had been converted prosaically to senior staff apartments in the 1960s. It was self-contained and stood alone with over two acres of gardens and a single carriage access from Tite Street in the southwest corner. Could this be transformed into one of Chelsea's premier houses without detracting from the primary purpose of the Royal Hospital? We sketched ideas for each of these options.

The idea of gaining planning and listed building consent for Gordon House and then selling a long lease gained traction, especially since it was not part of the original estate and had separate access. We began working up ideas to restore the main house back to a single-family dwelling. This had the potential to make a good house but not the spectacular one that the scale of the gardens warranted. Anything less than an exceptional property would fail to raise the serious capital necessary for the Long Wards upgrade. We had to do better.

Adjacent to the link point to the main grounds at West Road was the Sir John Vanbrugh orangery. This had subsequently been converted to a library and was no longer in use. Should this be returned to its original use and be ancillary to the house? It would add value and could not be separated without down- valuing the plot. The house was substantial but not especially large. The master bedroom suite would have to be of impressive proportions to attract top price. If this was to be accommodated, then additional guest or staff rooms would be needed. If we could propose a new mews building to the west of Vanbrugh's orangery the extra space could be provided and would improve the privacy of both the dwelling and hospital activities. The other prerequisite of mega-value houses was the inevitable underground swimming pool and spa facility and of course plenty of secure parking. Fortunately, there was sufficient garden space, no adjoining owners and hence the opportunity to create these amenities without undermining the original house. Our scheme drawings advanced, and we began negotiations with the RBK&C planners and English Heritage. Simon and Grace had remained involved as my support architects and produced a set of elegantly refined drawings that provided for a house of imposing potential. We understood the planning issues and a landscaping scheme was designed to limit overlooking between the property and homes on Embankment Gardens. Vanbrugh's orangery could have its original full height windows reinstated and a series of other important historic details of

Left:
The Royal Hospital Chelsea:
Great Hall undergoing restoration

Below:
The Great Hall completed
Photos © Adam Parker

the house reinvented. Part of the planning narrative remained the importance of achieving maximum potential value to pay for the essential ongoing improvements and long-term maintenance of the Royal Hospital. The consents were granted for what had the potential be one of the finest private houses in London. The sale was made to Nick Candy of the entrepreneurial Candy brothers. The Royal Hospital received around £70 million for the leasehold interest of the site. The money provided for the Long Ward works and for the long-term care of Wren's handsome secular institution.

18 ORIGINAL THOUGHT?

Louis XIV and Charles II were not the first benefactors to provide for the care of elderly ex-soldiers. In the year 1238 AD, Muhammed ibn Yusuf ibn Nasr secured control over Andalusia. During his reign, he sponsored the building of hospitals for the elderly, injured and blind, especially those who had served as warriors. Schools and colleges were built to advance education of the young, which he visited incognito to ensure the proper conduct of the management. Aqueducts and canals were built to irrigate the land which doubled agricultural production. He was a well-educated patron of the arts and sciences. In 1239, he commissioned an architectural project on the site of a small hill-top fort that would take a two-century dynasty to complete. At the centre of the Alhambra, the exquisite Court of the Lions is an expression of this exemplary governance. The 12 carved stone lions that support the centrepiece basin and fountain were a gift from the Jewish community to the Emir for his laudable tolerance born out of respect for different faiths.

Boabdil (Muhammad XII) was the last of the Nasrid dynasty. In 1485, internecine strife forced him to seek the protection of Ferdinand II and Isabella. He was regranted control of Granada and the surrounding mountains in 1497. Two years later, following a series of sieges, failed alliances and the growing power of the Inquisition, Boabdil capitulated and in October 1493, he departed to spend 40 reflective years in exile. For seven years, limited religious tolerance remained but thereafter the influence of the Inquisition tightened to a choice of conversion, exile or execution for all who held Muslim or Jewish beliefs. Tolerance was left in the dust, the Nasrid ideal left to rust.

One of Napoleon's generals tried to destroy the Alhambra at the beginning of the 19th century. Shortly after the Duke of Wellington supplied countless English elms that were planted around the base of the hill on which it sits. The trees have matured to form the shady forest park that now surrounds the foot of La Sabika. In 1829, Washington Irving travelled by horse from Seville to Granada. *Tales of the Alhambra* depicts his adventurous journey through the *contrabandista* inhabited sierra and his illuminating sojourn in Granada. At the time, the Alhambra had fallen into decay and was inhabited by all manner of impoverished humanity. It had become a desultory squat, home to invalid soldiers and myriad colourful characters. Irving befriended the lackadaisical governor and established his own quarters within the palace. He resided there for many months, collected stories and studied its colourful past. His research and personal encounters captured the enduring personality of the place and, despite the neglect, its immortal beauty. The publication of his *Tales* in 1832, encouraged the passion of English intellectuals and aesthetes on the Grand Tour and brought attention to the decaying structures.

Opposite:
A view from the hill of La Sabika

Above:
Hall of the Ambassadors:
Stalactite vaults

Right:
The Court of the Lions:
An elegant testimony to
religious tolerance

Opposite page:
The Court of Myrtles:
Water and reflection
.

Nasr's original brief for this new palace on the hill of La Sabika was that it should be a 'Paradise on Earth'. The result is about as close to that spatial dream as architecture has ever achieved. It is the connections and contrasts that are so sublime, from magnificent, decorated chambers to intimate, delicately detailed small rooms, some enclosed and so cleverly ventilated that the temperature never rises above 20 degrees even in the baking heat of high summer. Others are open sided to allow the breeze and framed views of the old city and mountain landscape beyond. Courtyards had long been at the heart of hot dry climate design, but the garden courts of the Alhambra do more than create comfortable human temperature. Some are colonnaded, others are held by almost blank walls decorated by climbing roses. All have water: sparkling fountains, still reflecting pools mirroring the sky or narrow rills irrigating the diverse flora. The supply was drawn five miles by conduit from the river Darro.

Some walls are plain lime plaster, others are highly decorated. Poems in Kufic script and floral arabesques in carved plasterwork embellish high walls above dado bands of five-coloured *faience* mosaic. These glazed surfaces exhibit almost all the mathematically possible classifications of repetitive geometric patterns. M.C. Escher, best known for his drawings of impossible perspectives, visited in 1922. He was enthralled, inspired and influenced throughout his own prodigious and original output.

Below:
Drawing of the vault over the Hall of the Two Sisters, from Owen Jones' *The Grammar of Ornament*

Opposite:
The vault over the Hall of the Two Sisters

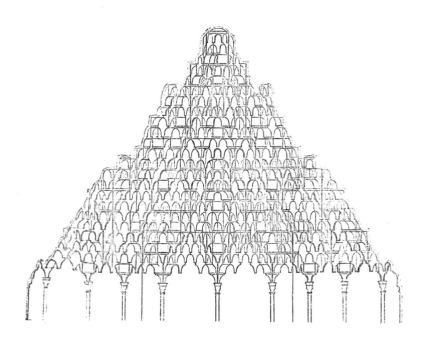

Section of Vault over the Hall of the Two Sisters, Alhambra

from Owen Jones.

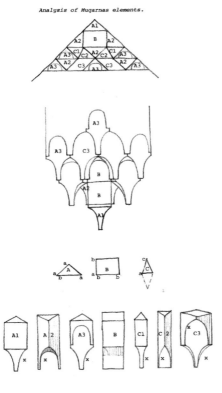

Analysis of Muqarnas elements.

The most spectacular decoration is that of the *muqarnas* or stalactite-vaulted ceilings. These appear as an architectural expression of the stars in the firmament above. Their apparent three-dimensional complexity defies geometric invention, for they are made of only seven different shapes of cast plaster. These are the 3D jigsaws to surpass all jigsaw suspended ceilings. Owen Jones, architect and author of *The Grammar of Ornament*, surveyed the vault above the Hall of the Two Sisters in the 1830s, and wrote:

The curves of the several pieces are similar, by which it will be seen that a piece may be combined with any of the others by either of its sides; thus rendering them susceptible of combinations as various as the melodies which may be produced from the seven notes of the musical scale.

Equally remarkable is that the faceted surface stops the reflection of standing sound waves that create the echo associated with domed ceilings. The complex textured surface of the *muqarnas* vaults cleverly provides a resonant acoustic for music performance without the distraction of unwanted echo. When architecture and music sing from the same mathematical hymn sheet, the outcome is indeed true harmonic and spatial beauty. Perhaps this is the closest to celestial architecture: the summit that architects yearn to climb, but often find so hard to reach.

Above:
Generalife: Water, a symbol of life

I have visited the Alhambra several times to seek peace and reflection. On each occasion, I have sat with eyes closed to contemplate the lives and events that the walls have witnessed. I ask myself: 'How come this palace of a different culture from my own evokes such powerful thoughts and emotions in my search to understand more of my lifelong specialist subject? What are the circumstances that create this as a place above others?' The starting point is its founder and patron, the client. Nasr had vision and a most challenging and clear brief. As an individual, he was learned, confident and determined. As a character, he had integrity and respect for others. Personal humility and wise governance brought about the safety of his subjects and longevity of the dynasty that he founded. The realization of great architecture requires the labour of a multitude of skilled trades. Acknowledgement of the value of teamwork and collaboration bestows dignity on those who labour. Pride and recognition motivate an artist or artisan to seek perfection in their work. Experiment precedes both failure and success.

Other essential components that generate great architecture are proportion and scale. These are accomplished through knowledge and application of mathematics, geometry and structure. When these ingredients are added to observation, intuition and the art of drawing then the design can begin. The architect should understand and analyse the context of landscape and climate to provide human comfort. The forces of nature are inherent to the setting of any architectural project: the rising sun, prevailing wind, extremes of annual temperature, the very soil from which the foundations will allow the edifice to rise and remain over time. The greater the application of vernacular experience of forms and materials coupled with knowledge of advances in environmental science, the greater the sustainable comfort that can be delivered for the occupants. The inclusion of nature will bring contact to context, while the opportunity for contemplation of nature may bring peace of mind for all who take time to enjoy the stillness of connection. Sunlight captured through openings may also frame views of the world beyond.

To the east, outside the walled enclave of the Alhambra, rests the *Generalife* (*Jannat al Arif*), the 'Garden of the Architect'. Elements of these gardens date from the days of the Nasrid dynasty Summer Palace, and though much is of later date, it houses a series of pavilions and linear gardens that retain the spirit and abundance of water engineering that characterizes the whole construction. It provides a place of contemplation with inspirational views of the Nasrid masterpiece. All the more remarkable is that the architect was recognised and honoured with a garden in his memory for posterity.

A successful place will stimulate the senses. Light, temperature, scents and sounds will each remind us that we are alive. Colour, sun and shade, the surface of materials, the melody of running and splashing water, the breeze in the leaves, birdsong, the fragrance of flowers are all integral to our emotional response to place. Water is vital to flora, fauna and mankind, its inclusion adds more than practical survival, it is a symbol of life, and symbols spark our subconscious. Surprise awakens awareness through contrast, changes of scale, from intimate to impressive, inside to outside. It is sequence that is key to the plan and art of place. Our senses are entertained, and we are drawn on to explore. Movement and exploration become a journey through time. Here, all these ingredients are in balanced abundance.

The power of such an historic place is not the sole domain of the Alhambra. The wealth of the world's historic architecture paints engaging pictures. The romantic origin and perfect form of the Taj Mahal endure as an exemplar architectural icon. Its elevated podium lifts it above *terra firma*. Four minarets frame space around its symmetric silhouette. Its silica infused stone absorbs and reflects the dynamic colours of the sky. It is a sublime pinnacle of architectural achievement, a love story in stone.

The silhouette of the Alhambra may fall short of that majestic achievement, but that is not the secret of the palace on the hill of La Sabika. The Alhambra is less of an icon, more a genius of place. Whenever and wherever we embark on a journey through a sequence of such inspired architectural spaces, we will see, feel, and experience it anew. That is the lasting joy of place.

Left:
Silhouette of the Castle on the Hill

19 THE CHIEF EXECUTIVES' LONELY HEARTS CLUB BAND

In the early nineties, the break-up with Alan Bayne and the pressures applied by the bank over our loan interest payments pushed my stamina beyond breaking point and I was hospitalised with stress.

I had heard of an organisation called 'Common Purpose'. The hypothesis was to bring together individuals from the public, voluntary and private sectors with themed workshops and visits to hospitals, prisons, fire services, charities and businesses to learn and exchange organisational thinking. In search of external stimulus and dissimilar company, I signed up. The insight into contrasting worlds and the issues faced by each proved valuable and thought provoking. Friendships formed as we all progressively opened up to the personal reasons that had brought us together. I christened the group 'The Chief Executives' Lonely Hearts Club Band'.

Jean-Jacques Pergant was the manager of the five-star Berkeley Hotel, situated where Belgravia meets Knightsbridge. He would subsequently take the helm of Claridge's and the Connaught on behalf of the Blackstone Group. His immaculate demeanour belied the questions burning inside his head. We became close and mutually supportive friends. Our new office at the Old School House was at the Southwest corner of Belgravia, The Berkeley at the Northeast corner. I would often escape at the end of an intense day by walking the mile to share a bottle of wine with Jean-Jacques in the refined air of the intimate Berkeley Blue Bar. At the Grosvenor office, the opinion was that I couldn't cross Belgravia without being within sight of one or more of our projects. It had become 'my patch', which was rewarding and brought professional satisfaction. J-J was questioning whether to set up his own hotel in Napa Valley or remain a well-placed peg in a powerful machine. I unburdened myself of the albatross of lonely leadership and my declining relationship with Susie. J-J had recently been through a tough divorce from his teenage sweetheart. We had a lot to talk about. We remained best friends until he moved to NYC in a senior role for Blackstone.

While J-J was still in London, he had commissioned a French, Beaux Arts-trained architect based in New York to redesign some key front-of-house areas of Claridge's. These spaces were original in their concept and stunning in their detail. I wanted to meet this man. His name was Thierry Despont. Around the same time, I was invited to Luttrellstown Castle, 25 miles outside Dublin. The huge estate had passed from the Guinness family to the Schlumberger empire, while the original castle-like house had been adapted to become a 14-suite private hotel. Private, because to stay there you had to book the whole place. It was where Posh and Becks had married. The grand house was set within pastoral grounds surrounded by two 18-hole golf courses and an unfortunate but out-of-sight log cabin club house. Our

Opposite:
45 Park Lane:
Double-height restaurant space carved out of the original concrete structure
© Adam Parker

171

brief was to insert, with sensitivity, a series of villas within the expansive acres. WATG, specialist American hotel architects, had already been appointed. They were best known for mega-hotels in Vegas, Hawaii and other resorts. Regrettably, I had seen their Dublin intervention, which I considered pastiche at best and crude of detail at worst. Beyond the luxury of being bivouacked in the Castle, I was unconvinced that I wanted to be part of an important planning application in association with a hotel design that I could not believe in. There are horses for courses. An historic Irish landscape is far removed from Las Vegas.

By the second or third visit, I had built a confident relationship with John, the project manager, whose reserved but genial manner bred open honesty. With an hour before we were to be joined by others for dinner, he laid out the American architects' plans on the top board of the grand piano and suggested it was time for a gin and tonic.

'What do you think?' he asked, with a mixture of deliberation and hesitation.

'I think I'll need that G&T and time to consider before I pass judgement,' I replied, hoping for the best and fearing for the worst.

John returned armed with two tall crystal glasses a few minutes later. The proposed hotel was lumpen, sprawling and even less appropriate for the landscape than I'd expected.

'Am I interpreting this correctly?' I asked, incredulous, but attempting to be generous. 'That a single roadway is driven in the arc of the ha-ha in front of the primary views of the Castle to reach the new hotel?'

'Correct. I wondered what you'd make of it.'

'If Heritage Ireland officers are remotely like our English ones, then my honest opinion is that this proposal is not consentable and rightly so. It would destroy the long-established aspect of the castle with a perfect view of limousines, delivery vehicles and refuse trucks trundling past. It would shatter the setting and provenance of the Castle with a sledgehammer.'

John's smile was approving of my bluntness and indicated that I wasn't alone in my judgement. What was the solution? Find a new architect with the sensitivity to design an architectural addition to this historic context. When John then asked for a recommendation, I stuck my neck out and suggested Thierry Despont. I had never met him, but I knew he had been responsible for restoring the Statue of Liberty and was also a gifted artist. Which is how we got together, a couple of weeks later, back at the Castle. Thierry looked like he had just stepped out of a Savile Row tailor's, though obviously with Parisian style and accent. Tad Sudol, his cool and less formal sidekick, held his own space. After the pleasantries of coffee on the terrace, Thierry suggested that just he and I take a walk to get to know the place and each other. As we talked, we soon found that we were on the same page regarding the importance of context and the delicacy of choosing the most appropriate location for the hotel. Before ending our promenade, we agreed that any new building should sit behind the Castle and connect to and be part of the neglected but intact walled garden. We both understood the vital importance of utilising the discreet microclimate of a garden courtyard.

'Have you ever heard of Yazd in Iran?' Thierry asked.

'I was there in '74,' I replied with a grin. 'It's spectacular.'

'You're the only person I've ever met who has ventured into the desert to explore Yazd.'

As ever, the shared experience of travel to remarkable places forged an immediate connection.

Thierry's gesture of getting to know me before discussing or presenting any of his elegant ideas was a generous compliment. Our design schemes subsequently emerged in detail and we began a very protracted process of negotiating the various consents. It had all the stages of the English process but shuffled into an order of Irish logic. Friendship with Thierry and Tad had been forged and we soon found ourselves working together in London. First off was a double corner site in Swiss Cottage north of Regent's Park. We prepared a refined design for mansion apartments which died a death on the altar of Camden planning politics.

Thierry was best known for designing some of the highest profile family houses in the USA. So, when the Mattel family bought the palatial Wyatt house in Kensington Palace Gardens, he was the best that money could buy. We worked together and I negotiated the historic building consent. By this time the Royal Borough of Kensington & Chelsea conservation officer who had persecuted us at Holland Park knew better than to pick a fight. The consents were granted uncommonly quickly.

Having worked on a multitude of projects in Mayfair but with none taken to fruition on Park Lane, the opportunity to collect a hotel on the dark blue Monopoly board squares just before 'Go' was too exciting to resist. The old Playboy Club, immediately south of the iconic Dorchester, had 14 years earlier been converted to the playhouse of the brother of the Sultan of Brunei, Prince Jefri, shortly before his fall from grace. The building was bizarrely contradictory. On the outside, it was gunpowder grey brutalist concrete; on the inside it had so much gold leaf that it had caused a world shortage at the time of its indulgent conversion.

It had lain empty for 14 years and Thierry was instructed to convert it to a boutique annexe of the Dorchester Hotel for their most exclusive guests. Thierry proposed that PD+P be the executive architects. As well as early ideas dialogue, this entailed being responsible for design coordination, regulation approvals and overseeing construction. We brought in a former fire officer who negotiated an efficient fire escape strategy, and I negotiated a beneficial party wall agreement with the adjoining building owners whom we had been advising. Together, these achieved an additional bedroom suite to each of the six upper floors. We had to reinvent the gloomy precast concrete cladding, but the budget was inadequate to remove and re-clad. The windows required improved soundproofing from the constant torrent of traffic that is the modern-day highway of Park Lane. The windows were solvable, but what to do to disguise that thundercloud-grey concrete?

'What about horizontal aluminium louvres set in front of the concrete spandrels?' I suggested during a design workshop at the Old School House. 'I once did a stage set for Roxy Music based on a similar idea.'

Above:
45 Park Lane: Before

Right:
A sense of arrival

Opposite:
45 Park Lane: After
Photos © Adam Parker

'We could curve them around the northern corner to make the entrance and at the same time speak across Park Street to the Dorchester portico,' Tad replied, picking up on the idea.

Thierry and Tad went with the idea and introduced an ace lighting designer from New York to complete the night-time transformation. As a final *pièce de résistance*, one of Thierry's huge planetary paintings was installed to command the grand high-ceilinged entrance foyer.

A complete mock-up of a bedroom suite was constructed off site to refine and perfect every detail of the Art Deco style interiors. Over 100 detailed refinements were made for the finished rooms. The idea of illuminated translucent stone for the backing of each bath proved problematic but was eventually solved and looked magnificent. There was a battle over the final account with the main contractor and a mountain of blame piled high. The disputed figure would not even have been petty cash to Prince Jefri. Whenever I turn north from Hyde Park corner onto Park Lane at night, the illuminated 45 Park Lane shines out on Monopoly Lane. The American lighting designer did us all proud and the gloomy concrete is transformed as an Art Deco tribute. It even beat the Bulgari to win the 'London Hotel of the Year' award.

Right:
Art Deco on Park Lane
© Adam Parker

A LONG WAY FROM PARK LANE...

Cliveden had been the country home of the Astor family since 1893. It stands above the Thames beyond Windsor within huge grounds, part manicured, part wild. Magnificent cedar trees line the approach, first winding, then opening out onto a formal axis; a perfectly contrived sense of arrival. As you draw up to the front portico, a valet greets you. He will park your car out of sight, however impressive or ordinary a marque. The entrance hall tells you that you have arrived in a place of tranquil elegance and refined affluence. The service is sublime, all effort has had prior consideration and is taken care of by others.

The Astor family are no longer the hosts. In 1942, they gave the mansion and land to the National Trust with a lifetime tenancy and an endowment of £250,000. In 1994, the whole estate was leased to a hotel operator, our client. It was the epitome of five-star hospitality. Our first visit was to consider, and happily be appointed for, the redesign of some of the back-of-house space into additional bedroom suites. Through this, we got to know and feel the atmosphere and character of the place and the operators themselves. They were pleased with the outcome. The next issue that they faced was that 37 rooms was not an economic model for staffing and maintaining a mansion hotel of this scale and calibre.

Set within the grounds, but away from the mansion and its views of the Thames and Windsor Castle, were the derelict remnants of the Canadian Red Cross Memorial Hospital. It had been built for the re-habilitation and respite of Canadian soldiers wounded in the 1914-18 war and had been rebuilt for use in World War II. By the late 1990s, 50 years on, nature had overtaken the Astor family's noble intervention. The hospital site was reached from the mansion via shaded lanes once used by Lady Astor and her friends to access the imposing indoor tennis court; a building that bore a close resemblance to a Florentine chapel, albeit in dark red Oxfordshire brick. The setting was overgrown, and now the lanes were mainly used by the gardening staff for access to maintenance workshops and storage sheds. My first glimpse of this atmospheric place had been whilst signing off the completed mansion bedrooms. The operating company wished us to explore the possibility of creating an annexe hotel and spa to add 80 rooms and hence a more viable future for the mansion as a luxury hotel.

I arranged to visit the site one spring morning at 11 o' clock and to meet Alan Baxter, the expert conservation engineer and chairman of the London Advisory Committee of English Heritage, along with Brian Harris, senior partner of a major firm of quantity surveyors: two experienced, wise, and friendly heads with whom to discuss ideas. I wanted to take time to gather my own thoughts before their arrival, so I left home early and was parked under an ancient cedar tree just before 9 a.m.

The ground was wet with a heavy dew and tall wildflowers glistened in the damp misty air. Between rows of orderly metal-framed ward blocks with broken windows and weeds, vigorous creepers reached for sunlight, entwining the rusting furniture and decaying structures. Old steel bedsteads, upturned chairs, trestle tables, tin lanterns, a broken wheelchair, a rotting leather boot or two: all littered the derelict scene. It was easy to conjure images of nurses in starched uniforms nurturing the wounded and dying soldiers who were so far from home. I wondered if the nurses had also crossed the Atlantic Ocean to care for their young countrymen, or whether these were local women from Maidenhead just down the road? I could hear the soldiers' cries of pain, the moaning of those waking from nightmares, unable to escape from the horrors they had observed in the Somme or Passchendaele; now damaged or dying in these secluded woods in Oxfordshire.

To me, there seemed only one design solution: to return the whole area of the hospital buildings to a wildflower meadow, and in the clearing at the lower end to place a memorial to the Canadian Veterans. Around the Astor indoor tennis court there was enough surface area to create a compact complex of courtyards, along the lines of an Oxford or Cambridge college, while the dark red brick Florentine chapel (as I preferred to think of it) would serve perfectly as the principal memory at the heart of the new setting.

Alan and Brian arrived at precisely 11 o'clock. We entered the tennis building and it was straightforward to see how this handsome extravaganza could be restored as a focal point for a new sporting facility. Out in the sunlight, we stepped carefully through the ward blocks, conscious of the broken glass. We moved slowly, sometimes in silence, sometimes observing small remnants: a chipped enamel water jug, a putrid beer bottle, an oxidised brass button. We talked as we stood in a clearing and looked back up the gentle hill across the rows of shattered roofs now woven with honeysuckle, ivy and Virginia creeper. They liked my ideas, the meadow and the memorial to the Canadian soldiers.

Back in our London office my small team began recalling and researching the quadrangles of our favourite Oxbridge colleges and the Oxfordshire vernacular. The new courtyards would be intimate, some formal, some less formal; sequences and links would be key. Our strategy was to consider the spaces between the imagined buildings before defining the architecture of the built forms. Another source of inspiration was the Inns of Court off the Strand, an exemplar of sequential spaces. We collected precedent images, planned suites of differing sizes, sketched sectional ideas, checked local roof pitches and the mix of materials, colours and textures.

The clients had a wonderful proposal after the presentation of our first ideas. Spring Cottage, within the estate grounds, was available from Monday afternoon to Saturday morning in a week's time. Why not stay there and advance the design at Cliveden by being near to the site? Why not indeed? Queen Victoria used to take tea there and it was the place Stephen Ward had stayed with Christine Keeler and Mandy Rice-Davies when they met John Profumo, with scandalous consequences that had brought down a government.

We arrived mid-afternoon laden with all the sketching materials we would need for our week of drawing. As you approach the cottage, a small window beside the front door frames a view through the building to the river beyond; an endearing detail of design that optimised its setting. After being served a classic English afternoon tea, we cleared the large circular oak table and started work.

Every day was a treat. Breakfast, lunch and tea would arrive with butler service. In the evening, we would dress for dinner and walk through the grounds to the mansion. The walk gave us an opportunity to consider subtly unobtrusive ways to enhance the lanes to allow electric golf buggies to take guests between the new annexe and the grand house. After dinner, we would continue drawing and talking until two or three in the morning.

By Friday evening we'd cracked it. There would be a main lawn with raised paths around a square in front of the west façade of the 'chapel'. *Cyma recta* shaped grass banks along the lines of Keble College would utilise and enhance the rising ground level. The south and west sides would be defined by one-and-a-half and two-storey accommodation wings. Along the north side, a range of oak trees would be retained to hold the space. The north wing would have open stairs along the lines of some of the Cambridge colleges. This discreet hotel annexe would have the

Below:
Pond Court:
Watercolour by David Birtwhistle

Above:
Reception building

Below:
Orchard Court opening to the meadow
Watercolours by David Birtwhistle

atmosphere and aesthetic of an Oxbridge College with a sequence of courtyards leading westwards. Pond Court was to have a large lily pool that would fill the entire space except for a walkway on two sides. The final Orchard Court would be open ended with a gentle splay to give an exaggerated perspective looking across the meadow to the memorial amongst the trees.

We enjoyed a celebratory Friday night dinner, confident that the scheme was one of our best. The client was delighted with our progress and subsequently commissioned a series of professional watercolour sketches to assist in communicating the scheme.

At the planning department, a very bright senior planning officer, Sophie, got the plot and was enthusiastic in her support of both concept and scheme drawings. Not only did she appreciate our approach but regarded the direct link via the existing lanes to the mansion as an essential component of the proposals. Rightly, she didn't want guests driving between the mansion and the annexe on public roads after boozy lunches or dinners. All was going swimmingly well.

The hotel operators had been in separate discussions with the National Trust over lease terms, and again we thought good progress was being made. We attended a high-level meeting at the National Trust offices in Queen Anne's Gate to present our scheme to a group of senior officials. It went satisfactorily, but the atmosphere was flat and unresponsive. We walked back through St James's Park to Ebury Street feeling disappointed and uneasy, especially since we were so confident in the quality of our concept and presentation.

Soon after, the National Trust advised the client that access to the mansion would not be allowed via the lanes but would have to be on the external main roads. This edict destroyed the notion of our scheme being an annexe to Cliveden and the whole connection was lost. Negotiations broke down and we called on Sophie to tell her we wouldn't be proceeding. She was as disappointed as we were.

The National Trust subsequently sold the site to a housing developer. Residential use would undoubtedly have created a higher land value than the hotel and it's obviously the Trustees' responsibility to maximise their assets. Unfortunately, in such circumstances, value is measured monetarily.

A few years later I drove past the site and a housing estate was being built where I had dreamt of creating a meadow and memorial. I haven't been back to Cliveden. I felt Lady Astor's gift to the nation and the memory of the Canadian soldiers had been badly let down. I know I'm not alone: all architects regret a favourite project that fell by the wayside.

20 SWAN SONGS

The Territorial Army had occupied the ten-acre Duke of York campus in Chelsea for 100 years. Before that, it had been a tough military-style school for orphan boys and girls since its construction in 1803. In the early 1990s there had been tentative discussions about the Ministry of Defence (MoD) selling off A Block, a rather dull post-war building fronting the King's Road. It was going to be difficult to adapt this to active frontage use and our view was that it should be replaced, even though it was in the Sloane Square Conservation Area, and thus defended by Borough officers. The barracks frontage, security railings and sentry blocks were just something to walk past to get from Sloane Square to the bustling King's Road shops. Whilst we were considering this stubborn issue, Stuart advised us that he had begun negotiations to purchase the whole ten-acre campus. The Treasury wanted the money.

There had been a series of public land sales by government ministries that had received negative press and criticism from the National Audit Office (NAO). Developers had bought land and flipped it at inappropriately substantial gain, most notably at the nearby Brompton Hospital on the Fulham Road. The NAO was out to stop further government embarrassment. So how was Stuart going to negotiate a single non-competitive bid for this very visible crown jewel in the MoD portfolio? Most people, including many within the Estate, thought he was wasting his time. This was useful for me, as I became one of his closest allies through the negotiations.

We started looking at ideas for the whole site. Several of the buildings were listed II★ and some Grade II and all ten acres were within the Conservation Area. Our brief from Stuart was to extend the urban grain. This meant creating a network of streetscapes with a variety of scales, some intimate, some more open with vistas to encourage the adjacent intensity of pedestrian movement around Sloane Square and the King's Road. We were to devise the potential for a rich diversity of uses. The spaces between the existing and new buildings should maintain the local pattern, scale and form to create a new pedestrian realm; it was definitely not to become a shopping centre. The task was to reinvent what was worth keeping and have a comprehensive mix of uses appropriate to each location. The running track and infield were to be maintained in use by Hill House School, who had enjoyed it as a sports field for decades. With ten acres previously out of public access, a cluster of historic buildings, the opportunity for new build interventions, a sequence of open

* Historic England (formerly English Heritage) defines the significance of historic buildings in three grades. Grade I: Exceptional interest - 2.5%, Grade II*: Particularly important - 5.3%; Grade II: Significant - 91.7%.

spaces and a wide mix of uses in the heart of Chelsea, we were presented with the potential of real scale placemaking.

A competition was held to select a landscape architect to join the team. Elizabeth Banks's firm fronted by Robert Myers were clear winners and were appointed to work with us. Robert proved studious with a logical clarity of creative vision. PD+P needed to expand our team, especially in the field of retail design. Philip Vernon, my childhood friend, had recently completed the Whiteley's retail and cinema complex on Queensway and was keen to join us from BDP, one of the biggest UK practices. It was fun to be working and sharing more time together after years of being increasingly distant friends.

The residents of the adjoining streets had joined forces as 'The Duke of York Residents Action Group'. Interestingly, this was before we, or they, had any idea of what scheme might be proposed; their action just reflected the inevitable fear of change, whatever it might be. The group elected Sir Derek Thomas as chairman and fortunately he acted with great intelligence and civility. Stuart agreed that he and I should meet Sir Derek monthly to advise on progress and consult over issues of concern.

The negotiations with the MoD advanced and what became clear was that a 'Subject to planning' bid would not be acceptable. The Treasury wanted best value for a scheme that would win consent. To that end, huge monthly meetings were held in the officer's mess conference room (big enough to plan a war) with the Estate, its consultant team, planning officers of RBK&C, English Heritage and the MoD planning and valuation advisors.

Our key masterplan strategy was to first design the spaces between the existing structures and then use them to determine the form, scale, and positioning of potential new buildings in the interest of resolving issues around public space, movement, vistas, scale, trees and so on. Secondly, to consider best uses for the retained historic fabric and any new buildings relative to the emerging spaces. Previous uses within the original and military buildings included dormitories, workshops, offices, classrooms, a drill hall, gymnasium, chapel, truck repair building and acres of tarmac for parking. New uses would be retail, restaurants and cafés, affordable and market residential for rent, offices, a relocated Garden House primary school, a medical centre, invisible underground car parking and a sequence of new public open spaces.

The Estate had the means to include a shop unit on the southwest corner of Sloane Square and relocate the tenant so that an arcade connection could be made at the eastern end of the site, thereby avoiding a cul-de-sac, the kiss of death for retailing. We opened an access lane opposite a busy corner of Peter Jones department store to create a vista to a mature tree adjacent to a new café on the corner of the left wing of the main HQ building. This added another point of visual connection. Important to the success of the main new public square was the removal of the 1950s military railings along the King's Road frontage, which in retrospect seems obvious, but was the cause of unnecessary debate at the time.

Left:
Duke of York's campus:
The plan unfolded
© Adam Parker

The most substantial new building that emerged was a replacement A Block, with English Heritage actively advocating a new building. This would face the King's Road, the new square, main pedestrian boulevard and linking lane: hence, a four-sided island building where each elevation faced a space of different character and scale. This was a challenging opportunity as it was the most prominent new building of the whole scheme and needed to be in respectful dialogue with the Grade II★ HQ without being pastiche. B Block located behind the King's Road frontage would have smaller start-up shops to attract new, non-chain retailers and 30 key worker flats above. The latter was a brave move but absolutely the right solution instead of hiding them away in the worst corner as so many developers do. Both we and Stuart wanted them to be the best affordable flats in London. B Block formed the north side of a new space opposite the drill hall and workshop range that would provide a 25,000 sq ft anchor store. In the centre of this space, we envisaged a contemporary version of a transparent steel frame market hall. We designed a mostly glazed, delicately structured central feature building with engineering design by Adams, Kara, Taylor (AKT).

We did not want a vast, unattractive servicing yard or tarmac delivery road. Robert Myers advanced the landscape design of the new public square with fixed stone elements that would define and contain traffic movements for early morning timed deliveries. Fountains were introduced within the paving for children to play in, and to give background sound and movement. Discreet historical storylines describing the history of the King's Road were carved and inserted in the paving. All mature trees were retained, and new trees planted in considered positions. We installed a network of floor boxes across the square with water and electricity to enable the future potential of market stalls. We knew that the new square needed

Above:
A place of pedestrian peace
© Adam Parker

to have its own café space with outside seating. There was lengthy debate with the planners and English Heritage over the location and size of any café relative to the setting of the main HQ building and important curved 'wing' walls that frame the Grade II★ composition at each end. Consent for what we wanted was not achievable at the time and what we had to settle for proved the least successful element of the scheme.

When we were designing the masterplan, several booksellers were opening big shops that were pointing to a new way of selling books with a café and a whole new vibe. We hoped that our anchor store might be that kind of bookshop, especially as Chelsea buys the most books of any borough in the UK. It would have been great as an amenity and for footfall. Regrettably, it was taken by the London Furniture Company in the first instance, but this did not work in the Chelsea market. It turned out to be the wrong kind of use for this key store within the scheme. When they failed and Zara moved in, at least they made a good fashion store that does bring in increased essential footfall.

Meetings with the planners, English Heritage, MoD, and residents advanced through nine months and by June 2000 we submitted a hybrid masterplan application for the whole site. This was 'Detailed' for phase 1 adjacent to the King's Road and 'Outline' for the central and southern parts of the campus. Consultation and meetings continued through the summer and autumn. Amazingly, consent was granted before Christmas in December 2000 and the Section 106 agreed as well★. The planning complexities and political sensitivities created a communication and working process that proved an exemplar with all parties being heard and getting what they wanted. The London Advisory Committee (LAC) of English Heritage were influential in their support of the proposals. Alan Baxter was chairman of the LAC and was especially enthusiastic when speaking up for the scope and design of the new build elements. When we were celebrating the opening of phase I and the new public square, he kindly commented, 'You are the only architects whose finished buildings look better than

★ Section 106 Agreements are formal Deeds made under the Town and Country Planning Act 1990 to secure planning obligations to mitigate the impact of a proposed development. They often result in protracted legal negotiations.

the optimistic CGIs (computer generated images) others present to win planning approvals.'

Construction progressed through the next two years with all the regular headaches of a major project. The new public square was opened in 2003, appropriately enough by the Duke of York. Shortly after, Lord Rogers wrote to Stuart congratulating him on at last creating a world class public space in London. I was chuffed when Stuart forwarded a copy of the letter, but it might have been even more pleasing if he had written direct, architect to architect. More importantly, the place is popular with people and delivered a series of new urban spaces with a broad mix of uses and lots of outside dining, whilst providing a traffic-free lung for the busy, linear congestion of the King's Road.

Some years later, a key local resident who had been influential in the planning debate wrote to Stuart with his thoughts following a visit to a café on the finished project. Chelsea is not William Blake's Jerusalem, but this kind note is a rewarding definition of what one is aiming to achieve as an architect:

I walked over for coffee yesterday at Gelateria Valerie and marvelled at what a fantastic success Duke of York Square has become. In the gorgeous sunshine, with the Saturday market booming, all the cafes packed, fountains playing, a Dixieland band banging cheerfully away, kids dashing about on skateboards or scooters, or dancing to the music, one 5-year-old Toscanini eloquently beating time with his drinking straw, what a splash of life and colour it's added to this corner of London!

Phase 3 was to include the Grade II★ HQ building, a new residential mews

Left:
Retail and restaurant therapy in the new Square
© Adam Parker

Above:
A colourful French food market comes to town on Saturdays

Right:
A Chelsea Pensioner soaking up the atmosphere
Photos © Adam Parker

behind and small flats in the former girls' dormitory building within the right wing. The main historic HQ layout had been a simple arrangement of four huge rooms at each level divided by a grand double staircase in the centre. The southern half had been for girls' classrooms and dining, the northern half for boys. Rigorous discipline meant that they had been totally segregated.

The stumbling block was to find the most appropriate use for this prominent classical centrepiece. Residential use would produce mega-high value but would mean inappropriate subdivision and crucial loss of public access. In the early 2000s, we had been appointed by Sotheby's auction house to review the efficiency of their numerous buildings in Bond Street and George Street and to create an extra new auction space and board room. It was a difficult task and revealed awesome inefficiency within a muddle of ad hoc links between the old buildings with different floor levels. This work triggered discussions about moving some of the auction rooms and experts' offices to an alternative location. We found ourselves investigating the possibility of Sotheby's moving to Duke of York HQ. The huge former classrooms were perfect as auction rooms and the top floor could provide good office space for the many specialist experts who advise sellers and collectors as well as providing cataloguing research and so on. The new wing that we had gained consent for at the rear of the HQ building provided access for very large items of art, sculpture or furniture. The scheme and discussions were going well, and it seemed an ideal use that would provide public access and useful footfall. Sadly, Sotheby's were simultaneously involved in a major litigation in New York over being part of a cartel. Christie's, their major competitor, had turned state's evidence. Sotheby's were unable to commit to the major decision to move and were, unsurprisingly, dragging their feet.

At the same time Charles Saatchi had fallen out with his landlord on the South Bank where his art gallery was located. I was on holiday when Stuart called.

'Guess who I've just taken around HQ?'

'I've no idea, I'm sitting by the pool in France.'

'Charles Saatchi. I've shown him around HQ and the auction house plans and it largely fits for his new gallery. He wants to take it.'

On my return, we began briefing with Saatchi's gallery manager. A dedicated team of us had spent nearly a year working up the structure and detail of the new link with lifts and stairs. This was crucial to improved circulation. English Heritage were insistent on it barely touching the historic fabric. The whole structure was to be cantilevered and hung from two concrete lift shafts to achieve this. The new wing had to be adapted to house Richard Wilson's iconic '20:50' work, better known as the 'oil room'. This was to be the only permanent installation. A viewing platform had to be created to look down onto the whole space, which was entirely flooded with black recycled engine oil. The oil was at once a reflecting pool, polished black floor, or mirror. The space had to be impeccably and minimally detailed to deliver the disorienting impact.

At the opposite end of the scale, Stuart was anxious that Eileen and Wal Jacques were ageing. For decades they had run the flower stall on the Sloane Square traffic

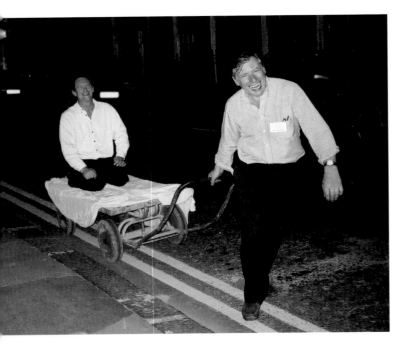

Above:
Cutaway view of the new Saatchi Gallery
spaces

Left:
It's a long story! Stuart Corbyn pulls an
architect

Below:
The Saatchi Gallery by night
© Adam Parker

island. Everyday they had to trolley the stand, equipment and flowers to and from a storage garage in Pavilion Road. Come rain, shine, snow and wind, they tended the stall. They knew residents and customers by their first names, always gifting a smile and local banter.

'You know the shop next to the arcade entrance to the Duke of York's. Doesn't it have a disused staircase on the side?' asked Stuart.

'I think you may be right. What are you thinking?' I replied.

'Could you carve a flower shop for Wal and Eileen out of the space? I'd like to find somewhere sheltered, out of the weather, where they can keep their gear,' Stuart suggested.

'We'll need to squeeze in a toilet, somewhere to brew tea and stack all the flower buckets. It'll be tight but worth a go,' I commented.

Sad to say Wal passed away and Eileen retired but their son, Brian runs *Jacques Flowers* in the space at the side of the arcade today.

The process of devising the masterplan and delivery of the whole Duke of York project was a ten-year-long opportunity to reinvent and create a series of new public spaces in central London. At times PD+P had over 40 architects, technicians and administrators working in a project office on site. For me, it was the fulfilment of years of learning and working in Chelsea, from hanging out as a teenage hippy, through first battles with conservation officers, dozens of buildings, new and reconstructed, that had helped to transform Chelsea and the Cadogan Estate. I guess that made it my 'swan song'. Or did it?*

When Stuart phoned, I never knew what to expect, often the call set off a whole new challenge. One of the most exciting came when my mobile rang one April afternoon in 2000.

'Guess what?' he chirped.

'I've no idea,' I replied as usual.

'I've just bought the First Church of Christ, Scientist on behalf of the Estate. I don't know what we can do with it, but I felt it was too good a building to become yet another overblown house. Much better to find an appropriate use to continue public access.' I agreed and we arranged to have one of our informative walk-arounds the next morning.

The main congregation space, which once held 1700 people, was spectacular despite the years of dust and the broken glass in the ceiling's decorative skylight. Most unexpected, for a church, was that it had a raked floor in the main space. In each corner of the building was a multi-storey turret with discontinuous floor levels. The original Sunday School room had intricate stained-glass windows which were bowed

---

* I was pleased that ten years on, the new chief executive, Hugh Seaborn, asked me to organise a design competition among emerging architects for a new café. Nex, a young practice, won the competition and, as I write, the new café is now open. I hope it adds to the life of the new square without dominating the open space.

out from a nearby bomb blast during World War II. This room had its own street entrance but was accessed down a flight of steps from pavement level.

Movement through the labyrinth of corridors, spaces, steps and stairs was disorienting. We needed a comprehensive computer survey so that we could understand our canvas. Traditional measurement by hand would take weeks and was unlikely to be sufficiently accurate with so many changes of level. The key issue was that we had no brief as to what use could be found for the unconventional old church. A laser survey was commissioned so that there would be an accurate 3D model to work from once we knew its future. In the meantime, Calvin Bruce, our conservation partner, and I visited numerous times to learn and feel the spaces, levels, features and character of this unusual but significant neo-Byzantine/Fatimid Portland stone edifice.

Some months later, Stuart arrived at our office after work.

'Did you know that the Cadogan Estate sponsors the Holland Park open-air opera season?' he asked, as I poured him a glass of wine.

'The Royal Philharmonic are the house orchestra for the season, and they don't have a permanent home. I've spoken to them, and they're interested in having the First Church as a base for their offices, library, instrument store and rehearsal space. If we can improve the acoustics they may even be able to use it for the occasional performance.' I was excited. Did we have another project?

'Didn't you learn a bit about acoustics when you were designing recording studios?' he added.

'Yes, but not a concert hall, that's a different ball game.'

Nonetheless, Stuart wanted us to work on it. He advanced discussions with the Royal Philharmonic which led to a brief and the confirmed commission to design a concert hall. We met with the orchestra and worked up a design around their requirements for library, offices, instrument storage, etc. We discovered that the existing raked floor had a void between the slope and the ceilings of the rooms below. We had been working on numerous projects with an inventive services engineer, John Case. He came up with an air conditioning scheme that utilised the floor void to supply freshly conditioned air to a supporting stem underneath each seat in the main auditorium. This was the most efficacious location for comfort levels and inaudible air noise. Space for the orchestra and a wider variety of artistic performances was enabled by extending the original stage. There was just sufficient head height to provide a large instrument store below the stage. The provision of a special lift made it possible to raise and lower a grand piano between stage and secret store. A huge, concealed roller-blind screen at the back of the stage could be unfurled for cinema scale projection.

Part of our brief from Stuart was to retain the original wooden pews around the three-sided gallery so that a substantial percentage of seating could be sold at lower prices (even though views of the stage and the acoustics proved to be as good from there as in the main hall).

One of our biggest challenges was to create disabled access throughout the building and all its various levels linking between the main auditorium and four corner towers. In the end, seven different forms of lift were installed to achieve this. On completion, the London District Surveyors made a special award for solving the problem. They understood how hard we had worked to achieve accessibility through the whole complex listed building.

English Heritage were supportive of our scheme and the proposed use. Having submitted the planning and listed building applications, we were dismayed that a vociferous group of nearby residents were objecting to the proposals on the grounds of increased traffic, noise and pedestrian movement. One objecting neighbour seriously proposed that Cadogan had enough money to restore the building and then leave it empty and unused. Should 'objectionable' neighbour better describe that attitude and the extreme self-interest that went with it?

As the building had existing use as a church, I suggested to Stuart that a short-term letting to an ecclesiastical group would not require planning permission. At the same time, we were acting for 'The Church of the Rock', a thriving multi-racial evangelical community who were looking for a temporary home during works to refurbish and extend their building in Tufnell Park in North London. Much as it would have been amusing to upset the self-oriented 'Nimby' neighbours, Stuart considered my suggestion perhaps a little too reactive.

Walter Lilly was the preferred main contractor with Matt Stag as site manager. Everyone enjoyed working on this special project and were delighted with the finished project. Matt rightfully won 'Site Manager of the Year' and the newly named 'Cadogan Hall' won the highest European conservation prize, a Europa Nostra Award. The building has proved a great success with a wide variety of music and events being staged in Chelsea, which previously had no such cultural venue. The adjusted acoustics have proved sufficiently effective for some of the annual BBC Prom concerts to be presented, recorded and broadcast from Cadogan Hall.

Six months after completion, I walked round to our latest pride and joy to investigate some snagging. Entering the back of the auditorium, a rehearsal was in progress. I sat down alone, watched and listened. A tenor singer dressed in jeans and black leather bomber jacket with his back to the auditorium was addressing a part orchestra of a couple of dozen musicians. They started playing and the tenor began to sing. It was José Carreras. I could hear every note even though he had his back to the auditorium. Unobserved, I let that privileged moment last for half an hour before silently leaving with music in my head and a proud smile from ear to ear.

For almost 30 years, Davis & Bayne and Paul Davis + Partners, the practices that I founded and led, were more than fortunate to design countless building projects across the 96 acres of the Cadogan Estate. I have covered only a small fraction of all that work here even in the longer chapters of this life in architecture.* For six of those years, I was elected as a national councillor and main board member of the Royal Institute of British Architects (RIBA). Amongst the architectural fraternity I was nicknamed "Mr Chelsea", a title that, whilst flattering, I wasn't entirely comfortable with; it made me sound more like a gangster or a hairdresser than an architect.

These were challenging times made enjoyable through collaboration with large teams. Together, we transformed neglected buildings, suffered the everyday headaches of construction projects, and celebrated successful completions. Restoration and façade retention made much of that work invisible on the street; so much the better to re-cycle existing historic architecture. The vibrant mix of uses has been kept and enhanced without the loss of the memory of place.

Having changed the inner shape and value of so many historic buildings around Sloane Square, when I spotted the Earl, Charles Cadogan, striding purposefully about his Estate, the *Racing Post* under his arm and a dapper trilby on his head, I liked to imagine that he might be inspecting some of the vision I had brought about. His Lordship spoke at the opening ceremony of every recently completed major project. It was a good opportunity to hear what was on his mind and he was always kind enough to mention me by name. Actually, he consistently called me 'Philip'; the first time he did it I didn't correct him – I had been called worse names. I came to expect it as 'our little joke'. Speech completed, he would confide that, before 1783, 'architects were frequently hanged on the gallows at Tyburn Hill'. Not entirely correct, that punishment was reserved for criminals, but not nearly as gruesome as the Pharaohs, who cut out tongues to avoid stories like mine being told, or Ivan the Terrible, who blinded Postnik Yakovlev, the architect of St Basil's, to stop him from creating another masterpiece.

* A complete list of our Cadogan projects is included as an Appendix (see page 245).

21 WITH A LITTLE HELP FROM MY FRIENDS

Nicky Haslam, the socialite and celebrated interior designer and I had recently completed a most stunning apartment in Chesham Place, just off Belgrave Square. The master bedroom suite was the most perfectly indulgent that I had designed. The plan provided an elegant separating vestibule for privacy and a boudoir-cum-study for breakfast or tea to be served, to write a letter or dress for dinner. It had his and her bathrooms which Nicky decorated to perfectly interpret the different personalities of Derek and Sheila Dawson, our clients who were moving back to London from Los Angeles. There were three walk-in closets, two enormous and double-height for Sheila, and one more compact for Derek. The bedroom itself was more than 50 square metres in area. It had a ceiling adorned with an original plasterwork cornice and centrepiece floating 4.5 metres above the silk carpet. The suite had everything a wealthy and stylish theatre-angel couple could wish for.

Most impressive had been Nicky's display of creativity and profound knowledge of historic interiors. The main drawing room had been neglected for years and had suffered water damage. The decorative plasterwork needed restoration and reinvention. We visited the historic architectural plasterwork archive at George Jackson's and selected mouldings from the correct era with further musical and theatrical detail motifs from the 1860s.

Nicky's arrival at a client meeting was always the subject of amused speculation. Would he be wearing his sharply tailored scarlet suit or appear dressed in a buttercup yellow New York fireman's outfit?

In contrast to his colourful attire and personality, Nicky proposed an all-white decoration for this important room, not minimalist modern but with layers of different shades of white. He subsequently provided copious images of white rooms in historic houses as well as his own informative sketches of how the room would look. A Parisian-style marquetry floor was chosen and formed a warm rich base, onto which Savonnerie carpets were spread. Nicky and Sheila selected the furniture and soft furnishings together, all in shades of white with occasional sparkles of silver thread. The result was ethereal and delicately peaceful.

The dining room scheme showed Nicky at his most creative: a room for night-time dinner parties at which Noel Coward would have felt at home. He had the walls lined in a simple silver paper, then directed the Czainskis, renowned *trompe l'oeil* artists, to hand paint exquisite pastel-coloured floral motifs, layer upon layer until only the remnants of the silver base sparkled through the horticultural canvas. It felt like being inside a Gustav Klimt painting.

Nicky and I were invited to an inaugural dinner, lit solely by candles and a softly glowing chandelier. It was an exceptional and memorable night, and our clients were

Opposite:
Rydinghurst sitting room
Photo courtesy of Nicky Haslam

delighted with the finished apartments. That was gratifying, but equally important was that Nicky and I had built a mutual respect and greatly enjoyed the experience of working together.

Ringo Starr and Barbara Bach had just bought the Rydinghurst Estate, near Cranleigh in Surrey, and had asked Nicky to create the design for the interior of this substantial house. Ringo wanted to appoint a local architect whom he thought would be inexpensive. Nicky was keen to involve me and had told Ringo that my fee would be no more than 10% of the build cost. So, a provisional meeting was arranged to dicuss ideas.

Nicky and I arrived early to walk the Grade II listed wreck. The rambling, mostly mid-19th century red brick assembly with *ad hoc* additions had previously been the holiday home of a Spanish aristocrat and was dreadfully neglected. As we stood in the ground floor rooms, holes in the ceilings framed views of broken melamine wardrobes in the bedrooms above. The sad condition of the floorboards called for careful placing of each step to avoid disappearing into the floor below whilst exploring the many rooms.

Ringo and Barbara arrived close to the arranged time in the inevitable polished black Mercedes saloon. Ringo bounced out of the back seat without waiting for the chauffeur to open it for him.

'Nicky told me you wouldn't be more than 10%,' he said, as an opener.

'How about 9.9,' I quipped in return, not knowing quite what to expect.

'Orll roight,' he replied, in that famous Liverpudlian accent. 'Let's go and see what we've got and you two can give us your ideas.'

It was a bright October morning and the downward slope of the extensive grounds looked like Richmond Park with trees neatly cropped by roaming deer.

'Nicky's told me you're the best, that's cool, but it doesn't mean we'll be friends forever,' Ringo continued, as we walked down.

I was only slightly taken aback. 'OK,' I replied. 'Let's just talk about the house and how you want to live in it.'

We spent a couple of hours discussing possibilities and priorities: a country house kitchen to hang out in with friends, a small study with an amazing sound system, huge clothes storage times two, a cosy private cinema and the most crafted sequence of rooms that you can imagine for washing down the dogs and Wellington boots after a muddy walk. Each priority seemed to carry equal significance in this informal but direct brief. There was a large separate single-room annexe building facing the long terrace that was to be a rehearsal and jamming space. Ringo wanted this to be unadorned, like an old village hall, except for power sockets every few feet for amplification equipment.

Both Ringo and Barbara seemed happy to let Nicky determine the style, imagery and atmosphere of the decor. Before leaving, Ringo said 'We want to move in by December next year, can you do it?' Somewhat shaken, but having been tested with impossible programmes before, I thought for a few silent moments.

'OK, but you'll have to let me do it my way,' I replied. I had already been musing on a maverick idea of how to go about restoring and transforming the handsome but ramshackle pile. Little did I know (and only found out much later) that his lawyers had told him it would be at least two years before they could move in. They were right: few listed building projects take less than 30 months, most often more.

'Let my accountant know your predicted build cost, I have a target budget in mind,' Ringo advised.

With which, he bounced into the back seat on the far side of the car, while Barbara kissed me on both cheeks and slid elegantly into the near side. The chauffeur closed her door and walked slowly round to take the wheel.

'We'll see you in a couple of weeks, cheerio,' they cried, smiling and waving. As we watched the car disappear down the long drive to the little bridge by the gatehouse, Nicky said, 'You'll be all right, Barbara likes you.'

Having watched the Beatles' rise to mega popularity as a teenager and revelled in each new album, meeting one of the Fab Four for real was like visiting New York for the first time. You imagine you know it, from countless movies, news bulletins, photographs and books. But on arrival, there's that surreal sensation of knowing and not knowing: the height, the resonance, the diversity from one block to another, the detail of the '30s skyscrapers, the overwhelming drama and shafts of light penetrating the vast scale of Central Station, more impressive than even the famous black and white photograph - the thunder and rattle of cumbersome yellow taxis trundling over potholes and steaming iron vent covers. But ignore your assumptions, that's never a good starting point. How was it going to be, working for Ringo: as I might have assumed, or an altogether different reality?

Ringo was even gentler than I'd imagined, unmistakable in his jeans, immaculate bomber jacket and neatly trimmed stubble. He was softly spoken and enjoyed a giggle, then suddenly he'd become serious and aloof, holding his distance. He seemed quite shy and unsure, at the same time holding a worldliness and perception garnered from the intensity of experiences that being a Beatle had thrown at him. There was an astute abruptness about him. He spoke in matter-of-fact clipped sentences which only came out when he was sure he wanted to add to the conversation. Barbara was as beautiful and high-cheekboned a woman as the Bond girl she had once been. They held hands a lot and she moved with the elegant control of a well-trained and accomplished actor.

Here was a project to get into and get on with.

That afternoon, I rang Ron Bates, the ginger-bearded Construction Director of Walter Lilly Construction, who were appropriately experienced and I knew well. It was they who had built the Chesham Place apartment amongst other of the houses we had designed. Ron agreed to meet me on site the following Saturday morning at nine o' clock.

For three hours we walked the building and on just two sides of A4 lined paper wrote a list of the key packages of work: brick and stone repairs, roof tiling and leadwork, windows, floor strengthening, plumbing, heating, electrics, plasterwork, and so on. As we went, we allocated budget amounts to each element.

Then we retired to the pub where we worked out the manpower and management resource ('prelims' in construction speak). Then we broke that down into a simplified schedule. We paused for a pie and a second pint. We reviewed and refined each of our best guesses. Next, we wrote a list of things that we had not included, such as the landscaping, new services intakes, specialist decoration, stable buildings, etc, on less than a single side of A4. The following week, I met Ringo's accountant and agreed the content of these three simple A4 sheets that were to become our control document for the project.

The reality was a little more complex, but it was to prove a highly successful strategy. Walter Lilly worked to a completely 'open book'. There was to be no quantity surveyor, there wasn't time. A QS would think differently; my approach would be regarded as too risky, this would require a foundation of trust. We agreed a list of the best specialist sub-contractors for each of the trade packages. We didn't go to competitive tender. Each specialist was asked to look at the work entailed and confirm if they could do their part within or better than our base allowance. If they could, great, get ready to go; if not, shout and tell us why and what they believed

Below:
Rydinghurst garden elevation and music annexe

their cost should be. Some things needed more discussion and negotiation. A week later, the scaffolding went up and shrouded the entire structure whilst the internal strip out began.

Although Rydinghurst was a Grade II listed historic building, we were able to commence repair works since consent was not necessary for that stage. While this progressed, we began all the drawings necessary for the alteration works that did require planning and listed building consents. We knew consent would take some months to be granted, so we pushed on with the extensive repairs. By April the following year, listed building consent was granted and we had eight months to complete the renovation. The team was going for it big time.

The atmosphere on site was like the old times, everyone was cooperating and helping each other, laughing and joking, whistling; progress was phenomenal. Proof of my belief that if you take away the time and cost of tendering, get people that you trust to know what they're doing, pay a fair price and pay it quickly, then you get A teams. The end result is the best workmanship and best value. The convention of competitive tendering is most often a false economy and never ends with the same figure that the contract started with.

Once a month, I would meet Andrew Crispin, Walter Lilly's project surveyor, to review and agree main and sub-contractor stage valuations. Within a day or two, I would meet Ringo's accountant and explain the figures and he would make payment, continually referring to our initial three pages of A4 predictions.

Through regular hands-on site inspections, queries were dealt with directly with each individual trade. Because the works were progressing so rapidly and efficiently, minor variations generally could be overlooked. Substantial variations were properly recorded, valued and paid for. In general, it is delay that costs everyone money and inevitably causes dispute.

Where there were major additions, such as those we had predicted and excluded on our third sheet of A4, these were costed and if necessary, additional management manpower brought in to avoid delays. There were substantial changes such as new gas and water mains having to be brought in half a mile from the main road. Ringo wanted 'moonlight' in the trees around the house. Nicky's specialist decoration and furnishings had always been outside our initial budget. Despite these escalations, we were keeping closer to programme than I could have hoped.

Early in October with only ten weeks to go Ringo took me to one side:

'D'you know, Paul, I reelly like fireworks?'

'Me too, saved all my pocket money for them as a kid.'

'I want to have a big firework party here at Rydinghurst on Guy Fawkes night, but I don't want to burn the house down before it's finished. Where do you think we should we have it?'

I suggested the walled garden that was well away from the construction compound and could safely accommodate a sizeable party. Which was lucky, as Ringo wanted a huge party with not just lots of friends but all the people who'd worked on the house as well. A huge bonfire was built, utilising the plentiful waste material on site. A stuffed guy resembling John, the site manager, was placed on top.

Come November 5th, all the site workmen and women, their partners and kids had been invited and proudly showed up. Although Ringo and Barbara are both vegetarian, there were stalls with burgers and sausages, hot soup, fish and chips and everything anyone could want on Guy Fawkes night. Among the throng of builders and their families was a host of rock n' roll aristocracy.

Ringo was in his element, chatting with everyone.

'Eric, meet Harry, he's been doing all the fibrous plaster at the house, he's a magician.'

Harry was of course knocked out being introduced to Clapton, his guitarist hero. He wasn't the only one.

A gigantic firework display exploded in the clear starlit sky above us and Ringo seemed a very happy little boy again.

Our target date to complete was 7 December. On 14 December, it was finished. Nicky's decorative scheme was in places colourful, delightful, and often humorous in detail. In a small vestibule opening onto the terrace, he had installed a faux-painted bookcase with antiqued book spines recalling the many Beatle song titles. Every room was comfortable and felt just as it might always have been. There were two enormous walk-in closets, a study crammed full of audio kit, a cosy private cinema and the most elegant dog and wellie boot washroom, just as had been imagined. The expansive informal kitchen/breakfast room was ready to deliver lots of cups of tea.

Where the wild deer still roamed, Ringo had secretly installed a life size sculpture of a rhino under one of the neatly trimmed oak trees down from the house. It was surprisingly easy to miss.

Within a month, the final account was agreed; it came very close to our original budget set out on those original two A4 pages. A further tranche of major changes as per the exclusions on our third A4 sheet had been completed and we were only one week late.

Fourteen and a half months after first meeting Ringo and Barbara at Rydinghurst, they moved in, just before Christmas. Amazing what you can do with a little help from your friends.

Below:
The Hallway
Photo courtesy of Nicky Haslam

22 ALL THE RIGHT REASONS

Dolphin Square was built on the Thames Embankment in the mid 1930s. At the time, it was the largest apartment building in Europe. The project was developed just after the Great Depression to provide affordable housing for people economically active in the City of Westminster. Ahead of its time, the building had its own *Dolphin* restaurant, swimming pool and shop. In the early 2000s, the Dolphin Square Trust (DST) decided to sell the remainder of the lease. It was sold to Westbrook, an American hotel and property group, in 2006. The DST established a Charitable Trust with an endowment of around £100 million from the proceeds of the sale. The purpose of the Charitable Trust was to continue to provide affordable new housing for people working in Westminster. Ian Henderson, then the Chief Executive of Land Securities Group, and Colin Redman from Grosvenor were appointed as Chair and Vice Chair of the new Foundation Trust Board.

One of the first sites that they acquired to deliver the targeted housing was on Vauxhall Bridge Road close to Victoria Station. The site had a planning consent for three large townhouses. Colin and I had been discussing new ways to deliver affordable housing and he generously put our name forward to the selection committee. Colin was part of the committee but had agreed not to speak because of our longstanding relationship. At the interview, I was asked, 'You have designed a lot of excellent housing, but most of it has been high value and a long way from affordable, why do you think you would be appropriate for key worker housing on this site?'

We had recently completed 30 affordable flats in the first phase of the Duke of York development, but my questioner was correct; circumstance had created the opportunities and our work had focused on the top end of the market. I was keen to redress that imbalance.

'My purpose and mission as an architect focused on residential design has always been to conceive homes that people will enjoy living in whatever their means. To deliver the best possible homes for key workers in Westminster would be a delight and a personal challenge integral to my passion for residential architecture,' I enthusiastically replied.

We were thrilled and excited when we were notified that PD+P had been selected from the shortlist.

The site on Vauxhall Bridge Road was just to the south of the extensive high-density low-rise Lillington Gardens, a seminal social housing scheme by Darbourne & Darke. All architecture students visited to admire and learn from it in the early '70s. This exceptional competition-winning scheme was characterised by a warm orange red brick and strong sculptural forms around a sequence of landscaped

205

courts. Our scheme needed to be in contextual dialogue with this development but certainly not be any kind of pastiche replica. To the west of our site stood the main entrance façade of St James the Less church in the Gothic Revival style by the architect George Edmund Street. Built in 1858-61, it was Grade I listed and regarded as 'one of the finest Gothic Revival churches anywhere'.* Along the east side was the heavily trafficked highway linking Victoria Station to Vauxhall Bridge.

As our ideas emerged, we debated the potential massing relating to buildings to the south and on the opposite side of the main road. We established that the site could take four and five storeys and that the depth could accommodate perimeter apartments with a central atrium, open to the air for ventilation and fire regulation compliance. A glazed canopy could create a covered courtyard for weather protection. Set around the sides of the atrium would be the stairs, lift and a wide access balcony. The main entrance would face north, thereby forming and activating a new public square celebrating the west façade of the Grade I historic building. We selected an orange red brick and during construction had the bricklayers hand batch the bricks to best reflect the texture and colour of the church. The apartments were briefed to be a mix of studio, one, two and three bedrooms. As many flats as possible should have external balconies. The design provided for a large communal roof terrace with seating and raised vegetable planting beds. Despite the budget limitations, the windows were of a high specification to reduce traffic noise. The original consented proposal for the site had proposed just three houses, our scheme created a variety of 39 dwellings for key workers and a small percentage for market rental.

Despite this worthy and much needed housing in an otherwise unaffordable borough of central London, we still faced an unnecessary and prolonged battle to achieve planning consent. One irritating issue was that to achieve the quantum of dwellings, we had no integral parking. Westminster wanted us to provide a certain percentage of residents' parking in accordance with their then current policies. Since the scheme was for key workers in Westminster and extremely well served by public transport, we stood our ground and did manage to negotiate the number down to just a few on-street resident parking spaces in conjunction with the then novel idea of having a shared car club. Reluctantly, the planners eventually accepted our case as we provided plentiful secure bike storage. Within a few years the Westminster policy changed to not allow parking provision within new developments in order to reduce car ownership and encourage use of public transport. Having dealt with the parking issue, the application was further delayed because we exceeded the Council's density guidelines. We were fortunate that the site dimensions suited the land-efficient courtyard atrium form, but it was surely better to deliver 39 flats to city space standards rather than just three large houses. Then we hit another regulatory barrier. All 39 flats had to have a fully wheelchair accessible bathroom (more space hungry than a well-planned conventional one). Whilst this may sound laudable in principle, the Trust were retaining ownership and management of the building. Hence, any disabled resident could be accommodated through time and good management. New market flats were not regulated to this degree. Every non-disabled key worker could have enjoyed more living space within the same flat area. Eventually consent was granted and the scheme was built.

The project won numerous major awards, but most importantly, the key worker residents clearly enjoy living there, a point proven by turnover being uncommonly low. Had I been eligible, I would have loved to rent one of the flats. It stands as one of my proudest projects for all the right reasons.

* Nikolaus Pevsner: *A History of Architecture*.

23 BLOFELD OR GOLDFINGER?

Pronounced Lu, Nick Loup's name is deceptive, French for wolf and phonetically Chinese. In his twenties, he looked like an English prep-school boy dressed in a smart grey suit. Thirty-five years on, he still does. Nick was always the brightest of his peers, hard to read, open and closed at the same time. Colin Redman was his mentor at The Grosvenor Estate. Nick and I worked and played hard together. We both learnt a lot from Colin.

Nick always appeared straight, formal and business-like, but his widest smiles came out in the noisy buzz of a nightclub at one in the morning. That was when his tie disappeared, the whiskey and vodka flowed, and he let his schoolboy haircut down. We became close friends through the mid '80s and early '90s, building projects and playing into the night.

By 1993, the recession was taking its toll on property development in London. My practice was heading for the rocks and Nick saw a future in the Far East. He left London to work for Jardine Matheson and made friends with some of the young Hong Kong Chinese property entrepreneurs. We kept in touch on his return visits to London. By '94, he was asked by the Duke of Westminster's property empire to set up Grosvenor Asia Pacific. At first, Nick acquired investment buildings to upgrade for enhanced rental income. However, the real target was to design and develop new prestige buildings. Nick had observed the Hong Kong preoccupation with branding, not just with trainers, fashion labels and cars, but property as well. Buildings were an essential expression of brand identity. So, what would the Grosvenor brand be? One evening over dinner and a bountiful dousing of Meursault, we laughed and talked over many different ideas. Suddenly, we hit it together; 'Bond, James Bond' –'Sartorial English sophistication and with the TOYS.' The penthouse suite should be where Bond's adversary would live. Dr. No, Blofeld, or Goldfinger always had the most dramatic, extravagant and innovative pads. We laughed a lot and the branding idea stuck with us both.

In '99, I got an excited and unexpected phone call from Nick.

'I've bought our first site for a new tower, it's in the middle of Repulse Bay, 15 minutes from Central and overlooking the South China Sea. How soon can you get over here?'

The idea of starting from scratch in a new city was both challenging and terrifying. The opportunity to design a new landmark building was so different from our work in Westminster and Chelsea, which had mostly involved adapting existing buildings. My appointment was a leap of faith from Nick since he knew that I had never designed a high-rise tower before. I was aware that I would have to convince his joint venture partners and investors that I could meet this new challenge.

Opposite:
Grosvenor Place reflecting pool: Stepping stones above the South China Sea

I cleared my diary and set off business class for Hong Kong. It was a long flight with time to think. The possibility of taking the practice international, to design something brave and different kept me awake all the way. I had no idea of the site or the city. I felt anxious and I was alone. What would I make of Hong Kong development expectations, and how would lifestyles differ? I planned to visit other recent projects to learn, evaluate and consider how I could design something relevant but better, to exceed expectations. My mind raced with stage fright.

How would Hong Kong, a new city, surprise me? Just as I'd found in New York, a place is never the same as its assumed image and atmosphere. The plane landed at Lantau, the huge new airport terminal designed by Norman Foster: a project so vast that the earthworks construction had been measured by satellite photography, an architectural league away from my own experience.

Nick was at the arrivals gate to meet me. As we walked to the car park, the clammy heat and humidity brought it home that we were in a different climate zone, a different place. The drive to Central Hong Kong takes about half an hour. The modern highway passes vast repetitive apartment blocks in bleak interstitial nowhere-land. Then suddenly the vertiginous intensity of Central Hong Kong hits you, urban highways wind up and over one another, high level pedestrian walkways link one giant complex to the next. Above it all, The Peak rises steeply to the south with more towers densely anchored into the hillside around Happy Valley. The buzz and energy of the place are manifest, somewhere between Manhattan and *Blade Runner*. Kowloon, old Hong Kong, is just across the bay, and the Star Line ferries carry hordes of workers back and forth between island and mainland. China is only a couple of hours to the north, and it hadn't been long since the centre of Far Eastern capitalism had reverted to Chinese communist government control. One country, two systems? Only time would tell. Another tension was in the air.

The Mandarin was the most luxurious hotel I had ever had the pleasure to stay in. With more staff than guests, the service was impeccable and inscrutable. Next morning, I tucked into a buffet breakfast to die for. I was ready to start a new working adventure. Nick had set up camp in a suite of offices on the 34th floor of Jardine House. The tower was best known as the 'Cheese Grater' on account of its silver metal cladding and repetitive grid of large circular windows. Introductions, coffee, then off to see the site...

As we drove out of the yellow tungsten light of the Aberdeen tunnel, the landscape had changed. It was verdant with tropical trees, and after a couple of minutes, there was the misty blue of the South China Sea. The coast road wound up and around the bluff to Deep Water Bay. The terrain and flora were suddenly more Mediterranean, the difference was the ashen, hazy lack of direct sunlight. As we approached the Hong Kong Golf Club, the affluence jumped out like the roar of a scarlet Ferrari. As the road climbed around the headland, the views and dramatically perched villas seemed akin to Southern California. Island Road dropped steeply into the wide, sandy expanse of the unfortunately named Repulse Bay. At its centre stood a colonial-style café and restaurant. Above and wrapped behind it, a long white apartment building with a dramatic square cut-out dominated the bay. I found out later that *Feng Shui* advice had determined the requirement of a 'dragon fly-path'. Or maybe it was just architectural licence?

At the end of the waterfront, we took a sharp left turn, up a narrow lane lined with small four-storey, tired-looking apartment blocks. At the end, just above the colonial restaurant, we parked behind the most worn-out vacant building. Richard Poon, who had acquired the site and joined forces with Nick, was already there to meet us with some of his staff. He seemed enthusiastic to hear my ideas before I had even grasped the new complexity that faced me. The plot was smaller than I had imagined possible to plant a 20-storey tower. Certainly, the views out over the sea were stunning and to the rear of the site was a steep hill, dense with broad leaf evergreen trees. Nick advised me that the location between the mountain and the sea brought auspicious *Feng Shui* without passing dragons. In front, the land dropped sharply down to the bay. The escarpment was overgrown with bushes and one elegant tree which looked like the specimen subject of a Chinese watercolour painting. My very first thought was that I wanted to preserve this tree as a key to the composition. Hong Kong developers and their developments generally disregard such arboricultural sympathy.

Left:
The retained tree, framed from the arrival driveway in the finished building

211

I paced out the plot, then strolled along the narrow access lane and was bemused as to how on earth a tall tower could be built with limited access to such a small parcel of land. We went back round to the restaurant for coffee and discussed the brief whilst enjoying the view from the terrace. Richard had a clarity of intent whilst being unexpectedly open to new ideas that broke established Hong Kong conventions. Among other things, he thought keeping the iconic tree was a great idea. This all gave me confidence and lightened the anxiety that I held about my lack of high-rise experience. The height had already been determined by the Hong Kong planning authority. The location in the middle of the bay was brilliant. What had surprised me was the permanent dull grey light on Hong Kong Island which seemed to deny both shadow and contrast. I started to feel that the bay needed a colourful centrepiece. Sculpturally, our tower would be taller than anything else around and hence an eye-catching beacon. As we returned towards Central, we parked on the headland so that I could take panoramic photos of the whole bay. Our discussions and numerous sketch schemes evolved and we concluded that it should be one large lateral apartment to each floor, with a high-ceilinged duplex at the top, complete with a pool on the roof-top terrace. Blofeld or Goldfinger?

Back in London, the design advanced, with the aim that every principal room should have the benefit of sea views. The point of arrival would be at road level with a discreet ramp cut into the rock beneath to conceal the parking. Lifted above this, we proposed a luxurious club house facility and projecting reflecting edge pool looking south over the sea. Above this and set back, 20 floors of apartments would climb skywards with each living room opening onto a generous central balcony. Current Hong Kong convention was to plan miniature bedrooms with floor to ceiling glazing that invoked a vulnerable sense of vertigo and rendered the rooms virtually impossible to furnish. I argued that the smaller secondary bedrooms should not follow this fashion, but rather have their windows set 3 ft (0.9m) above floor level. This more traditional pattern would enable more adaptable furniture layouts and a greater sense of security.

There was long debate over the external cladding, which needed to pass the stringent and formulaic Hong Kong building regulations. Eventually, we gained consent to use large terracotta panels that would give the scale and the strong, but subdued, warm orange colour that I had envisaged since my first site visit. Good local architects were interviewed to work alongside us as executive architects, that is, responsible for delivery. LWK secured the commission and the design advanced over a series of presentation visits with Nick's joint venture partners.

A start on site was made with the long process of piling and groundworks essential for anchoring a slender 20-storey tower in a climate subject to typhoons. Confidence in an experienced structural engineer was essential, as this kind of specialised expertise was way beyond my skill set. Once this slow stage was complete, the concrete frame rose rapidly. Although this was an exciting new experience to witness, it was also scary. I had never designed a tower before. How would the finished building look? Would it contribute to the seafront as I had imagined? Would the plan ideas suit the Hong Kong market?

The benefit of the time difference between London and Hong Kong meant that we would receive technical drawings from LWK in the morning, mark them up, then email them back at the end of our working day. The updated, corrected drawings could then be accessed by LWK at the start of their next day. It was like having two shifts operating through 24 hours.

Periodic site visits were riveting as the tower progressed upwards, enveloped in the ingenious, sustainable bamboo scaffolding that flexes in high winds and is wrapped in protective green netting.

Conventional Hong Kong marketing strategy was, and remains, to set up 'smoke and mirrors' show flats in Central, with the intent to sell as many 'units' as possible off plan before completion. Nick talked his joint venture partners into the very different strategy that he had learnt from Colin Redman: to act in the confident belief that that you don't show anyone or sell anything until the project is complete and as good as you can make it. Mark Humphrey had worked as Nicky Haslam's assistant on Ringo's house and was introduced to install a fully furnished show apartment in the completed tower.

Nick added the enjoyable idea of holding an extravagant launch party to mix potential buyers, luxury brands and the media. I invited Phil Manzanera to come out and play the Bond themes in his free-flowing electric guitar style at the side of the pool. At the time, Roxy Music had split up again and Bryan Ferry had been on his own solo world tour. The last show, in Hong Kong, just happened to be the night before our launch party. Happily, we all went to Bryan's gig at the Convention Centre, and he had the good grace to invite Phil up onto the stage to play a few guest numbers. Despite their acrimonious split, he accepted the invitation to the opening party the next evening.

Two days before the party, the first Aston Martin DB9 arrived in Hong Kong, and we borrowed it to be parked by the reception foyer. The tree that I had wanted as a feature from the outset was in silhouette, framed by an opening opposite the entrance foyer as foreground to the sea view. Mark had been designing furniture for Fendi, and there had been a Fendi fashion show in town that week. We invited the Fendi models to come to the party as poolside 'Bond girls'.

For good measure Nick had arranged luscious food and cocktails, more music and South American dancers in full carnival costumes. The party was set to start at 7 p.m. All was in place and looking great, but no guests had arrived. It was one of those apprehensive moments before a party begins when you have no idea how it is going to turn out.

Standing out on the edge of the cantilevered pool, Nick's phone rang. He turned white.

'What's up?' I asked anxiously.

'There's a traffic jam in the Aberdeen tunnel.' Nick's head was shaking in disbelief; his big gamble was about to crumble. As he listened, he repeated the caller's words out loud…

'The jam is being caused by the exceptional number of limousines leaving Central through the tunnel.'

Above:
The Tower in the Bay:
Adding some colour
to the hazy light of
Hong Kong

Right:
Early concept sketch

Far right:
Grosvenor Place:
Tower 1

We laughed nervously and looked up at our joint achievement. Our first tower in Hong Kong was a very long way from Chester Close.

A few minutes later, the flashy chauffeured cars began to arrive. The party was a major society event and went on all night. I got back to the Mandarin at 7.30 a.m., exhausted but satisfied.

Nick's original marketing strategy went further. During the party, there was a schedule of each apartment and guests were able to put offers against an apartment for a specific floor level: no offers were accepted, it was more about arousing interest. A couple of weeks later, a letter arrived at Grosvenor's office from Angela Ho offering to buy the whole tower. Angela was the fourth wife of Stanley Ho, the founder of Macau Casinos. She went ahead and did as she'd offered, giving Grosvenor and their joint venture partners an unusually large profit.

In March 2004, Grosvenor Place (as the project had been named) was entered for the 'Best International Residential Project' at the big MIPIM property convention in Cannes. Once the voting had concluded, our team went off to the main auditorium full of excited expectation to watch the awards ceremony.

'And the winner is... Grosvenor Place in Hong Kong.'

It was a proud moment for me to collect the award and I was grateful for Nick's loyalty and belief in me. I'd never designed a tower before, and most commercial clients only appoint architects who have a track record in a particular building type. The next day, Nick took a whole-page advert in the Hong Kong *Financial Times* with a photo of the tower and our name writ large. The overall success gave us instant provenance in Hong Kong and sufficient workload to open an office on Wyndham Street, a lively spot just up the hill above Central.

Having a presence in Hong Kong was instrumental in building a workload in mainland China and Japan as well as with more high-profile projects on the old colony island. These were exciting and challenging times. I made frequent visits around much of the Far East, looking, learning, and designing new projects.

This page & opposite:
Westminster Terrace
Grosvenor Tower 2:
Reception carved into the hill,
Design sketch of the base in
the hill and its spectacular night
setting

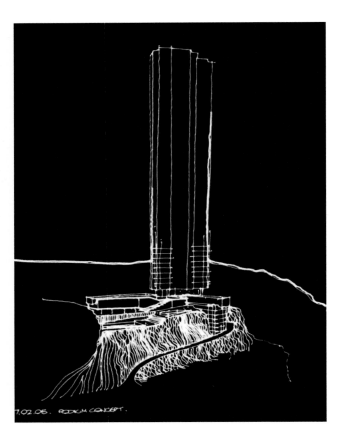

7.02.06. PODIUM CONCEPT.

24 DISTANT LANDS, DISTANT CITIES

In the early 2000s, the UK Department of Trade and Investment (UKT&I) were organising professional trade missions around the world to promote export revenue through the 'creative industries'. Having been excited and stimulated by visiting Hong Kong and designing our first residential tower there, I was hungry for more. With government subsidies, the idea of a UKT&I organised tour to Taiwan and Shanghai seemed a logical next adventure.

Taipei was a weird mixture of mega development and unappreciated historic urban gems. Taipei 101 was one of the tallest buildings in the world at the time. It wasn't my kind of architecture. The interior public spaces looked like an over-the-top film set for Flash Gordon; on the outside, cladding panels were falling off even though it was not long completed. The delegate group were then taken to visit the grounds and remnants of the Old Tobacco Factory. This was a vast walled garden within the city centre with an array of handsome but decaying structures, magnificent trees and overgrown pathways. I wanted to get involved and reinvent its potential as a great urban amenity. Sadly, we were advised that it would be unfundable in Taiwan at the time. To me, it had the potential of a Covent Garden or Duke of York campus, ideal for regeneration, reuse, public open space and a reinvented historic centrepiece; in short, imaginative placemaking.

What we did learn was that every Taiwanese city wanted to commission a 'Starchitect' to design an iconic art gallery, opera house or civic centre to attract architectural tourism. Everywhere we went, local officials asked about the impact of Frank Gehry's Guggenheim Museum in Bilbao and how it had transformed a declining industrial city into a 'must see' tourist destination. This was not the kind of commission that I was looking for. Perhaps I never had the imagination, but my ability and mindset lay more in the courage to design background buildings, places for people as part of a city rather than some egotistical focal point. The concept of conserving and reinventing the best of a city's history and memory as part of its future hadn't yet reached Taiwan. Worse still, the Old Tobacco Factory and its gardens were scheduled for demolition.

Next morning, we flew to Shanghai and our first visit was to Xintiandi, in advance of speaking at a major conference on the *Future of Cities*.

Ben Woods was an American architect out of an unusual mould. A former fighter pilot and restaurateur, he had won a competition to redevelop five or six decaying 1850s urban blocks in the French Concession of Shanghai. Having been involved in the regeneration of Times Square in NYC and the Art Deco district in Miami Beach, he moved to Shanghai and set up Shanghai Studio. Instead of razing the historic buildings to the ground, he set about renovating the grey brick

Opposite:
Stepping further East

Shikumen townhouses that formed the backdrop to the intimate network of pedestrian lanes and small squares known as Xintiandi. It was only recently finished when we visited on our first afternoon in the city. It had been an immediate success with new boutique shops, bars and restaurants opening. (It subsequently became a tourist magnet and an economic exemplar, with cities across China wanting their own Xintiandi.)

After the experience in Taiwan, this was a stimulating contrast to witness and demanded a thorough exploratory walkabout. Then it was time for liquid refreshment and there, straight ahead, was a bar. Less than coincidentally, it was the DR Bar (Design Research), and Ben was sitting in a dimly lit corner of his own achievement. We engaged in a wide-ranging conversation centred on our respective ideas of how we envisaged cities evolving, and the challenges he had faced changing opinions and values in Shanghai. The finale to our visit was in two days' time, when I was due to make the biggest public speech that I had ever had to present. Eager to learn about Shanghai and the inevitable debate over the breakneck change and development of the city, I asked him about the key issues.

I learnt that there was considerable argument and resentment over the forced municipal relocation of residents from whole neighbourhoods to facilitate massive redevelopment. Alongside the rise of the new middle class had come the fashion for BMW status symbols in place of bicycles. Much as this was understandable, it was also the inevitable cause of desperate pollution and coronary circulation congestion. The most controversial debate was over the city authorities selling off land for construction adjacent to the Creek, a popular waterfront public open space. These commercial development leases prevented public access to the riverside. I was mindful of the evolving success of London's access policy at South Bank, where all new development had to provide free pedestrian access to the south bank of the River Thames.

My head was full of ideas for the imminent conference. Absorbed in thought, I stumbled around the corner and there, sitting at another street café, was Will Alsop with a large glass of red wine in his hand. With his long, dark, unkempt hair and unshaven jaw, he looked more like an urban cowboy than a celebrated architect. But I wasn't surprised to see him there. He was well known for his radical, colourful and eccentric architectural creations, an *enfant terrible* in a suitable setting, a world away from the constrained, snail's pace, democratic planning process of England. We shared another bottle of red wine and laughed about making a living from selling design around the world. Whatever the idea being presented, self-belief is the quintessential ingredient.

That evening, our group visited the Bund: the wide riverside setting for the magnificent early 20th century stone bank and institutional buildings. These were rapidly being converted into a mix of bars, restaurants, galleries, flagship stores and offices. Some of the projects were very well executed and proving frighteningly crowded and popular with the emerging middle classes. Outside, the riverfront was buzzing with all manner of human life, rich and poor alike, a multitude enjoying the city's waterside.

The next day, we toured more of the city and learnt how each of the 19 districts all wanted to become the financial centre instead of focusing on the special nature of their location and historic character. Pudong across the river had just a few western-designed mega towers amongst dusty flatlands. That was soon to change. It was about to become the aspiration of all the other districts, a sea of wide boulevards and shiny glass tower blocks. Further along the river front, a vast area of docks with dozens of impressive but derelict cranes resembling skeletal dinosaurs was about to be cleared to make way for the 2010 Expo.

The Shanghai underground metro was being built at incredible speed having astutely recruited engineering expertise from the Hong Kong MTR. The rate of change in Shanghai was tangible. It felt like the Wild West in the East, amplified by the intensity of a nation, culture and city in transformation. Through immersion in this evolving city, I was rapidly able to pull together the material, ideas and narrative for the imminent big event. The stage and projection screen were huge. The packed auditorium seated 350 and was wired for simultaneous translation. It was by far the most professional set-up and largest audience I'd ever had to present to. I had a well-prepared set of images of great cities past and present, drawn from my travels around the world in different cultures and climates. London and New York were to be expected; Isfahan, as one of the first cities in the world with over a million people, surprised the audience; Kyoto, Granada, Siena, Rome, Venice, Vancouver and San Francisco delighted it. I had added in images of Shanghai to connect and contrast the comparative issues.

I talked about the great natural landscape features of cities, their rivers, lakes, topography and the precious amenity they provide to their citizens: how invaluable access to the Creek was for the Shanghainese and how the South Bank of the Thames had enriched enjoyment of the river for Londoners and tourists. Positive policies can bring about positive change. I compared the structure of Isfahan to New York and London and how trading, manufacturing, cultural and ethnic enclaves all group together to create commercial destinations, critical mass and individual character within a city. I offered my conviction that such groupings are the very basis of long-lasting commercial and social urban success. I used Xintiandi, Covent Garden and our masterplan for Duke of York's to illustrate how conserving and reinventing historic neighbourhoods can restore memory and generate new life within a city; how civic pride is borne of human affection for place.

My discourse expounded the importance of context and climate and how historic architecture had evolved to solve extremes of climate and landscape, thereby creating great places with identity and character. My treatise was, and remains, that grave mistakes can arise by importing architectural models from different climates, landscapes and cultures without re-interpretation for their specific context. I told the story of visiting that Muslim family in a Parisian designed flat in Tehran, where the only place to eat was on the floor in the hall because the layout took no account of indigenous family structures.

I talked about movement and public transport systems that provide the connectivity that is the electricity of a living city, urging my Chinese audience to keep their bicycles as well as satisfying their desire for new cars. I extolled the virtue of investing in public spaces, whether large or small, active or tranquil, underlining their value to the quality of urban life. I showed children playing in fountains, adults reading books under shady trees, crowded markets, skateboarders, *tai chi* exercisers and joggers in parks or just people sitting watching people.

I had no need for my notes, I had my beliefs and cinema-scale projected images to illustrate my thoughts. I told the story of cycling westwards at sunset alongside the river Thames from Chelsea to Barnes. This was a distance of six or seven miles crossing only three roads. I had dinner at a friend's home, drank too much and had to stay over. In the morning I cycled back to work next to the water, as the sun rose in the East. A tale of how uplifting living and working in the city can be with a bike rather than a car.

It was the best talk I ever gave. My free-flowing conviction and heartfelt passion went down better than I could have imagined. It felt as though I had at last joined a lot of dots and had truly escaped being that dunce in the classroom corner. The outcome was better than expected. I was asked to give a talk at Tongji University in Shanghai on my next visit and UKT&I used me as an exemplar of their successful programme to support ongoing government investment. I was the only delegate to win export projects from each of their overseas excursions.

The next UK Trade & Investment outing to Japan was well organised with a small group of British architects lined up to meet most of the top development companies in Tokyo and Osaka. In predictably formal settings, each party presented the scope of past and present projects. Our presentations were somewhat humbling compared to the quality and scale of Mori, Mitsubishi, and Sekisui House. I was excited to visit Kyoto to see the temples and gardens that I had only seen in picture books. It was worth it. The gardens have a tranquillity, composition, concept and detail that can only be experienced in the present moment: places of masterful calm, introspective contemplation and sublime abstraction of nature. The city itself is fascinating to explore, with arcaded lanes off the main street, lined with stalls selling every conceivable hand-crafted traditional artefact: the best knives, scissors and garden tools you will ever find anywhere.

Tokyo was like another planet, sophisticated, efficient but also unexpectedly uncosmopolitan. One was instantly identifiable as a westerner, an obvious outsider. The urban organisation and cleanliness of these cities were meticulous, as was the quality of their architecture and construction.

It largely felt like our small team were out of its depth. However, something must have clicked with Sekisui House, a major residential developer, since I was offered a scheme of two towers in Fukuoka, in the south of Japan. A subsequent four-and-a-half-day trip was arranged, and I was to travel over with Dave Hoggard who had set up our office in Hong Kong and moved there.

We arrived in Fukuoka on the Monday evening and were chauffeured to our hotel. Next morning, we were shown around the city and various of their projects. They were particularly proud of a huge 150-year-old tree that they had successfully relocated to be a landscape centrepiece. We were shown the site, a few blocks back

Above:
Entrance to Tokyo apartments

Left:
The scheme at night

Below:
Sitting room Interior
Photos courtesy of GPT TMK

from the sea front. Then it was lunchtime. As we were on the Japanese Riviera, we were offered the best possible fresh seafood. Along the middle of the restaurant was a long shallow bubbling clear seawater pool full of exotic fish. I like *sashimi*, but the sight of a platter with thin slices of raw white fish meat set around the fleshy skeleton of the donor sea creature still alive and twitching didn't appeal to my western stomach. Fortunately, most of the rest of the fishy banquet was cooked.

After the lunch, we went to their minimalist modern design offices. The top Japanese development and construction companies employ thousands of specialist architects, designers and technicians. They do 'design and build' to a level unequalled in the rest of the world. We were given a comprehensive detailed briefing on the project, the site, the mix and size of apartments. We were shown typical apartment plans and an explanation of the structural requirements to deal with high-rise towers in an earthquake zone. They covered the issues of site access, covered parking and orientation. No stone was left unturned. Meeting over, we were delivered back to our hotel. We were to meet them again for questions and answers on the Friday morning before returning to Hong Kong. Dave and I decided that with two whole days to spare, we should just get on and design it. Which is what we did, to the extent that by the Friday morning we had a fully advanced sketch design for our twin towers. We decided to present only part of our work to illustrate some of our thinking, but having designed pretty much the whole thing, we were able to ask precise questions to confirm whether our ideas were what they were seeking. They were fortunately aligned.

We returned to London via Hong Kong, quickly turned our sketches into more refined drawings, and sent them off to Japan. They liked the scheme and went ahead and built it. A couple of years later, we received copies of the marketing brochure for the completed building. The marketing material included the sketches that Dave and I had done on our initial visit.

Our first two towers in Japan had been built at arm's length, but much better was to follow when Grosvenor commissioned us to design a large mid-rise apartment building in Tokyo. This site was adjacent to Yoyogi Park with rooftop views of Mt Fuji. It would prove to be another joyous challenge with Nick Loup's supportive loyalty. We struggled in our first design meeting with Yasui, the local architects, as neither team spoke the other's language. We took an awkward break for lunch. On our return to the meeting, I brought out my sketching materials and began to communicate through drawing. The atmosphere took off because, as architects, we had a shared visual language. The finished project was a refined fusion of shared vision; enjoyable and, as it proved, highly successful: so much so that the joint venture clients wanted to immediately appoint the same team for a follow-up site.

Below:
Fukoka Towers sketch

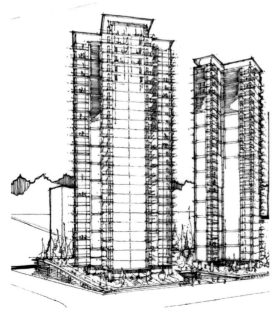

One unexpected outcome of my Far Eastern tours was that I was invited onto the UK Trade & Industry Advisory Board which met regularly in government offices on Victoria Street, only a 15-minute walk from the PD+P offices on Ebury Street. Following the recession and high unemployment of the early 2000s, one of the key topics for the Advisory Board was skill shortages amongst various professional sectors. The intention of the Board was to advise government on specific trades that should be allowed and encouraged to recruit into the UK from overseas. There were many skills within the NHS, farming, the sciences, and teaching that the country was lacking. The Home Office had wide-ranging immigration restrictions in place because of the high level of general unemployment. The UK and London were a world centre for architecture but were suffering from a serious lack of skilled labour. The Board repeatedly recommended inclusion of architects on the list because of the export strength of the profession amongst the creative industries. When designing buildings in different countries it is of considerable and obvious advantage to have staff that know the country and language. PD+P employed people from 17 different countries at the time. We needed more, as did any substantial architect's practice. The advice of the Board went unheeded by the relevant Ministerial Departments. Sitting on the Board became increasingly frustrating.

St Petersburg in Russia was the final government-sponsored destination that I ventured upon. The itinerary was structured to a very different format, centred on improving educational links between the UK and Russia. The British Council had organised a student competition to design a new pedestrian bridge across one of the many canals that criss-cross this historic city. Robert Hudson, on behalf of UKT&I and the British Council, asked Fred Manson and myself to judge the competition.

Below:
Ice shards re-freeze on reaching the wide waters of St Petersburg

We were also to meet the head of planning, to speak at a developers' seminar, and each of us was to mentor an architecture student workshop.

I had only met Fred once before catching the plane to Russia: he was a notorious maverick, of small build, with short-cropped silver hair, big round spectacles, and only slightly restrained punk clothing tendencies. Fred had been the head of the planning department at Southwark Council and had been the motivating force for The Shard to gain planning consent. He has a strikingly original brain, and it is no wonder that he has been working with Thomas Heatherwick in recent years.

A timed tour of the inner city was full of surprises and challenged all my existing assumptions. The river Volga was frozen solid with inexplicable gargantuan clusters of ice across an expansive horizon to a long, low bastion fortress. The maze of canals and colourful highly decorated buildings bounced reflections off each other. There were rows of market stalls with mountains of jumbled Soviet military memorabilia amongst cheap plastic toy trash. The biting cold and pale blue cloudless skies were sharper and brighter than imagined. The low-level April cross light illuminated every textured surface and decorative detail. Fred and I both bought black leather hats with fold down fur ear flaps. It didn't matter that we looked silly, at least our ears were warm. Robert whisked us off to the British Council to view the bridge competition submissions.

Fred and I first studied the drawings separately, and then prepared our individual shortlists. Next, we compared our opinions and quickly agreed that there was an outstanding winner. It turned out to be a young couple, Nadya and Alexander Gupalov. Their prize was to be two weeks' work experience at our office in London with their travel and accommodation paid for by the British Council. Our part would be to make their stay in London as enjoyable and stimulating as we possibly could.

The city planner's office was an expansive, sparsely furnished, high-ceilinged room straight out of a '60s cold war film. Victor was lanky and quietly spoken with good, only slightly broken English. He talked us through the epically-sized, tobacco faded map of the city that filled the wall at the end of the room. As we sat together in wide, well-worn leather sofas he discussed some of his plans and the difficulties that he faced in his beloved St Petersburg, not least because of the poor quality and maintenance of both the Soviet-era and recent developer construction. He also had the responsibility for maintaining the many historic palaces and squares, and the world-famous Hermitage Museum with limited funds. His was a gargantuan task.

He took us on a more detailed tour of this city of contrasts, with its vast, grey, decaying, Soviet-era housing estates and its recently built apartment buildings (incomplete though occupied). We visited gilded historic palaces that trumpeted the indulgent wealth of the tsars. Spreading wide and horizontal, St Petersburg was created out of marshlands. The river Volga appeared like shredded white chocolate on a luscious *gateau*. Victor explained that the dramatic angular shards had been formed as ice drifted towards the city, shattered into house-sized lumps and then, as the river widened, refroze into a single untraversable icescape. On the far side of this expansive art installation stood the sprawling fortress of St Peter and St Paul.

The low, wide bastion walls reach out over the riverbanks encircling a small but complete city within.

I was pleased to find that the student workshop I had been allocated was in a series of brick-vaulted spaces within the historic bastion walls. The brief was to design a new art gallery within these dramatic cavern-like spaces. Starting on Wednesday morning, the target was to mount an exhibition of the students' work on Friday afternoon. Two dozen senior students from three universities drifted into the temporary gallery vaults. First up, I had to introduce myself by giving an illustrated talk about my work in London and overseas. The students expressed little interest. I struggled to gain their attention and they continued to talk amongst themselves. Was it that I wasn't famous enough for them, that my work and observations were not iconic to grab their attention? All too soon it was coffee break time. I wanted to get them engaged and I wasn't sure how, but I had an idea that might just work. I spoke to the translator and asked her to carefully follow my words, tone of voice and pauses. I was about to take a big risk with something I'd never tried before, as I was desperate to get them into the room, engaged and onside.

Coffee break over, I asked them to move around so that they were sitting at different tables with no-one they knew. Then, I quietly but firmly told them to close their eyes, take a long deep breath and sit very upright, head stretched towards the ceiling. I'd never tried to lead a group meditation before and least of all with a translator to a bunch of unruly Russian students. Next, in an even slower and gentler voice, I suggested they focus on feeling their sense of touch through their fingertips, the clothes around their bodies, then touching their naked face. The translator carefully followed my tone of voice in a language that I knew not a word of. Then I asked them to concentrate on their hearing, in the silence, to listen for the furthest, most distant sound they could hear. It was like the world had stopped. Two dozen boisterous young adults became static in a void of quiet calm. Next step, they should concentrate on the sense of taste, to feel their tongues in their mouths and any residual taste from bitter coffee, sweet biscuits, or even their breakfast. As the slow seconds passed, it felt like they were going along with my weird experiment. Ten minutes in, I proposed that they very, very slowly begin to open their eyes, not to look out, but to just allow the warm tungsten light to land on the back of their retina: not seeing, but letting light in and feeling the sensation of light without looking outwards.

Gradually the group came back to life. I was staggered at the transformation, I had their attention, my gamble had paid off. I talked through the brief and the target of mounting an exhibition of their ideas in two and a half days' time. The energy in the room was now tangible. They brought out artists' materials and began to sketch ideas, some solo, some pairing up. When it came to lunchtime, most of them barely stopped; as I moved around the improvised studio, they were eager to discuss their initial concepts.

At the end of the afternoon, a crew from the local radio station turned up to interview us all. Next morning, I couldn't believe it, many of them must have worked all night. Sketches had turned into finished drawings. On their laptops,

Above:
Sestra River site zoning plan

Below:
One of many sketch views.
Drawing by Phil Radmall

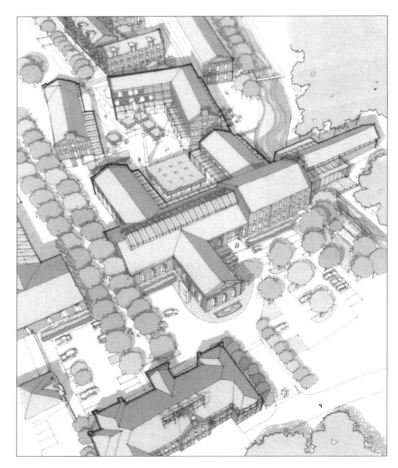

they had built complete 3D computer models. As Thursday advanced, their prolific output and energy built progressively. Unexpectedly, the radio crew reappeared and soaked up the atmosphere as the students enthusiastically explained their work and proudly showed their drawings.

On Friday morning the student group arrived in dribs and drabs, some switched on swiftly some looking like they had grabbed little sleep. By lunchtime, most of them were ready to mount the exhibition. It went up with the speed of light and in a couple of hours was all set. It looked fantastic, the quality of ideas, artwork, drawing skill and even models was outstanding. I couldn't believe how much imaginative work they had produced in so little time.

Back at the broadcast station, word of what was happening in the fortress must have got around. Just as we were standing back glowing with the students' achievement, a full TV crew arrived. They filmed the exhibition and caught the energy of what had taken place over those few days. That evening, the student workshop in the historic fortress had ten minutes' airtime on the St Petersburg television six o'clock news. The beers flowed and together with the students, their partners and even their tutors, we all had a well-earned celebratory evening.

Shortly after the St Petersburg trip, Nadya and Alex arrived in London. We showed them around our city, took them to other offices and gave them their own small project. They excelled. At the end of their fortnight prize, I asked them if they'd like to come back. Their pale blue eyes lit up.

'Yes, please, do you think you can arrange visas?'

With Robert's assistance through UKT&I liaising with the Home Office, two-year working student visas were granted. Once back in London, the presence of Russian-speaking young architects working with us was instrumental in winning a major commission to masterplan the vast, former munitions factory at Sestra River not far from St Petersburg. The site was a huge complex of historic industrial buildings, canals, and new-build potential. Pedro Roos and our young Russians came up with a great scheme and as time marched on, all was going well with Victor's support.

As their two-year visas came towards the expiry date, we applied to the Home Office to extend them. The answer was a disappointing 'No.' We tried again, but the same answer came back. Nadya and Alex had to return to St Petersburg. We tried to keep the project at Sestra River alive but without our Russian-speaking young friends in-house this proved hopeless. The massive project went no further.

The distressing side of this was that our government had invested in promoting the creative industries overseas. Studios and businesses like ours had travelled and worked hard to win international commissions and hence bring overseas earnings into the UK. To deliver a project in Russia with massive language and regulatory difficulties, it was essential to have staff from that country. Having been supported by one government department in winning the overseas work, the Home Office killed it off by the blind application of ill-considered, contradictory political policy. They did not and still do not look at 'every case on its merits', as they always state in government press releases.

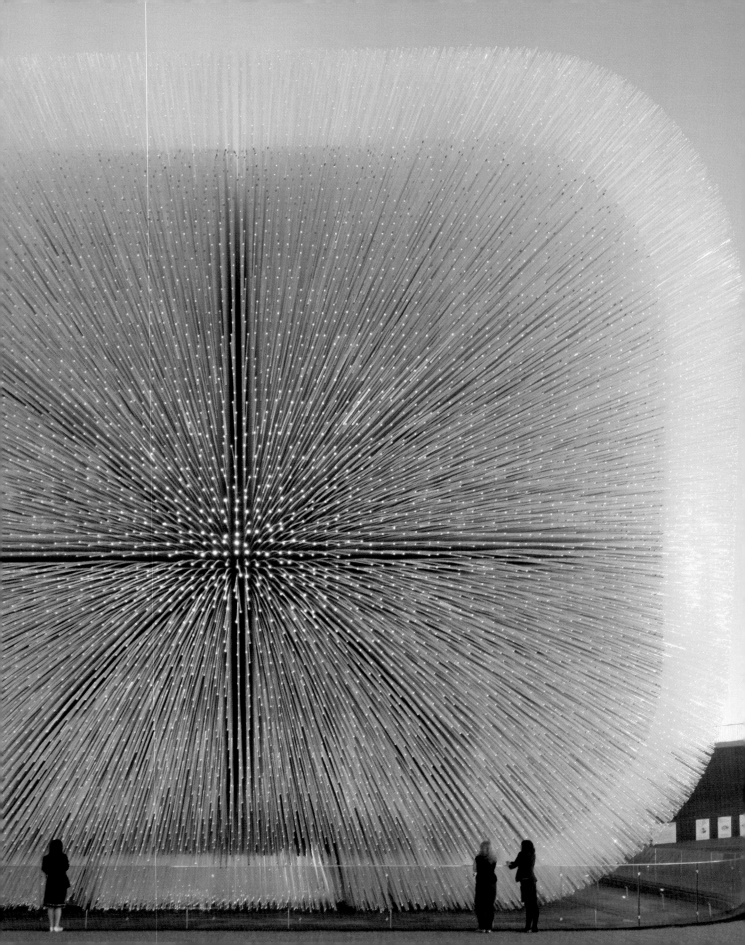

25 SPLENDIFICATION

The Chelsea Barracks site presented the largest new build opportunity so far on 'our patch'. The underused military barracks occupied 12.8 acres and was situated adjacent to Chelsea Bridge Road along the eastern boundary of Wren's Royal Hospital grounds. It connected the river Thames to Belgravia, Lower Sloane Street and only 200 yards beyond to Sloane Square. PD+P's office on Ebury Street was even closer. The Treasury was looking for funds and Chelsea Barracks was the most valuable disposable asset in the MoD London portfolio. Taylor Woodrow approached us, and we went for it. Unsurprisingly, all the big players were after it. Qatari Diar (QD) outbid everyone with an unmatchable billion-pound offer, Lord Rogers was their architect.

Controversy erupted when their scheme hit the press. As it advanced through the consultation stages of the planning process, vociferous local residents mobilised an effective campaign of opposition against the prospective steel and glass designs. Then HRH The Prince of Wales joined the debate and made his opinion known to the Qataris. They pulled the plug and time passed while the dust settled.

I was asked by QD to take a group of their executives around Belgravia and Chelsea to show them the character, scale and proportion of nearby streets and squares that might inform the approach to master-planning their site. The grand boulevard of Eaton Square would only be relevant to the main road frontage. In contrast, Chester Square had greater intimacy, especially the eastern half. As we walked, I talked about the linking subsidiary streets that vary in scale at each junction, thereby creating a natural hierarchy, degrees of density and a diverse mix of houses and apartments. The impact on value of green space and views over them was self-evident when compared to treeless streets. In Chelsea, we walked along the King's Road from Royal Avenue to Carlyle Square to illustrate alternative approaches to terraces and villas. Wellington Square presented one of the most compact and hence appropriately proportioned plan forms. Its obvious density struck a notable chord with the group. Sloane Court East and West were of relevant scale and only yards from their site. Ormonde Gate and Lygon Place demonstrated the enhancement of setting that the creation of a semi-private setback can have on the sense of place and value. The tour seemed to go down well.

I had had the good fortune to visit the Shanghai Expo in the summer of 2010 as part of an RIBA delegation. Thomas Heatherwick had won the competition to design the UK pavilion with his 'Seed Cathedral.' Before travelling east, Hanif Kara had explained the extraordinary geometry and structure that AKT had collaborated on that included 60,000 acrylic rods punctuating a huge invisible plywood cube. On the outside, the sculptural form swayed gently with the breeze, on the inside, the scale of the space was a surprise and sparkled with unimaginable beauty. Each of the 60,000 translucent rods held a plant seed illuminated by sunlight transported from the sky above the cathedral capsule. The setting of this poetic object was equally original. Each of the several hundred national pavilions exploded with massive site coverage and starchitect fervour. Thomas had created an open space where visitors could rest their tired exposition feet, chill out and enjoy informal cameo performances telling stories of British culture. The form of the space resembled the unwrapped paper of a precious gift. The welcoming amphitheatre of random folds tilted upwards at the edges to provide a sheltered route that gave access to the bridge link to the cathedral interior. Thomas was there to greet us and talk us through his creation. His enthusiasm, humility and puckish humour spilled over with every softly spoken word. It was a joy to hear him, to move through and quietly contemplate this original creation of space and geometric poetry. It had both joy and soul.

Left:
A magical space:
The interior of the UK Pavilion
by Thomas Heatherwick.
Photograph © Iwan Baan

Opposite:
The 'jewel' unwrapped:
The exterior and the site.
Photograph © Iwan Baan

Back in London after bouncing around the Far East, we needed to assemble a team to conjure a concept for the Chelsea Barracks competition. I was more than delighted when Thomas agreed to work with us. A base model of the site and environs was swiftly fabricated in the multi-faceted Heatherwick Studio workshops. We began playing with wooden blocks aiming to create a series of well-proportioned courtyards, squares and streets. DP9, our planning consultants, had their offices on Pall Mall. On leaving a meeting, I decided to walk back to Ebury Street via The Mall and St. James's Park. One of my favourite views in London is from the bridge over the lake looking east towards Horse Guards Parade and the silhouetted roofscape of Whitehall. It was a sunny day and I sat on the steps of Carlton House Terrace overlooking The Mall and the park.

What is so special about The Mall that makes it so much more than just another wide highway? Many such major roads are lined by tall plane trees. Here the scale of the trees not only define the avenue but also frame the views into the park, gifting a sense of distance as well as connection to a wonderful urban green space. Carlton House Terrace is set back from the trees and defines the opposite side from the park. It is the set back and the colonnaded podium that lift the terrace towards the sky thereby allowing a heightened scale that perfectly balances the longitudinal vistas of the park. It is this balance of proportion, scale and distance, the combination of formal rhythmic architecture, majestic shade trees, vistas to open natural park and connection to sky that make The Mall one of London's most admired processional routes. Behind the terrace, the neighbourhood of St. James's holds a rich mix of substantial buildings, streets, squares, intimate lanes and mews.

What if we talked to our friendly clients at the Royal Hospital and proposed clearing the overgrown understorey of trees along the west side of Chelsea Bridge Road? Doing so would open distant vistas through Ranelagh Gardens to the green acres that were the original river front arrival to Wren's composition. Then, if we set our mansion apartments back from the avenue of plane trees on the east side, we could create a similar grand gateway 'mall' linking Chelsea Bridge to Belgravia and Sloane Square. Light would be let into the gardens with the gift of green distance in place of the shadowy containment that then existed. It would be a vastly enhanced new threshold from the Thames into London.

Right:
Playing houses:
One of many iterative models

Below:
Carlton House Terrace, The Mall:
Splendid inspiration

Next day we were meeting at the Heatherwick Studio to play with our model. Thomas took to the idea and excitedly exclaimed; 'It's the Splendification of Chelsea Bridge Road, a new gateway into London and Chelsea.' The joy of transforming the ordinary into the extraordinary added energetic inspiration to our design dialogue. We were on a roll, on the same page and having fun with a new word for the dictionary. Our goal of placemaking took on a broader context than just the immediate site boundary.

When we came to present our scheme to a large committee of QD and interested individuals, the advising agents were of the opinion that too much saleable area would be lost by setting back from the roadside and trees. Our old rival, Michael Squire, was selected although the master plan principles of new garden squares and forms were similar. PD+P did win the consolation commission to design the private houses that now define the northeast corner of the site where it joins Belgravia. I was saddened not to be able to take a project forward with Thomas and felt that London had lost an idea for a splendid new celebratory route into part of its heart.

26 PARADISE AT HOME

The first time I visited the Temple Inns of Court was as a 15-year old. I was working in my dad's shop on High Holborn, the Visual Aids Centre. It stocked the fullest range of art and graphic materials. My passion for painting generated a deep knowledge of the products. An elderly lady barrister and amateur painter spotted my enthusiasm and befriended me and when she was off to court one day, asked if I might deliver her haul of equipment to her apartment in the Inner Temple. On my first delivery run, I wandered lost through the maze of courtyards, lanes and handsome buildings from across the centuries. The study of architecture never ends. Every time I pass through the historic gates something new is felt and learnt. Emotional response is one key, but often overlooked, function of architecture.

Decades later, because of my involvement with the UK Department of Trade & Investment and growing profile in the Far East, I was frequently invited as one of several guides to show respected groups of Japanese and Chinese architects and developers around a personally selected district of London. Others would show them around Canary Wharf, or occasionally the latest office towers in the City of London. When meeting up with them after their previous treks, the guided parties seemed at best underwhelmed, evidently bored, and difficult to engage. Japan had better, China had bigger.

The first time I was asked, I decided to take the group for a walk around the Inner Temple and Middle Temple Inns of Court, home and chambers to lawyers since 1320. These Inns of Court quietly embrace about 17 acres between Fleet Street and the Thames. Fleet Street has narrow pavements, bounded by tall buildings. The traffic is intense. Only a few feet from the curb, robust timber gates with castle-like strap hinges and exposed bolt heads open across narrow cobbled lanes designed for horse traffic. The moment one steps over any one of these few gated thresholds, time and noise evaporate. There is stillness, pace slows, the sky reappears, and an august sense of place takes hold of the spirit. The sequence of interlinked courtyards varies in scale, groundscape, formal and informal planting. This small quarter of central London is, remarkably, its own independent local authority. Over centuries of idiosyncratic stewardship, these acres have become an enlightened textbook study in evolved urban space: learned and intuitive placemaking.

The Temple Church is the earliest extant building. It was built and consecrated by the Knights Templar as their headquarters in 1185. Inner Temple Lane opens to frame a most intimate vista of the church. It leads the spectator close enough to touch the cold hard face of finely wrought stone. The circular nave emerges from a lower ground level, implying its earlier origins. It nestles between differing sizes of rectilinear courts and informal spaces that have grown around it over centuries.

Opposite:
Light and shade define solid and void
© Adam Parker

237

Above:
King's Bench Walk

Right:
Rebuilt in 1678

Above:
East gardens

Right:
Temple Gate:
Opening on Fleet Street

Below:
The Master's House
Photos © Adam Parker

Right:
The Temple Church
© Adam Parker

To the east, the Master's House sits with its simple flagstone path bisecting a perfect, very English lawn and flower beds. It resembles a fine country parsonage yet is situated in the heart of London. As one wanders westwards through the cloisters, you enter the delightful intimacy of Pump Court with its two almond trees mathematically spaced along the centre line. Then, crossing Middle Temple Lane, the vocabulary of the buildings is more varied, with origins across several centuries. Each is rich in detail. The spaces between are both held and defined by the diverse façades. The fountain, its basin, substantial trees, pastoral and manicured planting, changes in texture and level, all draw the observer onwards to explore from one interlinked space to the next. After turning east along Crown Office Row, the lawns of Inner Temple Gardens slope gently down towards the Thames, bounded by Paper Buildings and opening out to King's Bench Walk. This complex area of irregular geometry is lined on its Eastern boundary by the terraces originally built before 1548. They were rebuilt in 1678, having been destroyed in the fires of both 1666 and 1677.

Part of the brilliance of the sequence, the vistas, connections, and diversity of spaces that have evolved densely over the centuries, is the surprise and contrast when, with arms outstretched, the intricacy opens out across expansive sloping lawns to the breadth of the river and the distant South Bank.

After the first guided tour with Far Eastern delegates, I was pleased to be told: 'This was worth travelling from the other side of the world to enjoy.'

Left:
The Temple church, West door
© Adam Parker

241

27 CODA

Any memoir can only scratch the surface of a long life lived, hopefully, to the full. I was fortunate when young to live at a time in history when it was possible to travel to exciting places and cultures that have since become difficult to visit due to world politics. My 'Revell' slot car AC Cobra turned into a real one that I raced. I even had two Aston Martins. I married a beautiful girl, had three wonderful, healthy kids and – mistakenly – divorced. That was not part of the naïve teenager's dream.

I have lived in Chelsea whilst rebuilding much along the King's Road and Sloane Street. I worked for eight of the landed estates in London, contributing to their long-term stewardship. After years of challenges, I won the respect of planning and conservation officers. On the other side of the world, I learnt from different methods of construction and designed buildings relevant to local lifestyles. I won awards for places that people enjoy living in. At conferences, I was privileged to present my beliefs about cities in changing societies.

There has been real joy in collaborating with countless talented architects, consultants, and contractors delivering hundreds of lasting projects and breathing new life into a legacy of historic buildings. I made many friends along the way and enjoyed the trust of clients. As is the way in any architect's career, there were disappointments when schemes slipped away or failed to reach expectations. I founded an environmental consultancy with forward-thinking individuals to enhance the sustainability of our own projects and those of others.

My particular passion has been for residential architecture. I was lucky to learn a lot through a succession of commissions for private houses. Here, the dialogue with clients provided detailed insight into different lifestyles. Interpreting words and pictures into designs for families to live in was a stimulating challenge. Developing this understanding into plans for speculative homes for purchase or rent became my *raison d'être*.

Houses need people in order to become homes, just as songs need voices to be heard. Imagination reveals the unexpected. Memory binds us to place. The accumulated wisdom of the past is best not forgotten. Intuition, observation, reflection, and concern for context have anchored and driven my passion for making places. To these, you can also add conversation, understanding, learning, respect, dignity, and trust. These are not just words. They are the values and value of placemaking. Light, sound, water, space and people are the building bricks of place. Touch and scent are often forgotten but better when remembered. Passion generates the energy of conviction and perseverance. Self-belief demands careful consideration: very different from self-absorption, it easily slips into self-deception.

Let ego stand behind belief putting people and place before object.

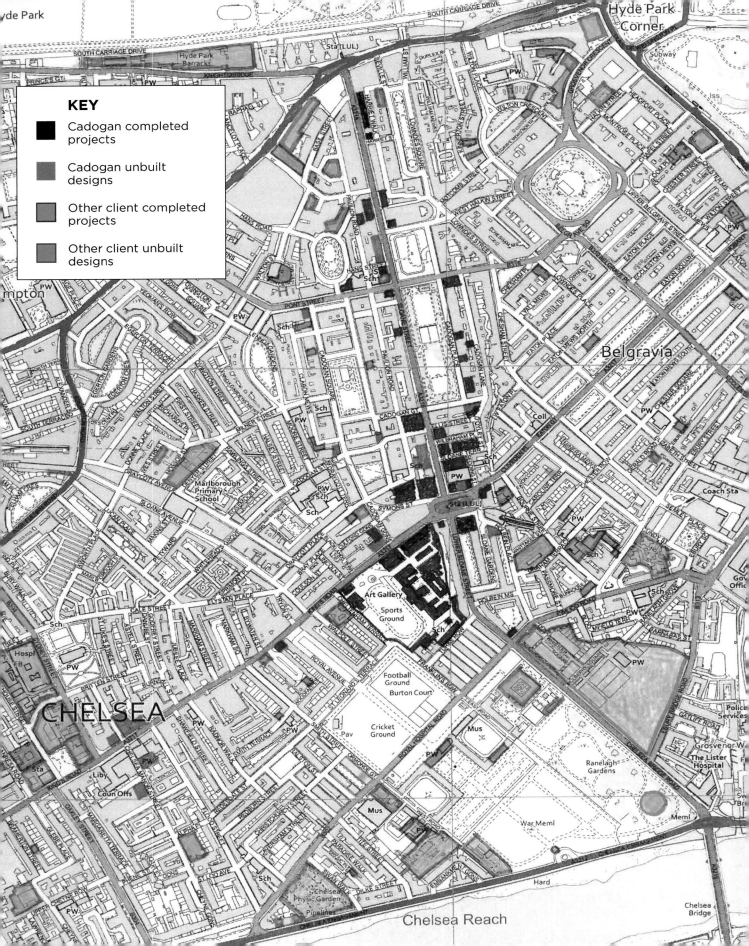

KEY

■ Cadogan completed projects

■ Cadogan unbuilt designs

■ Other client completed projects

■ Other client unbuilt designs

APPENDIX
CADOGAN ESTATE PROJECTS

1 Hans Street
[Corner of Sloane Street].
Listed building office refurbishment.
37-42 Sloane Street
Retail & office façade retention.
[Armani Store]
71-75 Pavilion Road
Knightsbridge NHS Medical Centre
New-build doctor's surgery.
74 Sloane Street
Pinks. Former bank listed building altered to create retail.
[Now part of Cadogan Hotel].
91 Sloane Street.
Refurbishment of flats.
120-122 Sloane Street + 1 Cadogan Gate
Medical suites & offices. Refurbishment.
123 Sloane Street
Restoration of original Henry Holland listed building to offices.
124 Sloane Street + 111 Cadogan Gardens
Offices & residential.
150-155 & 156-161Sloane Street
Major retail & residential refurbishment.
[Jo Malone, Stella McCartney, Paule Ka, Chloe, Dunhill, Mont Blanc].
1 Cadogan Place. Former Coutts Bank,
Corner of Sloane Street. Remodelling of bank to create Hermes store.
166-172 Sloane Street
Retail & office façade retention.
[Chanel, St Laurent, Pucci].
190/192 Sloane Street
Office common parts upgrade & subsequent office refit.
194-207 Sloane Street. Richmond Court
Removal of long canopy, new stone pilasters, fascias, and pavement tiling.
[Ferretti, Balenciaga, Tom Ford, Scervino]
[Protracted planning dialogue with RBK&C to alter shop fronts
to include first floor retail.]
141-145 Sloane Street + 15-16 Sloane Square + 257-261 Pavilion Road
Major retention of façades above tube line to create retail and offices with first stage
pedestrianisation of Pavilion Road.
[Pringle, Cartier, Tiffany, Links, Little White Company, Caramel, Heidi Klein].

Left:
Map of Projects on Cadogan Estate
and surrounding area, 1978 - 2013

2–12 Symons Street, 184–192 Pavilion Road + 19 Cadogan Gardens
Major re-construction above tube line with retention & reinstatement of façades.
Retail & residential apartments around podium courtyard with basement parking.
[GTC, The White Company, A La Mode, Franchetti Bond + 14 flats]

7 Sloane Square
Refurbishment of pub. [The Botanist].

13–14 Sloane Square
Structural alterations to create retail from bank. [Rag & Bone].

31 Sloane Square
Conversion of bank to create new shop. [Bamford and Sons].

35–38 Sloane Square
The Willett Building. Listed building major structural works to create new retail store.
[Hugo Boss].

50–51 & 52–56 Sloane Square. Blandel Bridge House
Retail & offices refurbishment in two phases. [Colbert, Basia Zarzycka, Emma Hope,
VV Rouleaux, Anta].

70–74 Cadogan Place
Planning and listed building application and appeal. Failed.

Cadogan Place, east side
Series of residential refits of listed buildings.

84 Cadogan Square, Stuart House
Listed building consent to revert to original major historic mansion.

61a Cadogan Square / 101 Cadogan Gardens
Change of use consent.

22–24 D'Oyley Street
New-build houses.

3 Cadogan Gate
Major refurbishment of ISVA offices.

39–45A Cadogan Gardens + [Culford Gardens house]
Major reconstruction and façade retention to create retail, offices & single house.

Duke of York Square
Ten-acre masterplan, consents & phased delivery of new public square, shops,
restaurants, cafes, offices, affordable and market rent flats, Garden House School,
underground car park, new residential mews and Saatchi Gallery.

4 Sloane Terrace + Sedding Street
Reconstruction of redundant telephone exchange to offices.

5 Sloane Terrace. Cadogan Hall
Restoration and conversion of listed former church to Concert Hall.

9–31 King's Road + 27A Sloane Square
Refurbishment of shops and flats above.

95 Lower Sloane Street + 94 Pimlico Road
Redesign of corner retail shops.

CADOGAN ESTATE SKETCH SCHEMES AND FEASIBILITY STUDIES:

126–134 Sloane Street. Liscarten House & Granville House + Pavilion Road.
Sketch scheme for new build retail and offices on Sloane Street with connection to Pavilion Road for local amenity shops.
Subsequently taken forward by Stiff + Trevillion.

8–12 Sloane Square
Restaurant & café options for hotel.

1 Sloane Gardens
Sketch ideas for conversion to new hotel.

34–42 King's Road
Sketch schemes for adaption of retail and residential above.

Sloane Square
With WSP option studies for enhancements to Square through improved traffic management and enhancements to public realm, pavements etc. prior to RBK&C proposals that were subsequently abandoned.

55 Sloane Street
Arne Jacobsen Danish Embassy.
Detailed review of comparative development options for cyclical rent review.

Major redevelopment of 196–222 King's Road retail, supermarket, cinema, residential
Started and subsequently on site by PD+P.

224 King's Road
Sketch scheme for corner bank building.

Chelsea Manor Street
Sketch scheme to open up two storey office building.

3 Chelsea Manor Street
Sketch alternative use studies for 1903 Cadogan Hall.

Footnote. There were also numerous other King's Road and Chelsea projects for the Sloane Stanley Estate, Martin's Properties Ltd., Brompton & Harefield Hospital Trust and Charity, Royal Hospital Chelsea, Chelsea Physic Garden, private developers, and householders not recorded in this memoir.

ACKNOWLEDGEMENTS

MY THANKS TO:

My tutor, Mark McCrum for encouragement and perseverance, Tim Epps for patient creativity on the design and layout, Paul Finch for reinstating my belief in a story worth telling, Adam Parker outstanding photographs, Sara Fox and David Attwood for meticulous editing and proofreading, Jonathan Wyatt for true friendship, Nicky Haslam and Thomas Heatherwick for the most imaginative fun and Ringo Starr for the best fireworks ever.

Along the way to Miranda Castro for a wedding that reconnected me to Phil Manzanera that led to recording studios, stage sets and the Roxy Music and Duran Duran years. To Roland Castro and Colin Redman for belief in a virgin architect, Stuart Corbyn for twenty-six years of patronage and to Nick Loup for inviting me to Hong Kong and Tokyo. Each had the rare courage to commission an architect to design projects that I had neither the experience nor track record to deliver. But then, my parents encouraged me be whoever I wanted to be. Mum personified hard work and cursed mistakes; Dad never took the same road twice when exploring city streets. He built a beautiful garden and let me pretend I lent a helping hand.

Most of all to Susie, Luke, Jessica and Henry Davis for their unconditional love through the best, happiest and most difficult years.

A LIFE IN ROCK N' ROLL & ARCHITECTURE
FROM THE KING'S ROAD TO TOKYO

PAUL DAVIS

First published in Great Britain by:
Prospero Press,
Highfield House, Tintern, Wales NP16 6TF
www.prosperopress.net

A CIP catalogue record for this book is available
from the British Library.

ISBN: 978-0-9928972-9-1

Set in Bembo and Gotham
Book design and layout: Tim Epps
Cover design: Henry Davis/Tim Epps/Jude Florschutz

Many of the illustrations in this book have been
sourced from the author's personal archive.
Considerable effort to track down copyright holders to
obtain permission for use has been made.

The author and publisher apologise for any errors or
omissions and will appreciate notification so that any
such corrections can be included in future editions or
reprints of this book.

Please contact:
info@mrchelsea.co.uk

Cover:
Photograph © Chris Mann.
Concept: Henry Davis

Frontispiece:
Frontispiece: Collage sketch by the author.

Introductory pages:
Photograph credits as body of text